The ACIM Mentor Articles

Volume 2

Answers for Students of A Course in Miracles *and* 4 Habits
for Inner Peace

ISBN: 9781726631891

Other Books by Liz Cronkhite

Non-Fiction

The Plain Language *A Course in Miracles*:

 The Message of A Course in Miracles*: A translation of the Text in Plain Language*

 Practicing A Course in Miracles/The Way of A Course in Miracles*: A translation of the Workbook and Manual for Teachers in Plain Language*

The ACIM Mentor Articles: Answers for Students of *A Course in Miracles*

4 Habits for Inner Peace

Releasing Guilt for Inner Peace: A companion to *4 Habits for Inner Peace*

Fiction

A Good Woman

You can learn more about these books at www.lizcronkhite.net.

Contents

Preface

In 2010 I published the first volume of *The ACIM Mentor Articles*, a collection of my newsletters between 2006 and 2009. For a while afterward I recycled articles already written. I concluded that book with an article written in April of 2010 explaining that I felt, at that time, that I had written all I had to say in that format. I then opened my articles up to questions from readers for the next few years. To distinguish my answers to readers from my usual short essays I prefaced these articles with "Ask". All but one of the articles contained in this volume are answers to questions from readers through 2014.

Some weeks I did not have a question to answer and recycled old newsletters so there is not an article in here for every week through these years.

In 2011 I published my book, *4 Habits for Inner Peace*. Some of my readers also read and referenced that book. So my articles going forward incorporated the language from that book as well.

The articles in this book have not been touched, but for some formatting corrections, and are as they were at the time they were printed in my newsletter. I have certainly evolved since they were written, but they honestly reflect my process at the time I wrote them. You may even note that my answers in 2014 are more advanced than my answers in 2011.

You, too, are evolving, and some articles will resonate with you more than others. And there will probably come a time when you put this book aside. Until then, I hope you find it useful.

If you wish to read or make comments on these articles you may do so at my blogsite, www.acimmentor.blogspot.com.

Liz Cronkhite
Las Vegas, Nevada 2018

1. Ask: Advice on sticking with the path (October 15, 2010)

"…my question for you has to do with the effectiveness of the Course *in waking up from this dream. Now, I've read of your own mind blowing experiences of God, which seem to have started early in your study. I've met a lot of people who have been working with the material for years (myself included) who have not had direct revelation. I've been studying other teachings that promise quicker results, but I still don't have anything earth shattering to report. Feeling a bit discouraged, but no matter how much I try to turn away from* ACIM, *I just seem to always be pulled back to it. Any advice you have on sticking with the path and releasing doubt would be greatly appreciated. Much love and thanks."* - Bryan in L.A. (October 15, 2010)

Despite my early experiences of revelation, Bryan, I didn't experience any comprehensive shift toward peace until I had been a student for over 20 years. A revelation is simply a glimpse of the Ultimate Goal of God. If I could stay There, I would not have returned to a perception of a world. Early on, I experienced Revelations as much as a curse as a blessing. On one hand, yes, they did reveal to me Truth and make it more difficult for me to deny Truth, but on the other hand, I sure did my best to deny Truth! Despite direct Revelations of God, I still had my doubts, maybe not about What was True, but about my wanting It. I was no less conflicted for having seen Truth; I was just less able to fool myself that the Truth wasn't True. And, as well, I still seemed to have two realities, Truth, Which I had seen, and the world, which was still very real to me because I had not released all of the layers of deep-seated belief in, and attachment to, it. I am still bumping into those false beliefs and undoing them, on deeper and deeper levels.

I'm telling you this so that you know that it is a process, and that your doubt is not because you have not had a Revelation, but because, on some level, you do not yet wholly want God.

You answered yourself with regard to sticking with the path—you keep being drawn back to it. This is because you know, on some level, that it is your way to peace. You asked for it, and you received it. God is always in your mind, and you know God. This is what you have to trust. The doubt that you experience is the resistance of the ego, which will never accept Truth, and will always tell you to doubt. You may be listening to it now, but, as you learn to not identify with it, you will reach a point where you hear it, but you no longer listen to it, and, finally, when you completely release the personal thought system from your mind, you will not hear it at all!

Peace came for me after years of earnestly opening my mind to God each day and returning my mind to God throughout the day—just as the lessons in the Workbook teach us that first year. In other words, peace came when I made a commitment to peace by choosing it again and again throughout each day. Returning my mind to Truth became the focus and purpose of my mind (therefore, my life). This shifted my attention (identification) away from the ego, and the shifts toward peace that came were not earth-shattering, but subtle and profound, until one day I looked up and realized that peace had come to stay in my awareness. It was not time, nor was it direct Revelation, but *willingness* to keep Truth in my awareness, and to work through my obstacles to peace, that resulted in the comprehensive peace that I experience now.

2. Ask: Trouble forgiving (October 29, 2010)

"I have a person in my life that I am having a lot of trouble forgiving. Usually, when I have a problem with a person, I usually find something good to concentrate on. By doing this, I have something to hold on to when there is a conflict. But with this new person, I can't find any good in them. Sorry if that sounds harsh but that is the total truth. This person has done a lot of harm to people. It's hard to ignore that—I know I'm supposed to believe that the world is an illusion and there is no loss, but it's very difficult to see people being victimized. Is the Course *saying I literally made this person up? I am torn between the two concepts of cowardice and forgiving. Sometimes I feel like the* Course *is asking us to "back down" which, in my mind, could easily be seen as an excuse for cowardice. I think about this in terms of dealing with this person in the world. In other words, sometimes I feel like I should confront her, which brings up feelings of fear. Then I use the* Course *by thinking I don't need to confront her after all and that Jesus will some how take care of it on a different level. Is this just an excuse for not doing anything?*

I hope this is clear. I no longer talk to this person, by the way. I know this isn't the best way toward peace but it's the best I can do for now. Many thanks." - Anonymous

This is a great question, because you bring up a type of circumstance that is so typical for *A Course in Miracles* students, and because so much is misunderstood about true forgiveness. You also missed a miracle, which is also very common for early *Course* students, and I will get to that in a few paragraphs!

True forgiveness means recognizing that only God is Real. This is not something that you can grasp intellectually. This comes from allowing God into your awareness over and over until God is a real experience for you. So, the first thing that you must cultivate is your awareness of God. Then, for a while, you will seem to have two realities: God and the world. This is when you can really start to forgive, because you will be able to let go of what seems to be happening as you turn within to God and remember that *This is What is Real.* Then, what seems to need forgiveness will fall away from your mind.

True forgiveness, then, is not about seeing the "good" and overlooking the "bad" in a personal self; it is letting go of personal-selves-as-reality altogether. This is why the personal thought system (ego) considers the *Course* so radical!

On some level you *do* project the forms that you seem to experience with a body (itself a projection of your mind), but form is never the issue, because all form is neutral (has no meaning in itself). For your peace of mind, the projections with which you need to be concerned are your *projections of meaning* onto the forms that you see. These projections are the source of your conflict. So, it is never the form that you have to forgive, but the story that you have for the form. The stories that you have for others are there to reinforce your identification with a personal self, both by making the personal self seem real, and then by reinforcing the particular story that you have for it. These stories all, in some way, tell how you are a victim of others. (You feel attacked, abandoned, betrayed, misunderstood, etc.). This is simply the way that the personal thought system thinks, and you cannot change it. That's why you have to release the personal thought system altogether, and you do that by forgiving its projections of meaning over and over and over again.

For example, this woman of whom you speak behaves in a certain way. Since you were not specific, I am simply going to call her behavior "abusive". When you are centered in God, you will find that you can simply observe that her behavior is abusive and recognize that she behaves that way because of something going on in her mind; it has nothing to do with you. You can then decide to be around this behavior or not. But, when you are centered in the personal thought system, you will "take it personally" and make her behavior about you ("she's attacking me"). If you do the latter, it will play into whatever story the personal thought system in your mind has for your personal story ("People are always so mean to me", for example).

Remaining in uncomfortable situations is self-torture, not forgiveness. The same can be said for seeking out uncomfortable situations just to forgive them, which some *Course* students feel they need to do. (Sometimes you are obligated to stay in uncomfortable situations for a limited time, and these you can use to remind you of God.) Forgiveness is commonly misunderstood, because the personal mind teaches that love means sacrifice (which makes the forgiver a victim again). Your choice to no longer speak with this woman is a miracle, not a failure! A miracle shifts your mind toward Oneness with God (peace), away from separation from God (conflict). You chose forgiveness and peace, and it showed up as your choice to take care of yourself by avoiding an abusive person. I'm going to guess that you missed this miracle because you probably expected forgiveness to show up either as the abusive woman changing her ways, or you somehow finding her lovable.

A miracle always occurs in your mind, and it always brings you peace of mind. If a change of mind is all that is needed to bring you peace, then the miracle will not necessarily result in a change in the world that you perceive. But, your change of mind (choosing forgiveness) happened to result in you changing your behavior (choosing to no longer speak with this woman) to bring you peace.

If you find that you still cannot let go of this woman, then you need to further forgive your thoughts about her. You will need to look at how your story for her ties into your story for the personal self with which you identify, and release it in the recognition that the personal self *is not you*. It's just a story in your mind with which you choose to identify.

Always be on the lookout for the ways that the personal thought system tries to "spiritualize" the personal self. Inner peace is the result of your awareness that you are One with God (Eternal Love, Peace, Joy), not of you being a certain type of person ("good", "kind", "righteous") to please God. The personal is totally irrelevant to God, because it is not of God; it is only a story in your mind. This is what you recognize when you truly forgive.

3. Ask: How do I forgive what I am not? (November 5, 2010)

"This week's story on forgiveness was very enlightening. You said that most people who find another troubling is because the "other" has somehow said something that connected (not well) with our "story of me" (ego) and has made us feel like a victim. What if the people you don't want to be around have what you think are qualities you don't have? Not because there is anything wrong with the person (being abusive, etc.) but their personalities just seem to drive home the "story of me" that you think is "wrong", such as, not being outgoing enough, not being family oriented, ...these are the people I don't want to be around, not the obviously nasty ones.

This always is my problem...comparisons which make me feel like I'm lacking, no one is ever "bad", really, they are "good", it's just that I feel bad because I'm not like them...self-assured and outgoing etc. I've never seen this problem written about and I wonder if others have it. Thank you for listening." - Anonymous

Yes, others have this problem! I had it myself. But, before I get to the heart of the question you are asking, I want to address a couple of other points in your email, just for clarity.

First, addressing what you say in the first paragraph, what bothers you is never what someone says or does, but what *you think about* what they say or do. You are the one who takes their words and/or behavior "personally" and makes it a part of the story that you have for the personal self with which you identify; it is therefore you who choose to make yourself feel like a victim.

Also, in the second to the last paragraph you say that no one is ever "bad", they are really "good". Actually, all personal selves are a mixture of "good" and "bad" (these designations are, of course, subjective judgments). When *A Course in Miracles* says that you are Perfect, it is not speaking of you as a personal self, but in Truth. If you want inner peace, the goal is not to "perfect" the personal self or to make it "good" or more God-like, nor is it to learn to deny what other personal selves are really like. The way to inner peace is to let go of personal selves altogether in the recognition that *they are not reality.*

This segues neatly into the answer to your question…All personal selves are insecure; it just shows up in different ways in different personal selves. This insecurity is the result of the inherent guilt that is part of the personal identity. You cannot identify with a personal self and not feel guilty, because the personal identity is meant to be the negation of God. When you believe that you are a personal self, you believe that you have attacked God by making a part of God not-God. You feel that you are "bad", which leads to feelings of unworthiness, which manifest as some form of insecurity. Most often, this shows up as one feeling that they are "less than" in at least some aspects of their personality; in some personal selves, this shows up as an overblown sense of worth, which is meant to compensate for their insecurities.

For me, this problem of feeling less-than did not fall away all at once, but over time, as I learned to step back and simply observe the personal mind's thoughts, then turn away from them to re-center my mind in God. The more I opened my mind to God, the more I experienced God, and the more God became real to me. I realized that God in my mind is completely untouched by what the personal mind does, and that God is What is permanent and unchanging within me, so God is What is Real within me. I became more and more aware that who I thought I was as a "person" was completely irrelevant, because it is made up of passing, shifting thoughts—it's not me! All personal selves, either "mine" or "others", have become less relevant to me, because they are not the Truth. I can just observe them, let them be, and let them go.

The confidence I have, then, has not arisen from a "fixed" personal mind that has overcome its insecurities, but from the awareness that *only God is Real.* I've found that a lot of what I thought I needed to fix in my mind has simply fallen away by my centering my mind in God, rather than in my trying to "work on" what I saw as "problems". In fact, "working on" something only holds it in my awareness! When I attend to turning my mind to God, what causes me pain falls away naturally and effortlessly. So, when the personal mind prods you with insecurities—or, anything else, for that matter—simply recognize what is speaking, that it does not speak the truth about you, and turn within to God, Which *is* the Truth about you. Your insecurities, and anything else that is an obstacle to peace in your mind, will fall away naturally in time.

(If you have completed the Workbook and you want to know how to keep your mind centered in God, go to my website, www.acimmentor.com and click on "4 Habits for Inner Peace).

4. Ask: How can I choose to not suffer? (November 19, 2010)

"How can I choose not to suffer? In my head I can but I still feel the pain of rejection." - AM

In Truth, you cannot suffer, but you need to be in touch with the Truth in you to be able to turn toward It, away from suffering. So, before you can stop suffering, you must cultivate your awareness of God within you.

In your mind, you have two thought systems. One comes from God—what *A Course in Miracles* calls the "Christ Mind" or "Holy Spirit" in you. This is the Part of your mind that knows that you are One with God (eternal, limitless love, peace, and joy). The other thought system is what the *Course* calls "ego", and I have translated as "personal mind" or "personal thought system". This thought system is the opposite of God in every way. Its foundation is guilt, therefore fear-of-God, which manifests as anxiety, anger, insecurity, irritation, worry, etc. It is your identification with this thought system that leads to your suffering, so the obvious correction for your suffering is to stop identifying with it. But, you cannot be without an identity, so you will only stop identifying with a personal self when you identify with God. This means that God has to be more than just a nice idea that you've read about in a book; God has to be a real experience for you.

If you are already conscious of having experiences of God—what the *Course* calls miracles (indirect experiences) and revelations (direct experiences)—then, when you are caught up in the negative emotions of the personal thought system, you can turn inward, away from them toward those experiences of God. At first, these will just be memories of occasions when you've been aware of God through revelations and/or miracles. You remember those experiences and remind yourself that the Source of those experiences is What is real, not what is appearing before you, or what you are thinking about what is appearing before you. For myself, I use the phrase, "Only God is Real." This turns my mind back toward those experiences. When I use this phrase and feel myself take a deep breath and relax, then I know that I've made the connection to Truth. From there, I'm able to just observe the personal thought system's thoughts without taking them on as my own. I rest in peace, and the thoughts that cause my suffering fall away automatically in the recognition that they are not about anything real.

In time, the Presence of God will be more than just rare occasions that you can remember—It will always be with you, and turning toward It, away from the world and the personal thought system's stories for you in the world, will become much easier.

If you are not conscious of having had experiences of God, then you need to invite them into your awareness. Simply open your mind to God: "I'm willing to experience You." These words are for you, not for God, Which is always right here within you. If God is not in your conscious awareness it is because of your obstacles to being aware of God, not because God isn't here. Your willingness has to be a *feeling* of truly being open. It does not have to be perfect; you don't have to be without fear or doubt. Simply open yourself, then let go and trust. Miracles will come into your awareness and show you that God is with you.

Miracles can take many forms: A sudden awareness of the Presence of God with you; an insight that shifts you toward peace; a change in perception about a situation that shifts you toward peace; a spontaneous feeling of peace or joy that is unconnected to anything happening "out there"; guidance from the Holy Spirit; an awareness of Oneness with God or another. It always happens in your mind, and changes you; it may or may not show up "out there" as something in the world of form changing. Miracles are the experiences that "prove" to you that

God is Real and within you; this is why they are necessary. (This is why it is called *A Course in Miracles*!).

The more that you center your mind in God, the more miracles you will experience, the more real God will become to you, and the less effect the personal thought system will have on you. Return your mind to God again and again throughout the day; don't wait to suffer to do this. Any time that you have a quiet moment, turn your mind inward and remember that only God is Real. As God becomes a real experience for you, painful thoughts will be something that you release easily, and you will no longer suffer.

5. Ask: Forgiveness can take different forms (November 26, 2010)

"In your October 29th newsletter, there was a question about forgiving and how the person had trouble forgiving an "abusive" person. In your answer, you suggested that "forgiveness" can take different forms, and that choosing not to speak to someone might be "a miracle, not a failure". This perspective helped me a lot, after I felt into it for a while. I agree that this might be a way of letting go, and free myself and the other person from grievances and other attachments.

However, there is one thing that is still puzzling me. It seems to me that there are people where choosing not to speak/interact is not an option. Close family members, for instance. What about my 4 year old son? What about my mother? It seems to me I can't just choose to not to speak to them, or stop taking care of my son, although I must admit that I sometimes feel like it. On the other hand it seems that not having all options would contradict the idea of forgiveness and miracles. What are your thoughts on this?" - Anonymous

This is a very good question, and I wanted to address it in the article you mentioned, but it was already so long!

When you choose to forgive, you are asking for a miracle. A miracle is a shift in your mind toward an awareness of God (love, peace, joy); how this shows up is an *effect* of your change of mind, but is not the miracle itself. So, the miracle (your awareness of God) is the same every time you choose one, but how this manifests in the world of form is always perfectly suited to that specific form. The result in the world can be a change in the attitudes and/or behavior of the personal self with which you identify, a change in another's attitudes and/or behaviors, a change in the situation, what you need showing up at the perfect time, etc.

The point of that part of the article was not that you always need to walk away from someone who is disruptive, but that you should not pre-judge how your choice for God will show up in the world. In that case, the woman chose to forgive, and what she was inspired to do was to cut off contact with someone with whom she did not have to be around. This may or may not be how another would be inspired in a similar situation, or even the same person would be inspired in another situation like that one. The form that a miracle takes in a mind that perceives itself in a world depends on what is needed at that time in that particular situation. For many, learning to set healthy boundaries with others is how miracles will show up for them for a while. For others who don't need that lesson, the miracle will show up in another form.

And in a situation where you have to be around someone disruptive – at work, for example – or with someone with whom you do not want to cut off all contact – in your family, for example – the miracle will show up, again, in whatever form you need at that time in that situation.

You do not have to decide or choose how a miracle will show up; in fact, you don't want to. This will just close your mind to seeing the manifestation of the miracle. Your choice for a miracle will result automatically in it manifesting in your perception of a world, just as your choice for the personal self (ego) manifests automatically in your perception of a world! When you choose to forgive, you can trust that a miracle has come, and you "need do nothing" but simply sit back and watch it unfold perfectly in your mind and/or in the world that it perceives.

6. Ask: Disease and healing (December 3, 2010)

"Would you please comment on disease—how our thoughts create it and how we heal again. Thank you." – AM

You are mind. Diseases of the body are no different than any other appearance. The world, the body, diseases of the body—all of these are thoughts in your mind. They are the *effect* of your mind, which is their *cause*, but they are not you. They are "illusions", because they are not your Reality.

God is your Cause and Reality. God is Limitless, Formless Being, or Mind, extending infinitely and eternally. The experience of God is boundless love, peace, and joy. God extends only God, so as God's Effect, you extend God infinitely and eternally. In God, then, Cause and Effect are One and the Same, but in your belief that not-God is possible, you are cause of effects unlike God. When you identify with (give your attention to) a personal self in a body in a world, then, you believe that you are limited, time-bound form. This is not true, so it is painful. Also, to believe that not-God is possible, you must believe that you attacked God and took part of God away from God. This means that your identification with a personal self is one of inherent guilt and fear of punishment. Your pain and guilt and fear manifest in your awareness as an anxious mind and a dis-eased and dis-ordered body.

As a thought in your mind, the body is healed, then, by your decision to have it heal. This can happen spontaneously, but most often this is done through what *A Course in Miracles* calls external "agents" (medicines, doctors, treatments, etc.) showing up to give form to your decision to heal the body. But this is not real healing, because the real source of your dis-ease and dis-comfort is your belief that you are a personal self in a body in a world. To focus your mind on healing the body, then, is to do nothing real. It is to keep your mind mis-identified with what-it-is-not, because, healthy or sick, a body is never you. Even when the body is healthy, your mind is still conflicted if it is identifying with the body. Eventually, dis-ease and dis-order will return in your awareness again.

True healing, then, is your learning to identify with your True Cause and not with the erroneous effect (the body) of your belief that not-God is possible. To do this, you must withdraw your attention from the body and the world it seems to inhabit. You must look inward at how your own thoughts contribute to your sense of peace or conflict, and correct those thoughts that lead you to feel conflicted by affirming God as your Reality. As you focus your attention inward, and return your mind to God again and again, God will become more and more real in your experience. You will find that, as an effect of your healed mind, the world that you perceive, including the body, will improve. But, ironically, this will no longer matter to you, because you will realize that they are not your cause, and they are not you; they are meaningless. You will have inner peace, and what more is there to want?

7. Ask: The Mind/body split (December 10, 2010)

"I have a point on which I would love some clarity. When one's newborn is sick and needs antibiotics for pneumonia, wouldn't the most recent message from the Course *concede that one not identify with the illness as the ill body is not God Consciousness? Therefore, leading one not to treat the sick infant? When a woman bleeds every month she must take care of her body? The mind/body split has me perplexed... I can be in full loving consciousness, living out of the Love Consciousness not the fear consciousness and have a back spasm that necessitates a focus. Is one to deny this?"* – Anonymous

I'm not sure what you mean by "most recent message from the *Course*", but *A Course in Miracles* is quite clear on your first question about treating an illness or not: You (or anyone that you are caring for) do not need to suffer. Take whatever is necessary to ease your discomfort or pain. The appropriate course of treatment to pursue will come into your mind as a manifestation of your choice to no longer suffer. The answer that you receive to anything that you perceive as a problem in the world is an expression of a miracle (your awareness of God), and to refrain from accepting this guidance is to deny the expression of a miracle.

A healthy body is no more God Consciousness than is an ill body. God Consciousness is an awareness that only God is Real; the body does not enter into this awareness at all. You are never a body, so it is just as erroneous to identify with a healthy body as it is to identify with a sick body. Moreover, a healthy body does not "prove" that you are aware of God anymore than a sick body "proves" that you are unaware of God. The "proof" that you are aware of God is inner peace. You can be just as aware of God when the body in your awareness is sick as when it is healthy. You can have inner peace no matter what is going on in the body or in its world.

The purpose of any spiritual path is inner peace, which is a state of *mind*, and what happens in the physical universe is quite irrelevant to inner peace. In fact, what causes one to be in conflict instead of peace is that one attends to what is happening in the world that they perceive, rather than to their state of mind. Inner peace is the result of your awareness of the Truth (God) within you; conflict is the result of your choosing to attend to (identify with) what is not-Truth (the personal self, body, world).

The mind/body split is this: You are mind (cause); the physical universe that you perceive, including the body, is an idea in (an effect of) your mind. This is why you only need to attend to (identify with) your mind, and you don't have to give the world any thought. When you do, you end up back in conflict, because the body is not you, and the physical world that you perceive is not your reality.

Your sense of peace or conflict is always the result or your thoughts. "Attending to your mind" means noticing when you are not at peace and undoing the thoughts that are obstacles to your awareness of God. God is always right here within you, so, if you are not aware of God (at peace), it is because you have thoughts that are obstacles to this awareness.

You can trust that when you center your mind in Truth (God) that what the body in your awareness needs will show up as a manifestation of your mind's Perfection. By "what the body needs" I mean not just for its health, but enough money, loving relationships, meaningful employment, etc. By "show up" I mean that what you need will come through others, through opportunities presented to you, through inspired thoughts, through the Holy Spirit's guidance, etc. You will simply know how to direct the body. You don't have to give this any thought. If you want to be at peace, your only part is to center your mind in Truth, and *trust*.

When you are in a Loving place in your mind and the body has a back spasm it is the personal thought system trying to get your attention. And it works! Just laugh, and take something for the pain. All that it means is that the personal thought system is still in your mind, and that you still have some attachment to it, or it would not affect you. But this is nothing! It is not real. Only God is Real. You do not have to take anything else seriously. If you do take what is happening to the body seriously, this only indicates that you want the body to be you. And this desire, too, is not real. The Truth (God) in you is not touched by anything that happens in the body or in its world, or by your desire for the body and its world. When you know this, you will be at peace, and nothing else will matter.

8. Ask: Spiritual partnership (December 17, 2010)

"...I am friends with, and see so many people on this planet now, who are so striving to be in a healthy, committed spiritual partnership. They have drawn to them people who seem perfect for this dance of love and yet the feeling isn't mutual and has all the additions of "I love you, but, not in the way you love me" etc. Then the victim comes out, why am I not good enough? On and on the inner ego screams. And we feel alone and know that we aren't.

Can you comment on how we can keep our inner balance and peace in the days where the person we think is the most wonderful for us as our beloved spiritual partner really isn't the one?" – Anonymous

Your real "spiritual partner" is the Holy Spirit (the Truth in your mind). If you want inner peace, which is a state of *mind*, this is the relationship that you must make your primary relationship. When you do this, relationships in the world then become extensions of your relationship with God, in that they all become the means for you to attain inner peace by your learning in them how to choose peace. In other words, your larger goal of inner peace makes all of your relationships "spiritual partnerships". This includes relationships that do not go the way that the personal thought system in your mind has decided that they should go. If you single out only certain relationships in the world to be "spiritual partnerships", then you make them idols, and obstacles to inner peace.

You will find that when you center your mind in God, you have peace, and personal desires, for a certain kind of relationship as well as for anything else, fall into the background. You do not have to deny personal desires, but simply trust that, if they do not naturally fall away in your awareness of your Wholeness in God, they will be fulfilled at the perfect time in a form that is meaningful for you, and that serves your larger goal of attaining inner peace.

9. Ask: Psychoactive drugs and *Course* "purists" (December 24, 2010)

"Thank you for your recent blog entry (December 10, 2010). It is very helpful and rings true with what I understand the Course *to be saying about the mind/body 'split'. I have one question— and others may have the same question as well—does the same thinking also apply to medications that address problems such as ADHD and depression? At the end of the day, if I feel peaceful about my decision to take psychoactive medication isn't that all that matters? Then again, I can see that maybe some* Course *'purists' would consider that a cop out and just show that we haven't been going to God often enough. As you can see, I have conflict about this issue..."* - MP

Of course, psychoactive drugs are no different from other drugs which you take to ease your suffering or discomfort. There is no reason for you to suffer, not just physically, but psychically, or with the chaos of ADHD. Just as with physical illness, you can trust that, as you center your mind in God, you will be guided to the medicine or treatment that is right for the body.

Becoming wholly aware of God is a *process*, and there may come a day when you feel that you can put drugs aside, and, if it does, it will happen naturally, and you will not do so out of a sense that you "should", but out of the simple recognition that you no longer need them.

Ah, this question is a fine example of how the personal thought system (ego) tries to insert guilt into the process of spiritual awakening. Your conflict is the result of your sense of guilt that you may be doing something "wrong" by taking psychoactive drugs. Behind this guilt is the belief that God is an authority that you have to appease through righteous behavior or be punished. This guilt, and the false belief about God underlying it, are good things to uncover, because these thoughts are obstacles that must be undone if you want to be at peace. I hope that some day those *A Course in Miracles* "purists" also realize this for their own peace of mind!

Whenever your thoughts dwell on behavior, you can be sure that you are thinking with the personal thought system, because only a body "behaves". The personal thought system wants to keep you identified with a body; it wants to keep you feeling guilty. But, since God is Mind, it is only your mind which is One with God, so it is only your mind to which you must attend to be at peace. A true path of spiritual awakening is one of a growing awareness of God, which happens wholly in your mind. What you do or do not do with the body is totally irrelevant to God and to your awareness of God, so to your sense of inner peace.

When you find your mind drifting onto behavior – yours or anyone else's – remind yourself that God is not an authority that you have to appease, but the One Being That simply *is*. God is always in your mind, and has never left; it is you who are distracted by something else (the personal thought system), which causes your sense of conflict. All that you need to do to be at peace again is to release this distraction and rest in God.

10. Ask: Removing blocks to Love (guilt/fear) (December 31, 2010)

"Can you talk about what the Course *says about love and removing blocks to love (guilt/projection)?"* – Anonymous

A Course in Miracles teaches that you do not have to learn Love, earn Love, or attain Love, because Love is always within you. So, if you are not aware of Love always, you must have obstacles to this awareness. To be at peace, then, you must seek for and remove your obstacles to your awareness of Love's Presence within you.

God is an experience of Formless, Boundless Love, Peace, and Joy. This is your natural State of Being. "Love", then, is another word for God. Your obstacle to being aware of your natural State of Being is your belief that you are something else, which takes the form of you thinking that a personal self in a body in a world is your reality. Underlying this belief is the belief that you have "attacked" God to make this separate "reality", so at the heart of your identification with a personal self is guilt, and fear of punishment from God. You cannot identify with a personal self and escape this guilt and fear; they are the very core of the personal identity. This is why you have to release the personal identity to let go of guilt and fear. Guilt and fear also serve to maintain the personal identity in your mind, because they make you fear turning inward, where you would find God and undo the personal thought system.

The personal thought system (ego) does not want you to be aware of the guilt and fear in your mind, because, when you do become aware of them, you want to undo them, which would undo the personal thought system. (This is why it is so resistant to you being a student of the *Course*!). The way that the personal thought system deals with your guilt and fear, then, is to project them away from your mind. Now, it seems as though there is a world that is guilty and fearful, and you are an innocent within it. This works well for the personal thought system, because projection keeps guilt and fear in your awareness while keeping you from looking at their source within you, so you cannot undo them.

So, in order to become aware of Love-as-Reality again, you must begin by observing how your own mind works. The physical universe that you perceive is neutral—it has no meaning in itself. All of the meaning that you see, you project there. When you are in the personal thought system, rather than see the world as neutral, you take personally what occurs in it and you tie it into the "story" that the personal thought system in your mind has for the personal self with which you identify. This story usually takes some form where you are a victim of cruel others or a harsh world, where you are "innocent" and others are "guilty", or where you are "right" and others are "wrong".

As you take responsibility for these thoughts, the world that they make for you, and the sense of conflict within you that results, you are able to forgive them (let them go) in the recognition that they are not about the Truth (God) in you. Forgiveness of the personal thought system's projections of guilt and fear, then, removes from your mind the obstacles to your awareness that Love is your Reality, and you are able to rest again in Love and Peace.

11. Ask: Guilt after a suicide (January 14, 2011)

"My son, 42, was addicted to heroin. He committed suicide over a year ago using both heroin and carbon monoxide. Some days, guilt overwhelms and haunts me. My 'head...brain...right mind' knows better, but somehow the Ego takes over. Help. Thank you." – BA

I am very sorry for your loss. No parent expects to outlive their child. I hope you have around you the support that you need as you go through the grieving process. Both the disease of addiction and suicide tend to leave a lot of guilt in their wake, which only adds to the pain of grief.

All guilt represents THE guilt at the core of the personal thought system (ego): The belief that you have separated from God. This belief takes the form of you believing that the personal self and its world are your reality. This is why the personal experience is so painful. You cannot escape guilt when you identify with a personal self; the only way out of pain and guilt is to release the personal thought system from your mind altogether. Then, only the Truth and Its peace, are left in your mind.

It is when you go through the worst personal experiences that you are closest to the very core of the personal thought system. This is why guilt is pounding you right now as you experience this horrific loss. If you find that you cannot simply observe the personal thought system's guilt and let it go as you rest in God, then you need to find out exactly what the personal thought system is saying to you. When you cannot let go of the personal thought system's thoughts it is because you believe them. These thoughts are tied into the story that the personal thought system has for you as a personal self, and they give form to the guilt that you feel. They will be some form of how "bad" or "wrong" you are for things that you did or did not do for your son. Ask the Holy Spirit to join you in looking at the specific thoughts that you have about your relationship with your son. These guilt thoughts can be on many layers. Some with be conscious; others will rise to the surface as you become willing to look on them and let them go.

To overcome guilt, you have to be willing to release the story that the personal thought system has for you. In Truth, you are not a personal self; you are One with God. When you go through an experience like this, it gives you an opportunity to forgive the thoughts that you have for yourself as a personal self. In essence, you do not forgive individual incidences about which you have thoughts that you need to release; you must forgive, or let go of, the whole story that you have for yourself as a personal self.

True forgiveness means recognizing that you are One with God and that nothing else is real. It comes only as God becomes more real to you. You have to develop your awareness of God before you will be able to forgive the thoughts that cause you pain. As you become more aware that God is Real, you will live in a state of forgiveness, which is really the recognition that there is nothing to forgive.

Looking at guilt thoughts can seem like a frightening process, because, before you see that the thoughts that cause the guilt are not real, you believe them. So, remember as you embark on this process, that what you will find is that the guilt that you feel is not justified. Also – very importantly – remember those experiences of God that you have had, whether a direct experience of God through Revelation, or an expression of your awareness of God through a miracle: Guidance from the Holy Spirit, insights and changes in perception that shifted you toward peace, answers to your spiritual and practical questions, etc. Even being a student of *A Course in Miracles* is a miracle, because you asked for peace, and the *Course* came into your awareness as the means to help you attain peace. Revelations and miracles are the "proof" that you are not separate from God; God is still right within you. They undo the very premise of the personal thought system's argument that you are guilty. Guilt is never justified; it is always caused by the mis-belief that you are separate from God.

12. Ask: Impatient to experience the Holy Spirit (February 4, 2011)

"I have just recently found and begun to study the Course *(about 6-9 months ago). I find myself so impatient to develop a feeling of connection to the Holy Spirit/God. It seems that the harder I try, the more it eludes me! I am feeling very frustrated. Can you offer any advice to alleviate this sense of pressure that I have imposed upon myself? I also have a dread of having to endure countless future lifetimes if I don't "get it" during this one...Thanks for your help."* – L.D.

You will be relieved to know that it does not take many lifetimes to attain inner peace. In fact, it doesn't even take one lifetime. It only takes an instant.

You have never left God, so you always have inner peace. What is missing is your *awareness* of the inner peace that is always within you, and that only takes a moment to choose. Inner peace results when you are aware of Truth (God) within you, and you can invite Truth into your awareness right now. In fact, only right now *can* you be aware of Truth and be at peace.

There is no past or future, and the idea of birth into a body has no meaning either once or many times. (M-24.1)

The idea that it takes time to be at peace is the personal thought system's (ego's) way of putting distance between you and God in the form of time, of discouraging you from even trying to find inner peace, of validating itself by making it seem that you find peace through its story, and by trying to assign to itself an aspect of Truth – eternality – by having you believe that it has a real existence that lasts many lifetimes. The personal thought system is never real; it never really exists. It is only an erroneous idea in your mind *right now* which makes you unaware that you are always in God, so it is only *right now* that you can put it aside and be at peace.

You have already invited Truth into your mind; this is why you are studying *A Course in Miracles*. In time, it seems to take time for peace to unfold in your awareness, but you can circumvent this, and the frustration that this seems to make you feel, any instant that you choose, by turning inward to Truth. Each time that you sincerely open yourself to Truth, you lessen your belief in time, and the hold that this belief has over you.

Practicing coming into the present to be with Truth will bring up your obstacles to peace. These are beliefs and attachments that make you fear God. For peace to grow in your awareness in time, all that you need is the willingness to work through your obstacles to peace with the Holy Spirit.

Simply rest in the present with God, trust, and let the process unfold. Your becoming more and more aware of the Holy Spirit and being at peace (this is the same thing) is inevitable, because you already have peace, and, in your perception that you are in time, you've already chosen it.

13. Ask: Discrepancy between the Bible and the *Course*; also, One Mind (February 11, 2011)

"I 'm submitting a couple questions to Ask ACIM Mentor. Thanks for your time.

a) The Bible says God created man out of the dust from the ground and breathed life into him and made him a living soul. This gives the impression the Bible is speaking of the physical body as well as the soul. ACIM *states the body is not a creation of God but an illusion of personal self of our own making. Can you please clarify the discrepancy?*
b) If all of us are many expressions of the One and share one Mind and we have no private thoughts and our seeming differences of form and our seeming separateness from one another are really illusions concealing our shared Source and oneness, then why are all thoughts and beliefs not in harmony?" – RR

God is the One Being that *is*, without form, extending infinitely and eternally. Being All-that-is, God also contains the idea of Its own opposite, which can only ever be an *idea*, because All cannot have an opposite. The nature of All-ness undoes the idea of Its own opposite the instant that the idea seems to occur. But, since the idea of not-God contains the concept of *time*, *within* the idea of not-God it seems as though the opposite-of-God began a long time ago, and will be undone in some indefinite future. However, in God, this idea has never occurred.

The part of God's Mind in which the idea of not-God seems to occur is what *A Course in Miracles* calls the "son of God". The son of God is always a part of God, but it projects not-God: limited, time-bound form, or the physical universe, including bodies. Onto these billions of bodies, the son of God projects its split mind, so that each mind seems to be a replica of the son of God, split between God and not-God, the latter taking the form of a unique personal thought system (ego).

So, the physical universe and personal selves, or "souls", that the Bible attributes to God, the *Course* explains is really only a projection of an idea that can never have reality—it is an illusion that only seems real within itself.

What you think of as your mind, then, though it seems to be individual, is really just a projection of the son of God's mind, split between God and not-God. The God part of your mind is real and eternal, and is completely untouched by the not-God part of your mind. The not-God part of your mind is the projection of an idea that can never be, so it really has no beginning or ending. It is just an erroneous thought in your mind that you can release right now to be aware of God in your mind again.

The reason that seemingly-individual minds are not in harmony is that they are not supposed to be; as representatives of not-God, they are meant to be the opposite of Harmony. But, if you observe personal thought systems (egos) long enough, including the one with which you identify, you will begin to see that the content of each is the same: All are insecure, selfish, self-centered, defensive, anxious, etc. The only difference is the degree to which these traits predominate in each personal self. For example, one is more anxious, another more defensive, and so forth. You will begin to realize that, even in its replacement of diversity of form for the Oneness of God, not-God cannot get away from a twisted sort of oneness! When you see this, you will begin to understand that there is only one mind.

Only God in your mind is Universal, which means that God in what seems like "your" mind is the same as God in what seem like "my" mind and is the same as God in what seems like "their" minds. When the *Course* says we are One Mind, this is to what it is referring, not to the personal self and its thought system. When you are aware of God in your mind, then you are in Harmony Itself, Which is the Universal part of every seemingly-separate mind.

When the *Course* says that you have no private thoughts, what it is saying is that the thoughts that you seem to think with a personal thought system are not your real thoughts. But, certainly, when you want to believe that you are a personal self in a body in a world, you think that your private thoughts are your real thoughts, and this is what blocks your awareness of God in your mind. This is why, to be at peace, you must learn to forgive (let go of) personal thoughts, so that God can arise in your awareness again.

14. Ask: Is Oneness a double-edged sword? (February 18, 2011)

"I have been feeling so much the sense of oneness with all I see and it is most pleasing when I see good things happen to people, animals, plants, world, environment, etc. because it brings such joy because I know I am them they are me. But what really brings pain is when I have this sense of oneness with people, animals, environment when horrible things happen to them and I truly feel horrible and a sense of helplessness and grief that doesn't leave me, for the same reason I see them as me and me as them. For example, wish everyone was a vegan so billions of animals don't have to be tortured and then horribly be murdered in slaughter houses, when the earth is being poisoned daily with all the chemicals and trash and deforesting done to it, when I see children and animals abused and big pharma, and corporations destroying everything for the almighty dollar, and its endless the victim victimizer scenarios that plague my mind. I truly want all to be well and happy, so in this case isn't this feeling of oneness a double edged sword when on the one hand it brings me such joy and on the other such pain. How do I see all this horror

and feel good about it? Even though I totally can intellectualize that this world isn't real and I believe this with all my heart. But while in the world I must have a dream and I would rather all my dreams be in the positive rather than negative realm. I would rather be well than sick, rich than poor, happy than sad, see peace than war, see life rather than death, rather see me and others in comfort than suffering, etc." – JB

A Course in Miracles describes the kind of thinking that you do with a personal thought system (ego) as "upside-down thinking". What this means is that the personal thought system teaches you that the world is not just an idea in your mind, but that it is in fact reality, and that it is your source—that your experience of peace or conflict is caused by it. This is "upside-down" because it is exactly the opposite of how your mind really works. In fact, you first choose the thought system – personal or True—that you want to experience, and then you either project conflict (personal) or extend Love (True) from your mind to the world.

When you experience God's Love (Oneness) within yourself, you are detached from the personal thought system, its world, and its thoughts about its world. They are irrelevant to you, because you recognize that they are not about anything real. You experience a joyful, uplifting liberation from the limitations of a personal self, a body, and a world. The world may still be in your awareness, so the experience of Love extends to embrace all that you perceive all at once. This occurs no matter what is appearing and how the personal thought system would judge it. As Love extends from your mind, you recognize that It is coming from within you, so you recognize that form is not real, and what is appearing has nothing to do with your experience of peace or conflict.

You are not being told that to be at peace you must learn to see horror and feel good about it. You are being told that to be at peace you must be willing to recognize that all form, and the personal thought system's thoughts about form, are not real. This awareness comes as God within you becomes more and more real to you, not as a nice idea, but as an actual experience. This takes time to develop, and if you find that you cannot detach from the world, then first you must focus on developing your awareness of God within you. (If you have completed the Workbook, look at my website, www.acimmentor.com, under 4 Habits for Inner Peace).

You are never in a world; it is only ever an idea in your mind. If you want peace, then your choice is not between a dream of a world that the personal thought system judges as "good" and one that it judges as "bad", but between continuing to dream of a world and to awaken from all dreaming. The "happy dream" to which the Course refers is happy because you recognize that what the body's eyes show you, and what the body seems to be experiencing in the world, is not real, so it does not matter what is appearing. It is still a dream only because you still perceive a world. The gentle path of awakening that the Course lays out is one where you will first experience the Peace of God within you while still perceiving a world, then you will put the world aside completely, and only the Peace of God will be left.

15. Ask: Discrepancies between the Law of Attraction and the *Course* (February 25, 2011)

"I am glad some are asking about the discrepancies between the Bible and the Course. *I have just finished reading the* Law of Attraction *channeled by Abraham through Esther Hicks. Here also there is a wide discrepancy between the descriptions of who we are in physical bodies as described by Abraham, being a definite and determined decision to come "here" as the forefront of thought and extend All-That-Is, and the* Course *which states that we have no choice but to*

come "here" until we are healed and no longer need to.

Another major discrepancy is the advice on how to live: LOA suggests we focus our thoughts as far as possible on what we want whereas the Course *suggests the exact opposite: do NOT formulate and ask for anything. If you are familiar with the above writings would you please give us your thoughts on these issues…"*– RC

I, too, like it when students bring up discrepancies between other spiritual teachings and *A Course in Miracles*. Bringing these discrepancies to the Holy Spirit was how the *Course's* teachings were clarified for me, and also helped me to understand what I was experiencing as I practiced the *Course*. When used with the Teacher of Truth, contrast is a wonderful way to sort out Truth and not-Truth.

I have not read *The Law of Attraction*, nor have I looked deeply into the teachings of Abraham/Hicks, but I can address your questions. It is not important what a teaching actually says; what is important is how you read it, and that is expressed through your questions.

The *Course* does not teach that you have no choice but to come into the world until you are healed and no longer need to. The world is an idea in your mind, not a place where your mind goes into a body. If you are implying by "until you no longer need to" that seemingly-individual minds reincarnate, then the *Course* also does not teach this. As I quoted a few articles ago, the *Course* states directly that many lives apart from God have no more meaning than one life apart from God. Each personal self is a projection of *one mind* that seems to be split between God and not-God. Since it is all one mind, some seemingly-individual minds merely tap into other "stories" for personal selves in that one mind and decide that they were their own individual past lives. This is why many claim to be the reincarnation of the same people!

I'm going to use here the metaphor of a dream that the *Course* uses to clarify this further. The one split mind is what the *Course* calls the son of God, or the "dreamer of the dream". Each seemingly-individual mind in the "dream" is only a "figure in the dream" of that one mind—just as when you dream during sleep, each figure in your dream is really just a projection in your mind.

Even though you think that you are a dream figure, in actuality you are the mind behind the dream – you are the dreamer of the dream. Every mind is, which is why every mind is really one and the same. The "illusion" is that there are many minds that are different from each other. You only become aware of this, however, when you choose to "awaken". The process of awakening makes you more and more aware that you are not a dream figure, but the dreamer of the dream. In other words, you are Limitless Mind, not a mind in a body in a world. You will never grasp this idea with the personal thought system's intellect, because it cannot understand this. But you will come to understand this as you practice turning to God in your mind and releasing (forgiving) the world.

Which is why, if you are serious about inner peace, you will not be interested in dreaming a better dream (focusing your mind on manifesting what the personal thought system in your mind—ego— wants), but in awakening from the dream (being aware that you already have everything and that the perception of lack is only a dream).

When you focus on what is showing up in the world, you engage in what the *Course* calls "upside-down" thinking. You teach yourself that the personal self is not just an idea in your mind, but what you are. You think that the world causes your sense of peace or conflict, when in fact peace and conflict are states of mind that you choose. You confuse cause and effect— the world is your cause and you are its effect—when in fact, you are the mind that causes the world that you perceive.

What this means in practice is that when you center your mind in the conflicted, erroneous thought system (ego), you project away the power of your mind and think that you are helpless. You think that you are a dream figure in a nightmare that is the making of a separate, unknown mind (sometimes called "God"). But, when you center your mind in Truth (which you may choose to call "God"), you reclaim your power, and the dream that unfolds in front of you manifests the peace of your mind. You recognize that it is a dream: an effect of your mind; not your cause, nor your reality, so you have no need to try and control it.

So, it is always the case, as *The Law of Attraction* teaches, that the source of the world that you perceive is you. But LOA (as well as many other similar teachings) then contradicts itself by reinforcing your belief that the world causes you by telling you that, if you want to be happy, you must control what shows up in the world. You cannot be both cause and effect; either the world causes you or you cause it. Attend to what is showing up in the world, and you remain in conflict, confusing yourself with your dream. Attend to maintaining your peace of mind, and you will remember What you are as the dream fades from your mind.

16. Ask: Overcoming martyrdom in relationships (March 4, 2011)

"I have just been dropped by a friend. She's no longer talking to me. She thinks I "dissed" her – I can understand her interpretation of events but it's an interpretation and not a fact. It's interesting how she just stopped communicating without even telling me she was angry so I was just left hanging. I could go back and ask her for her side of the story, beg her forgiveness, etc but it's hard work—and I don't think I've done anything wrong. I'm familiar with this place and have fallen on my sword many times in this kind of situation. Usually, I would rather take the fall than lose the friendship. But I'm sick of doing it and to be honest, my instinct is to just leave it. Still, it's hard to think that a friendship is over. Any advice? Thanks." – SD

What stands out to me in your story is that you think that to maintain a friendship you have to be a martyr. It was never a friendship to begin with if you can only maintain it by "falling on your sword". It was a power game.

From what you have written, it sounds like you said something that your friend misinterpreted. This is inevitable between personal selves (egos). Every personal thought system sees through the filter of its own story for itself. All personal selves see themselves as victims of a harsh world, each in their own way. You must've said something that played into the particular victim-story that she has for herself, which apparently has nothing to do with what you intended when you spoke. You are responsible for what you said, but not for how she heard it.

All that you can do in this situation is to clarify your meaning: "I'm so sorry you heard it that way. But what I meant was…." Now it is up to her to release her interpretation of what you said, or not. If she chooses not to, then you have to wonder if it is such a loss to lose someone from your life who is unwilling to learn and grow. It is very hard to be around others for very long when they are not willing to accept that they made a mistake and to learn from it, Also, her not talking to you and not telling you that her feelings were hurt is another sign of immaturity, and also that perhaps she doesn't value the relationship enough to want to clear the air between you.

What you have to look at in yourself is this pattern of martyrdom in relationships. It seems clear that the personal thought system in your mind has decided that your "story" is that you have to sacrifice yourself for others in relationships. Some or all of these three things are occurring: The personal thought system in your mind interprets others' behavior in such a way as to make you feel that they are demanding your sacrifice, it creates situations in relationships so that you have to sacrifice to maintain the relationship, and/or it attracts or is drawn to people who will demand sacrifice from you as the cost of the relationship.

Understand that the personal thought system in your mind is not going to change. As was said above, all personal selves hold some variation on the theme of victimhood for themselves. The most that the personal thought system might do is change in which situations it feels like a victim, but the victim-aspect of its story for you will always be there in some form. But, when you decided that inner peace was your goal, you began the process of letting go of the personal self as your identity, because your misidentification with it is your obstacle to peace. Your True Identity is in God.

Keep in mind that you will only let go of the personal identity when you have some experience of God as Reality. You cannot be without an identity, so you will not let go of the personal thought system until the Truth in your mind is real to you. Once It is, then you will find the willingness to begin to let go of the particular story that the personal thought system has for you. So, you may have to allow this pattern of sacrificial relationships to continue as you put your efforts into building your awareness of God first.

Once God is real to you, you will find that you will be able to step back and observe what you are thinking and feeling when you are with others. When you start to feel that you are going to have to sacrifice, stop and look at those thoughts. Look at what is really happening, as opposed to what the personal thought system is telling you is happening. Is another really asking for sacrifice, or are you just expecting them to? When you are strongly drawn to others, check in to see if they are like others in the past with whom you played a game of sacrifice. If you find that you are repeating the pattern, stop, and either break the thought pattern that will lead to you making a martyr of yourself, or drop the person who is going to demand that you make sacrifices for the relationship. If you have trouble with any of this, ask the Holy Spirit to help you see what is going on in your mind. It takes willingness, time, and patience with yourself, but you can learn to avoid the pattern of sacrifice and have true, mature friends in your life.

17. Ask: From lack to Abundance (March 11, 2011)

"I have a problem reconciling ACIM *teachings with doing daily tasks making living in Commerce. Say, I am a salesperson. I need to be aggressive, persuasive, not take NO for an answer, follow up on my competition to know what they are doing to counter it to my advantage, maximize my profits by up- and cross-selling, etc, etc, etc. I do it honestly, delivering what's promised, don't lie and cheat etc, etc. Say, this is not coming from my greed or wanting to live a decadent life, but because I need to do it to stay in business and earn physical living i.e. pay the mortgage, taxes and the whole slew of other bills you are aware of, and the family/society is expecting/demanding me to deliver. But this feels and sounds like I am coming from LACK, or WORRY (FEAR) of not being able to make my living and fulfill the expectations of my family or society.*

ACIM *tells us to be/live in the Mind of ABUNDANCE, but, as I mentioned before, it is hard for me to make that switch, from LACK to ABUNDANCE." – RM*

God is formless being, extending infinitely and eternally. God is All, so God is Abundance in the truest sense.

The universe of form, which is not-God, is the idea of the opposite of God in every way: It is time-bound, limited form. It is the idea of lack, limitation, and loss given form. So, in the universe of form, you cannot have it all at once. You have to trade one form for another form: You have to trade the body's attention, time, energy, education, skills, and experience for money, which you then trade for things that the body needs to live in the world.

So, when you look out at the universe of form and think that it is reality, you are indeed in a mind-set of lack, and you will inevitably worry. But this is not reality; God is Reality. The universe of form is only an erroneous construct of reality in your mind. So, you have the choice to attend to it, or to attend to the Truth (God) in your mind. When you bring your mind back to Truth again and again, you become aware that Abundance is Reality, and that the universe of form is only a bunch of meaningless images passing before your mind.

You cannot have two realities, so you have to decide to which you want to give your attention: The universe of form (seeming reality) outside of you or God (Reality) within you. You do not establish which is actually real, but you do make real to you that to which you give your attention. When you attend to form, lack and fear are real for you, but when you attend to God, you know that you have Everything. You experience within yourself a feeling of abundance, and an awareness that all is perfect, whatever is appearing in the universe of form.

Attending to God within you does not mean that you neglect the body's life in the world. It simply means that you give your awareness of God priority. You take time to commune with God everyday, you return your mind to God again and again throughout each day, and you use every situation that you encounter in the world to remember that only God within you is real. This takes willingness, discipline, and time to become your way of being while you are still aware of a world, but the reward is inner peace.

Inner peace is an experience of wholeness, so it is an experience of abundance. When you have inner peace, you have no needs. Your awareness of Abundance within then manifests in the universe of form as everything the body needs showing up: loving relationships, meaningful employment, enough money, etc. So, give Abundance (God) priority in your mind, and abundance will show up in your awareness.

18. Ask: Do you need codes so you are not left behind? (March 18, 2011)

"What is one to make of those folks who claim to vibrate at a high frequency because they are connected to the light? Some offer to transmit the new "ascension codes" to the rest of us (for a fee), so we can vibrate at the right frequency as earth is making a shift.
I've read testimonials on these types of websites of how these services have changed a person's life for the better. Do we all receive these "codes" so we're not left behind?" – Anonymous

What you make of those who teach what you describe is up to you, but let me explain to you your relationship to God:

There is no time, no place, no state where God is absent. (T-29.I.1)

God is Formless Being extending everywhere, always. God is All that is. Being All, God must also contain the idea of Its own opposite, but, since God is All, God cannot have an opposite. The-opposite-of-God, then, can never be more than an idea, and this idea is undone by God's All-encompassing nature as soon as it is thought.

However, as the opposite of the Eternal, not-God contains the idea of time. In the idea of time, it seems as though not-God began long ago and will be undone in some indefinite future. So, there is a part of Mind that thinks it is in time, and seems to be split between What it is (God) and the idea of not-God. (*A Course in Miracles* calls this split part of Mind the "son of God"). Since God is Eternal, Formless, and One, not-God manifests as a universe of time-bound, diverse form. The split mind, then, is projected into this universe of form as many minds, or personal selves. So, in every seemingly-separate mind, God still abides beyond the personal thought system.

God, then, is always in your mind, whether you are aware of God or not. You cannot have more or less God, or more or less of a connection to God, than any other mind, because all seemingly-separate minds are really just a projection of one split mind. You may have more or less of an *awareness* of God than others, but this has no effect on God at all, only on your state of mind. The more aware you are of God, the more you are at peace.

So, you do not need to attain, earn, vibrate, ascend, or have special codes to be aware of God, nor can you be "left behind", because you have never left God's Mind, as God has never left your mind. God is the Constant in your mind; everything else will fall away when you release it.

All that you need to do to be aware of God again is to invite God into your awareness, because God is always right here in your mind. To *keep* God in your awareness, you need to look at your blocks (guilt, feelings of unworthiness, attachments, etc.) to being aware of God so that you can release them. These blocks take the form of thoughts that you believe in. Some are conscious; some are unconscious; none of them are real.

So, you don't need anyone else to give you anything so that you can be at peace. All that you need is to turn inward to God, and to be willing to release your obstacles to being aware of God. It is that simple.

As for the testimonials: When you have a headache and you decide that you no longer want it, you take a painkiller to give form to your decision to no longer be in pain. In this case, some have decided to change their lives, and they give credit for the changes to the codes. However, codes will not bring lasting transformation to inner peace. That only comes from an awareness of Truth (God).

19. Ask: What comfort is there in the *Course*? (March 25, 2011)

"People are probably aghast at the idea of two Danish teenaged girls being held hostages by Somalian pirates. What is going to happen to this family? What would Jesus do if he were the father, unable to keep his daughters from being ravished in front of his eyes?... Does ACIM's teachings have anything that would be of comfort to the father of this Danish hostage family?

Also, the quake in Japan where hundreds died—if a student of ACIM were in that situation where all the familiar landmarks around him where being swept away how would he cope with it? And how do we onlookers safe... miles away look upon this tragedy? Surely, with pity, but what comfort is there in ACIM's assurance that all this is illusory and we are all safe (even the ones who drowned) in God's bosom?" – DH

I cannot answer for what Jesus would do in any situation, but as a student and teacher of *A Course in Miracles*, I can answer both of these questions from my own experience.

Until you experience God as Reality, the words in the *Course* are nice, but not truly comforting. You have to go beyond merely trying to intellectually grasp what the *Course* says to sincerely inviting God into your awareness, and practicing what the *Course* suggests in your daily life, for it to bring you comfort. This is what the Workbook is for.

After you have completed the year of lessons in the Workbook, if you want peace, you must still apply the daily practice to which it introduces you: Formally communing with God daily, turning within to God several times a day, calling on the Holy Spirit for guidance, and extending Love in your awareness to remember that you are Love. If you make these habits the focus of your life, then, in time, God will become a real experience for you, not just a nice idea that you've read in a book. You will then be able to turn away from the universe of form and inward to God and remember that only God is Real. This awareness *does* lead you to see that the universe of form is an illusion, so it *does* comfort.

Unless the father of those hostages or a person in the midst of the destruction caused by the earthquakes and tsunami in Japan has had an experience of God on which to call, it is unlikely that they will find real comfort in anything. The only reality that they will think that they know is the one appearing before the body's eyes. Certainly, you cannot tell someone who thinks that they are in the midst of horror that the horror is not real, unless they know God within themselves. Then, you can remind them to turn within and bring their mind back into the present with God as much as possible, to allow things in the world to unfold in the recognition that it is not their reality, and to trust that if they need to take action, they will know what to do when the time comes.

Whether you seem to be personally in the midst of a crisis or are merely affected by observing one, it is the same: Your peace is disturbed; you are in conflict. So, if you want inner peace, the response is the same in either case: Turn inward and invite Truth (God) into your awareness so that you can know that only the Truth is True.

20. Ask: Why does the *Course* emphasize many brothers? (April 1, 2011)

"...I am in Chapter 27, The Healing of the Dream. In section VII it discusses how to look upon our "brother" in the dream of our creating. If there is only one Son of God, then why is there emphasis on multiples (or dream figures?) of the Son as brothers when in reality there really are no brothers?" – RR

A Course in Miracles meets you where you are when it first comes into your awareness – experiencing yourself as a personal self in a body in a world with other personal selves in bodies (brothers). Simply reading in a book that there is only One Mind is not going to transform you to an awareness of One Mind. You must have experiences that shift your awareness to Truth. So, the *Course* teaches you to use your experience as a personal self with many "brothers" to undo this experience and become aware of One Mind. It does this with the Holy relationship.

The Holy relationship begins with one other, where you learn to observe your mind and to recognize how, with the personal thought system (ego), you look on this other through projections from a story that you have for a personal past for you. You then consciously choose to overlook these projections, and to come into the present with Truth (God, Christ, the one Son of God, Holy Spirit—all the same) instead. Once you have done this successfully with one other, you extend this practice into your relationships with all seeming-others that you seem to encounter. In time, after practicing this again and again, you become aware that what you thought was "you" and what you thought were your "brothers" are just passing projections of your mind, and that only the Truth is Constant and True.

So, the words and symbols in the *Course* meet you in your identification with a personal self with endless "brothers", but the *practice* of the *Course* takes you beyond the projection of a personal self and brothers to the actual awareness that there is only One Mind.

21. Ask: Overcoming resentment (April 8, 2011)

"I'd really like your Course *related advice on something. My husband and I have been separated for two years but are still living in the same house because we can't afford to live separately. We have a son with learning difficulties who has two years left of high school. I'd like to try to remain in the house for another two years until he is finished school. I really need to forgive my husband though, because I'm finding the situation, my almost constant reflection on our relationship (most of which was awful and abusive), and the circumstances that lead to our separation very difficult to get past. Birthdays and holidays are cruel reminders of the family that I wish we could have been. I am stewing in a pot of resentment and hate, although I have, a few times, been able to get to a place of peace and forgiveness, through following the* Course. *I find it difficult to make those times last though.*

One of my former Course *teachers remarked that I'm in the perfect place for learning forgiveness. Everyone else tells me I should get out. I need to finish my schooling before I leave, or else I'll have to forgo that, and for me, that's just not an option. Something inside me tells me that I AM in the right place for a major shift in forgiveness, only my ego seems to be fighting that with everything it has got. I'd really appreciate your wisdom here."* – Anonymous

First, because others will read this and there is much misunderstood about forgiveness, I want to make it clear that you never have to stay in a situation just to learn forgiveness, nor do you have to go looking for painful situations in which to put yourself just to learn forgiveness. True forgiveness recognizes that only God is Real, so if you hold onto or seek situations to forgive, you make them real to you, which is the opposite of forgiveness! Moreover, as you center your mind in Truth (God), you will find that forgiveness often manifests as you leaving behind unloving and painful situations, and if you insist on staying in or on making those situations, you are missing the lesson of forgiveness entirely.

True forgiveness, then, can only really be practiced in the authentic unfolding of the life that is natural to you. In your case, for your own practical reasons, you are choosing to stay, temporarily, in a situation that is uncomfortable. But, you are experiencing much more than just a situation that is not ideal. As you stated, your almost constant reflection on a painful past, and your stewing in resentment and hate, are keeping you in conflict.

If you want inner peace, then, you must address what is occurring in your mind. Inner peace is the result of an awareness of Truth, and nothing else. It does not come from an idealized situation in the world. In fact, it works the other way around: First you find peace of mind, then it manifests in your awareness as a peaceful and happy life for the body in the world.

Your obstacle to being aware of Truth, therefore to being at peace, is your attachment to the story that you have for yourself as a personal self in a body in a world. Right now, the specific aspects of that story that are disturbing your peace is the story that you have for your marriage, its ending, and your continued relationship with your husband. It is good that you have had some experiences of peace and forgiveness, because that means that you are in touch with the thought system in your mind that knows Truth. Now, you have to be willing to let go of the story that is keeping you from *maintaining* an awareness of Truth.

You can use your situation to stay in hell, or, as the other teacher suggested, as a rich opportunity to become more aware of Truth and find peace. Aside from communing with God daily and touching Truth again and again throughout the day, specifically, when thoughts about your husband, past or present, cause you to lose your peace, recognize that they are what are causing you conflict, and choose to put them aside. They do not represent the Truth in you, so they are not the way to peace. Come into the present and turn within to God, and remember that God within you is all that is true. As you touch God within, the specific thoughts that you need to release (forgive) the painful thoughts that you are having about your husband and your situation will come to you.

This is a process that takes time and patience. As you choose peace over conflict again and again you are going to bump into your obstacles to peace. These are thoughts of guilt; fear of God; your desire for, attachment to, or belief in the universe of form as your reality, etc. But, bringing these thoughts forward, looking at them, and releasing them is the only way to peace.

22. Ask: Overcoming addictions (April 15, 2011)

"Could you please address overcoming addictions from a Course *perspective…"* - Anonymous

As not-God, the personal thought system is the opposite of God in every way: It is the ideas of conflict, lack, dis-order, dis-cord, dis-ease, etc. given form. There is no such thing as a perfect personal experience. Some personal selves manifest diseases and disorders of the body; some manifest diseases and disorders of the personal thought system, like addiction, depression, psychosis, or other mental illnesses. All personal thought systems are at least neurotic, because guilt and fear are at their core. No personal thought system can ever be whole, because, as not-God, they are all the opposite of Wholeness.

Above all, remember that you have one problem, and that the problem has one solution. It is in this that the simplicity of salvation lies. It is because of this that it is guaranteed to work. – (W-80.5)

In Truth, you have no problems. All problems that you perceive, then, are problems of the personal self. But, you are not a personal self; it is only an erroneous idea in your mind. If you want peace, then, you must recognize that your identification with a personal self is your one obstacle to peace. Each seemingly-specific problem is only a symptom of your one problem of identifying with a personal self. So, if you want to be free of a problem, you must be free of its source: Your goal must be to let go of identifying with a personal self altogether. Then, healing of what seems like specific problems will follow.

True prayer must avoid the pitfall of asking to entreat. Ask, rather, to receive what is already given; to accept what is already there…The form of the answer, if given by God, will suit your need as you see it. This is merely an echo of the reply of His Voice. The real sound is always a song of thanksgiving and of Love…You cannot, then, ask for the echo. It is the song that is the gift. Along with it come the overtones, the harmonics, the echoes, but these are secondary. In true prayer you hear only the song...God answers only for eternity. But still all little answers are contained in this. (S-1.I.1-4)

You are mind; the personal self is a thought of yourself projected from your mind. As an *effect* of your mind, the content of its story unfolds from the content of your mind: When you identify with it, disorder is the content of your mind, and this manifests as disorder in the personal self and its "life" unfolding before you. But, when you choose to identify with Truth, then wholeness is the content of your mind, and this manifests as whatever the personal self needs in the universe of form—thoughts, books, people, doctors, programs, processes, opportunities, etc.—showing up to bring healing and peace to it and its life. When you center your mind in God, you will find that many disordered and diseased thoughts, traits, habits, etc. fall away naturally from the personal self with no effort on your part.

So, you overcome addiction the same way that you overcome any aspect of the personal experience: You return your mind to Truth again and again. As long as the personal thought system is in your mind, it will manifest disorder in the personal self and its story, but, in time, as Truth becomes more True to you, and you become less attached to a personal identity, discord will manifest in your awareness less and less, until, finally, the personal self and its universe of form will be completely gone from your mind, and only peace will be left.

23. Ask: Does God want to experience not-God? (April 22, 2011)

...a) I have been reading about "A Course in Miracles" and here is what it says:
We are all one with God. Sometime (which never happened, since time is an illusion), there was this tiny mad idea of separation (duality). From that tiny mad idea, we bought into a dream that we were separate from God, and that's basically how the universe as we know it was formed (the Big Bang). None of this is real, however, and when we wake up, we'll have an experience of oneness with God again; an infinite, eternal Oneness.
b) Another thought system, which I believed to understand so far, puts meaning and purpose behind this "illusion". God is said to have desired an experience of him/herself objectively, either as a fun game (hard to play Ludo by yourself), or according to some beliefs, as a means of continued evolution and development. Thus, The One sent out parts of him/her-self into an illusion of duality, so that The One could experience him/her-self as that which is "God yet not-God". We will always have a distinct identity (individuated), yet becoming more and more "Godlike" (removal of the false sense of separation) for the rest of time, and thus, God's completeness and perfection is constantly in a state of expansion, growth, and movement. There is no "endgame", just bigger, better, and more complex Oneness and movement within the Oneness.
Are these really the same or different? – MK

These two concepts are different, and they do conflict.

First, for clarity, I want to clarify what *A Course in Miracles* teaches.

God is All, and being All, God must contain even the idea of Its Own opposite. But, being All, God cannot have an opposite. So, the idea of God's opposite can never be more than a "tiny, mad idea". This idea, then, is undone by God's All-encompassing nature the moment that it is thought. (It's a lot like if I, as a person, think "I'm a frog." What happens to that thought?

Nothing. It's so obviously untrue that nothing happens. So it is with God and the idea of not-God: Nothing happens. God doesn't even have to make the effort to dismiss it, because it is so obviously not true).

However, since God is eternal, the idea of not-God contains the idea of time, and in the idea of time it seems as though not-God began a long ago and will be undone in some indefinite future. Since God is one, formless, and limitless, not-God projects into time a multitude of limited forms, some of which are direct projections of its own mind (personal thought systems, or egos). So, you don't really "buy into" the idea of not-God; you are really the one mind that wants to think that not-God is real. It seems as though there are many minds to which not-God is happening, but really there is only one mind that has taken many forms of not-God. If you want to be at peace, you must learn that you are the mind making the choice to see not-God as real; it is not being done to you. Otherwise, you will think that you are powerless to undo it.

You may consider the story of the Big Bang as the seeming-beginning of not-God or you may accept or make up any story that you want for time, because it is never anything more than a story. It has no reality. The past and the future are just ideas in your mind right now. You also do not have to wait for some future time to experience your oneness with God, because God is always in your mind. You can undo your belief in time right now by turning inward to God in what the *Course* calls the Holy Instant. In the Holy Instant, you step out of time and experience God in this moment. In fact, you must do this if you want to be at peace.

There are several fallacies in the second concept that you mention:

The idea that God has made the personal experience because It needs to have "fun", learn about Itself, evolve, develop, or grow implies that there is lack in God. But God is All, so complete. Moreover, since God is All, God is everywhere, always, so there is nowhere into which God could extend or grow.

The idea of distinct identities in God contradicts the idea of oneness. The term "oneness" means that God is the One Being that is; in God there is only God. Clearly, differentiation is the opposite of Oneness, and obviously so is the idea of a multiplicity. What would a multiplicity of One be but that very One?

There is also nothing to become more God-like. God within you is already whole and perfect. God is all that is real in your mind. Not-God is only an idea, and an idea that is meant to be the opposite of God, so, to be at peace, you do not "fix" this idea; you put it aside. The way to peace is not transforming, but releasing (forgiving) that which is not peace.

These fallacies arise as one tries to grasp God by squeezing God into the limitations that he or she knows through the personal thought system (ego). Of course, they are also trying to make the personal self real by implying that its attributes (lack, individuation, transformation) come from and are a part of God. Those who teach these ideas have either not yet experienced God, or, what is more common, they have experienced God, but then they allowed the personal thought system to decide what the experience meant; they didn't stay open and allow the experience to teach them. The Truth is very threatening to a mind that is very attached to a personal identity, and a split mind's first response is to try to integrate Truth into what it thinks that it already knows.

When you do have an experience of God, through direct Revelation, or through a miracle, it is never in or through the personal thought system. In fact, the experience teaches you that you are not a personal self, because it makes you aware of another part of your mind that can observe the personal self. This other part of your mind is so manifestly real that you realize that you are not a personal self, but a mind thinking of a personal self. Only then can you make the choice to put the personal thought system aside, and follow this other part of your mind, Which is Truth.

24. Ask: Healed in the presence of a teacher (April 29, 2011)

"I was recently healed of a persistent resentment while in the presence of a person who has dedicated her life to teaching ACIM. It was like a feeling of warmth and deep healing of that old wound/habit just by being in the presence of her love. What do you think happened? This was not intellectual; it seemed to be some sort of radiant experience. Of course in the Bible, it is mentioned that for example the woman was healed by touching Jesus's robe. What do you think happened? I have heard of folks being healed just by being in the presence of Teachers of Love of different religions. How would this be explained by ACIM? Thank you." – EH

You were healed because you chose healing. All forms of discord— physical, emotional, and/or intellectual—are of the personal self, which is a thought in your mind. So, all healing occurs in the mind of the one who thinks that discord is occurring. You were open to seeing peace and love in this teacher, which reflected the peace and love within you, and you were healed of a particular resentment

The Bible story that you mention is a metaphor for this: In a woman's desire to be healed, she touched the Christ within (love, peace), embodied by Jesus in the story, and was healed.

25. Ask: Isn't the "dream" part of God, too? (May 6, 2011)

"a) I know I'm a part of God. Yet I cannot deny that there is a body which is my vehicle in this life. So there must be a purpose or reason for which this energy from God manifested in this form (my body, mind, spirit in this lifetime). I need to perform a "role" in this life to fulfill that purpose. Why do I need to perform a "role" in this dream/illusion we're living in?
b) Secondly I'm a part of God (drop in the ocean) and God (the ocean) is all there is anyway, so everything including my body, mind (including the idea of separation that leads the mind to create the sense of personal self or ego), spirit - these all are part of God as well. So are all illusions and dreams, part of God - aren't they? Because God is all there is. So why do we need to wake up from the dream or illusion as that is also part of God?" – MK

If, as a person, I think, "I am a frog", that idea is not a *part* of me; it is just an idea that is over the instant that I think it because it is so manifestly not true.

So it is with God and the idea of not-God: Because God is All, God's Mind contains the idea of It's Own opposite (the universe of form and all thoughts about it). Yet, being All, God cannot have an opposite. The opposite-of-God can never be more than an idea, and it is so manifestly not true, that, to God, it is done the instant that it is thought. It is only within the idea of not-God that not-God seems to be real.

There is no intention behind the idea of not-God; just like God, it merely *is*— or would be if it could be at all! It has no reality, so it has no purpose or meaning, except what the mind thinking about it wants to give to it. This is why *A Course in Miracles* emphasizes the importance of the Holy Instant. In the Holy Instant, you turn inward, away from the universe of form, and touch God, and you realize that God is What is Real, and the universe of form, and your thoughts about it, are nothing. The more that you practice the Holy Instant, the more that the Reality of God takes hold in your awareness and the unreality of the universe of form becomes obvious.

You are indeed a part of God, but you are not a personal self in a body in a world. Like God, *you are mind*, and, for now, you think that you are a personal self in a body in a world. Your belief in and attachment to this idea is the source of your conflict. You do not "have to" wake up from this illusion, unless you want inner peace. Becoming aware of the Truth (God) within you, then, is something that you do because you love yourself and want to be at peace, and for no other reason.

So, you do not "have to" give a purpose or role to the personal self with which you identify, unless you want to. The *Course* gives you the purpose of forgiving, because it recognizes that when you come to it you will be almost wholly identified with a personal self, and will feel a need for one. As always, the Holy Spirit uses ideas in not-God (in this case, a desire for a purpose) to lead you out of conflict and into peace. As you practice your purpose of forgiving, which means getting in touch with God within and letting go of your belief in and attachment to the universe of form, you will find the personal self with which you identify is inspired to play different roles in the world over time until you realize that you are mind, not a personal self. Then, you will stop thinking in terms of purposes and roles, but only in terms of maintaining the peace of your mind. For a while, the personal self will seem to continue on, but you will recognize that it is not you, only a thought in your mind that requires little attention, because, as an effect of your mind, its needs are met as a manifestation of your awareness of peace.

26. Ask: Does it take years to learn the *Course*? (May 13, 2018)

"... I am 64 years old, have melanoma and have just started ACIM *and am on lesson 25...I have read others that say that it takes years to learn the* Course *and I may not have that. I know that nobody knows how long they will live but my case seems to be different than say a 25 year old. Do you have any comments about that?"* – DH

A Course in Miracles is a self-study course for inner peace. Inner peace is the result of an awareness of Truth (God) as Truth, which you may have had before you picked up the *Course*, or which may have begun for you when you picked up the *Course*. In my own experience, and through my own observations of others, it does seem to take at least 20 years after first becoming aware of Truth for one to reach *comprehensive* peace, and longer still for one to reach *complete* peace, if this is their goal. In any case, all students of the *Course* begin to have a more peaceful experience as soon as they start seriously studying it, and their peace increases as they go along.

I'm going to make an assumption here, which is always a tricky thing, but I think this is what I am reading in your question: You fear that you must attain something that the *Course* offers – perhaps peace - before the personal self seems to die or there will be unpleasant consequences for you after the personal self seems to die. There is a false belief behind this thought, and it is that you are a personal self, and that the personal self "continues on" after this "life". This idea is just the personal thought system's (ego's) way of making you believe that it is eternal. But it is not; it is only a passing thought.

"The ego is nothing more than a part of your belief about yourself. Your other life has continued without interruption, and has been and always will be totally unaffected by your attempts to dissociate it." – (T-4.VI.1)

God is all that is real in your mind. God is completely untouched by not-God (the universe of form, including personal selves) in your mind. God has no beginning or ending: It is here in your mind before you thought of the personal self, It is here as you think of the personal self, and It will still be here when the personal self falls away. What is eternal in your mind is not personal or individual; It is Universal.

"Nothing real can be threatened. Nothing unreal exists. Herein lies the peace of God." – (T-Intro.2)

God is unchanged and unchanging; your belief in and attachment to the universe of form is only an obstacle to your awareness of this, that is all. So, you "need do nothing"; you are already whole and perfect in God.

You might ask why you would bother with something like the *Course*, which helps you to undo your obstacles to being aware of God, so leads to peace, if you don't *have to* do it because it does nothing real. There can be only one reason: Because you love yourself, you want inner peace.

27. Why didn't forgiving work? (May 20, 2011)

"I feel angry at "Joe" and I'm attacking him in my mind. Then, I remember to choose again and follow ACIM steps of forgiveness. First, I recognize my anger or attack thoughts. Then I recall that ideas leave not their source e.g. my rage is actually a projection of my belief that I'm separate from God and take responsibility. Third and last step, I ask the Holy Spirit to take it from here by healing a grain of my mind. Twenty minutes later I feel angry at Joe again about the same issue. Did forgiveness fail to work? Could it be that since my anger is really about my own guilt over thinking God is still separate, that it's irrelevant whether I project onto Joe a 1000x or a 100 different people 10x, it's all the same. Each attack thought episode is an opportunity to "bring home" to my mind projected attacks and give them over to the Holy Spirit. Or am I just making excuses for Course forgiveness that really doesn't work and I'm just deluding myself? If I'm not kidding myself and these described decisions are in line with ACIM forgiveness, why can't I forgive "my" whole personal self world by saying "I withdraw all projected guilt and turn it over to the Holy Spirit" at once and experience immediate and lasting peace? Can you comment on this whole scenario please?"- J

What you are experiencing is very common for new, practicing students of *A Course in Miracles*. Let's look at each of the issues that you bring up:

1. It is good that you stop to recognize that you are experiencing anger and attack thoughts, and that these, not what another says or does, are the source of your rage. But, it takes a long time to learn to generalize and really understand that the real source of your anger comes from deeply-rooted guilt and fear over a belief that you have separated from God. At first, it is best to focus on only what the personal thought system (ego) is telling you right now is the justification for

anger. Those thoughts will tie into the story that it has for you as a personal self. In fact, their purpose is really just to reinforce your identification with a personal self. The deeper thoughts about guilt from separating from God will come up later, after you have worked through layers of false beliefs about yourself as a personal self.

2. When you give something to the Holy Spirit, what you are really saying is that you are turning away from the personal thought system, and turning your mind to the thought system in your mind that comes from Truth. For this to really work for you, the Holy Spirit has to be a real experience for you, not just a nice idea. Only from the Holy Spirit within you can you look on the personal thought system's story for you with detachment.

3. True forgiveness means recognizing that only God is real. Until the Holy Spirit is real to you, you will not be able to let go of (forgive) the personal thought system's story for you, because you will think that it is your identity. So, if anger returns, this indicates that you have not really let go of (forgiven) an idea that you have about yourself, either because God is not yet a real experience for you, or because you do not want to let go of the personal story that you have for yourself. Before you can truly forgive, you will have to develop enough of an awareness of God to be willing to release your attachment to a personal story. This may mean working through layers of fear of God first. Then, when God is real to you, forgiveness will happen naturally.

4. Yes, all projections of guilt and anger are really the same, whether they are over the same person or situation or over many different people or situations, because at the core they come from your guilt and fear over the belief that you have separated from God. And, yes, each episode of unforgiving is an opportunity to turn your mind to your True thought system, the Holy Spirit.

5. The *Course's* method of forgiving does work, and you are not deluding yourself; you probably just do not yet experience God as real, or trust God enough yet, to be willing to let go of the personal story that you have for yourself. You are never really attached to a particular incident of unforgiving thoughts, but to the story about yourself that they support. So, instead of struggling to forgive, work instead on building your awareness of God first.

6. When God is real to you and not just a nice idea, and you are truly willing to let go of the personal identity and its world, then you will indeed let go of it all, all at once, and have lasting peace. You can prepare for that moment by becoming aware of God, working through your guilt toward and fear of God, and rooting out of your mind all of the ways that you are attached to a personal identity. Peace first comes and goes, then comes to stay, then comes to be all that you experience.

28. Ask: How does one get to the point of experiencing God and peace? (May 27, 2011)

"...(see the last paragraph for May 20, 2011), you advise making God real to oneself. I have been a student of the Course *since 1992. I still am not able to "make God real" to me, or for that matter, Jesus. On the other hand, I do realize that I am not truly willing to let go of my personal story and I am experiencing fear and anger much of the time, especially at my husband of 40 years. Periods of peace are now less frequent than before I began the* Course. *How does one get to the point of experiencing God and Peace?"* – PM

Actually, I do not advise *making* God real to you, but allowing God into your awareness. This is done simply by being willing to have God come into your awareness, and shows up either as a direct Revelation of God (very rare among individual minds, and within an individual life) or a miracle (very common, and necessary to become aware of God).

(It is not necessary for Jesus to be real to you for you to have inner peace. The story of Jesus is simply a metaphor for spiritual awakening, and it is no more real than any other personal story. But, some find the idea of "God" or "Christ" or "Holy Spirit" too abstract and need a concrete form to think about, and "Jesus" is a symbol offered for them to use).

A miracle can show up as a sudden shift in your internal experience toward peace or joy, or as an awareness of wholeness, regardless, or in spite of, what is appearing in the world. It can also be guidance from the Holy Spirit; an inspired answer to a question, spiritual or practical; a sudden insight into Truth; an awareness of Oneness with what seems like another; or an unseen experience of comfort in a time of crisis or despair.

Miracles have a cumulative effect. The more you experience miracles, the more God becomes a real Presence in your life, the more you trust God, so the more you have inner peace.

It is not uncommon for students to feel like they experience less peace after they start studying the *Course*. Inner peace is the result of being aware of God, and when you make the conscious choice to have inner peace, you run into your obstacles to being aware of God, therefore, to being at peace. These obstacles are the guilt and fear inherent in the personal thought system (ego), which comes from the belief that you have attacked God and will be punished; your attachment to a personal identity, which the personal thought system tells you offers you something more than Everything; and your projections of personal traits (anger, inconsistency, untrustworthiness, etc.) onto God.

So, what you need to do to allow God into your awareness is to look at the fearful thoughts that come up when you attempt to commune with God, to call on the Holy Spirit, or to extend Love. These thoughts represent beliefs that block your willingness to allow yourself to experience God. Often, you simply need to bring these beliefs to light for their obvious falsity to become apparent to you and to be released. Some beliefs, however, you will need to address again and again, reminding yourself, for example, that God is not an authoritarian being that you have to appease through righteous behavior, but the One Being that simply *is*. The belief in guilt takes many insidious, and often subtle, forms, but, as you work through many layers of this false belief, you will become more and more willing to trust God and to allow It into your experience, and peace will naturally follow.

29. Ask: Probing questions about God... (June 3, 2011)

"Lesson 65 of ACIM *- Workbook for students says: "God gives only happiness, therefore, my function is happiness." Speaking for myself, after witnessing the March 11th, 2011 Japan's massive 9.0 magnitude earthquake followed by 30 feet high tsunami... I am wondering just how can people be happy and fulfill their goals and function of happiness under these devastating situations? I've been pondering on these probing questions while practicing the daily lessons of the* Course.
Does God really love us?
Does God have a different plan of survival for us?
Does God exist?
Does God have a different Will than what we will for us?
Does God have nothing to do with what we will in life?
Does God not want us to make this world a better place to live?

Does God have nothing to do with such disasters?
Can you please explain for me?" – JJ

I addressed the specific issue of the earthquake and tsunami in Japan in an earlier article, and that answer ties into the answers for your other questions. You may wish to read it after you read these answers at (#19).

1. God is the One Being that *is*; God is Reality. God is Love, and in God, there is only God, so God's Love is never *directed toward*, but simply *is*. So, the Truth in you, Which is God, is Love. Love is your natural state of being. The idea of yourself as a personal self in a body in a world is the misidentification in your mind that is an obstacle to your awareness that you are God's Love; it does not come from God. You only have to be willing to put this idea aside, even for only a moment, for you to become aware of God's Love within you.
2. God has no plan of survival for you, because God only knows God in you, and, in God, you have no beginning and no ending, so you have no need for "survival". The personal self, being only an idea, also has no need for a plan for survival, though, when you identify with it, you think that you do. Because the personal "life" that you perceive is an effect of your mind, when you center your mind in Truth (God), what you need to do or know to take care of the personal self will come into your awareness as an effect of your awareness of Truth. So, while God does not take care of the personal self, your awareness of God does.
3. If by the word "God" you mean an experience of wholeness, then, yes, God exists. God is the Truth within you, and it is an experience of boundless love, peace, and joy. But, if by "God" you mean an authoritarian being that made the world and that you have to appease through righteous behavior or be punished, then, no, that god does not exist.
4. Because God is the Truth in you, your will is not separate from God's Will, but, when you identify as a personal self in a body in a world, you think that you have a will that is separate from God's Will. This is your source of conflict.
5. If by "life" you mean the personal life, then God does not have anything to do with what you want for that life (it's not really appropriate to use the word "will" for the personal life, because it is only a faulty desire; you can never make it real). But, again, your *awareness* of God within you has an effect on the personal life in your awareness, which is itself only an effect of your mind. All that you have to do is attend to your awareness of God, which will result in inner peace, and the personal self's life in the world will manifest peacefully.
6. God does not know of the world, so it is irrelevant to God whether or not you work at making the world a better place. But doing so will be an obstacle to peace for you, because you will be reinforcing the world as real in your mind, as well as reinforcing in your mind the idea that the world causes your experience of peace or conflict. Inner peace is the result of being aware of God within you, and nothing else. This is why you can be at peace in the midst of a hellish, chaotic world.
7. God is formless being, so God has nothing at all to do with the universe of form, or anything that happens in it, like natural disasters in the world. Natural disasters occur according to the "laws" of the universe of form (in this case, plates moving over the surface of the planet); they are not personal. Even though the universe of form is the idea of the opposite of God, everything in the universe of form has no meaning in itself. So, you choose how you want to look at anything that happens in the world. You can use appearances of discord, like natural disasters, to

remain in conflict by giving them meaning, or you can use them as reminders to turn within to God and remember that only God is real.

30. Ask: Why do you need your learning most in upsetting situations? (June 10, 2011)

"As a student of the Course, *I've learned that you'll need your learning the most in situations that appear to be upsetting rather than in those that are already calm and quiet. Why is that? Can you explain for me?"* - JJ

It's not that you *need* your learning only when confronted with discordant appearances, but, perhaps, that you *choose to use* your learning only when confronted with discordant appearances.

The only way to lasting inner peace is through an awareness of Truth (God), but when one first becomes aware of Truth and experiences peace, they are not likely to accept yet that this is the *only* way to lasting peace. So, at first, when you are in pain, you are likely to turn to Truth only after you have exhausted all of the other ways that you have sought to relieve yourself. Then, when Truth brings you the relief that you want, you let It slip from your mind until you find yourself in pain again. In other words, at first, you use an awareness of Truth as a band-aid, rather than as the whole way to peace.

But, in time, it will dawn on you that really only an awareness of Truth brings you the peace that you seek, so you will call on It sooner rather than later when you find yourself confronted with an obstacle to peace (guilt, fear, attachment, projection). And, finally, it will one day occur to you that you do not have to wait for discord to bring Truth to mind; you will want to be aware of It as much as possible to stay in peace. Your commitment to inner peace will have deepened, and your whole life will be about maintaining inner peace. You will return your mind to Truth again and again throughout the day, and you will turn to It as soon as possible when an obstacle to peace arises in your mind. At this stage, there will be no distinction for you between appearances that once would have upset you and appearances that are calm and quiet, because you will choose to be always aware of Truth and at peace within.

31. Ask: The personal story, victimhood, and roles... (June 17, 2011)

"Can you please explain further these comments you made?
What do you mean by "victimhood"?
What do mean that I am attached to a role I play?
What is my personal story?
I have to look at the story I have about myself. What does that mean?" - JJ

The personal thought system (ego) in your mind has a story for you. *A Course in Miracles* refers to this as your individual or personal past. This story begins with your birth into the world and includes your childhood, adolescence, etc., all the way up to now. This is your "personal story" and it is not an obstacle to peace in itself but functions as one when you identify with and are attached to it because it is not reality.

In Reality you are One with God, so you are formless being. But you have an idea in your mind of a form (body) in a universe of form. It seems like this idea began at the "birth" of the body, but really it is just an idea in your mind right now. In itself this idea is not an obstacle to peace. You can choose to simply observe it as you rest in peace within. When you do so its story will unfold harmoniously as an effect of your peaceful mind. But when you identify with this idea your mind is in conflict because it is not Truth. Your mis-identification with the personal self then manifests as a discordant story for the personal self.

You know that you identify with and are attached to a personal story when you feel that it defines you and that you have to defend it. When you identify with it you feel under attack by others, the world, and sometimes even your own "nature". In other words, you are an innocent "victim" surrounded by cruelty and you are powerless. You are hurt easily and you take everything personally. You see everything that happens around you, like neutral events and other people's actions and words, as being about you.

The personal identity is one of roles: victim, savior, parent, professional, artist, intellectual, etc. Some roles, like "parent", are facts and are not obstacles to peace unless you so define yourself by them that you cannot let them go. Some roles, like "victim", are interpretations that always function as obstacles to peace because they are the result of you projecting your own thoughts onto others.

The personal thought system projects from its personal story into the present to perpetuate the roles that it has assigned to you. For example, let's say that your personal story is that your father left your family when you were a child, leaving your mother to struggle to support you and your siblings. You have grown up thinking of yourself as a victim of abandonment. You view your relationships with others through this filter. You expect abandonment and interpret others' actions through this expectation. You may also be attracted to others who are likely to abandon you so that you can perpetuate the victim role.

You will also take on other identities and roles from these earlier parts of your story. You were poor as a child, so your story may be that you feel destined to be poor. Or maybe you have risen above poverty through hard work and see yourself as a "survivor". Perhaps you were the eldest child and because you had to take on more responsibility as a child, as an adult you still see yourself as the one who has to take responsibility for others. Your reaction to your childhood story could also be the other way: Because you took on more responsibility as a child you do not want to take on any now.

Inner peace is the result of being aware of the Truth (God) within you. When you first invite Truth into your awareness you experience a magnificent peace, but you soon find that it is hard for you to maintain an awareness of Truth and to stay at peace. The reason is your belief in and attachment to your personal story for yourself. So when your peace is disturbed you must look at this story and all of your conscious and unconscious beliefs in and attachment to it so that you can recognize how this affects you now. As the Truth becomes more real to you, you will find that you can let go of this story because you have Something with which to replace it. In time you will simply rest in Truth within and let the personal story unfold in front of you, without judgment on it or attachment to it. You will recognize that it is not you, but only an idea in your mind.

32. What is meant by "extend love"? (June 24, 2011)

"I wonder exactly what is meant by "extend love" or how one extends love. Is it a loving intention toward the person, or a wish for them, or what? Can you give an example?" – JO

"Extending love" means replacing unloving thoughts in your mind with the awareness of Love in your mind. For example, your peace of mind is disturbed while watching something on television. Your peace is gone because you believe that what you see is reality. You extend Love in this situation by turning inward to Truth (God), feeling Love's Presence within you, and remembering that It, not the images appearing, is What is Real.

It may take you a while to accept that only your own thoughts cause you pain. So at first you may feel that you need to extend Love "out there" to the images that seem to be causing you pain. Or you may extend Love to another who is sharing their painful story with you. You can do this by imagining the situation or the person in a Loving Light. Or you may use some other image to symbolize Truth. The idea is to replace what you are seeing or hearing with an image or idea that reminds that only the Truth is True. In time this practice will make you aware that the source of your pain is not the image that you are seeing or the story that you are hearing. Only your own thoughts can disturb your peace of mind. So if you want to be at peace you must extend Love in your awareness, which means in your mind.

33. Ask: Beauty and Ugliness: How did this amazing design come about? (July 1, 2011)

"...Having accepted (maybe as blind faith) that this material world in which we 'dream' ourselves is an illusion, I find myself looking with wonder at the natural world around me, here in the peaceful country close to the sea. Everything seems miraculous...I could go on marveling for pages and only touch the edges of the wonder. But then I tell myself this is all illusion. That God 'doesn't know about it'. So how did all this amazing design come about?...I had to visit the nearest city. As the bus took me further and further into the busy streets, the grubby buildings, the crowds blind to each other as they rushed in and out of shops-the illusion idea wasn't hard to grasp..." - MDT

The universe of form is projected by what *A Course in Miracles* calls the *son of God.* This is the part of Mind that contains the idea of not-God (illusion/ego). It is split between God and the idea not-God. Your seemingly-individual mind is made in the image of this split mind. When you see beauty and ugliness in this projection you see the duality of your split mind. Keep in mind that other seemingly-individual minds will see the projection of form differently. For example, a city lover may see the city as beautiful and the countryside as tedious.

You are experiencing the personal thought system's (ego's) equating of what it values with "reality". What it judges as "good" or "beautiful" or "right" it says is real. What it judges as "bad" or "ugly" or "wrong" it says is unreal. This is its attempt to spiritualize not-God.

Reality (God) is formless being extending without limit. It is an experience of wholeness and boundless love, peace, and joy. When you hold onto any of the universe of form as real you hold onto an obstacle to being fully aware of God. This makes it an obstacle to complete peace for you.

The *Course* does not ask you for "blind faith". You do not have to pretend to accept what you clearly do not experience as true. That is lying to yourself, which is not conducive to inner peace. The *Course* teaches you to invite the Holy Spirit into your awareness so that you can learn What is True and what is not true. When you are aware of God as Truth you are not attached to what the personal thought system judges as beautiful and you are not disturbed by what it judges as ugly. You recognize that only God is eternal and that all form passes. This is beautiful indeed!

34. Ask: Why is the Course so Christian? (July 8, 2011)

"...I've found that the Course's *context has been a problem for students who have non-Christian beliefs (Muslims, Hindus etc). Why does a universal message such as* A Course in Miracles *have to come in a specific religious framework? And, does that not inevitably breed separation and at the same time denying the universally of specific religion?*
Indeed, the Christian language of A Course in Miracles, *not to mention the presence of Jesus throughout the material, can pose a great challenge for students of other cultures. If my personal-self is looking for a way to invalidate the material or throw up obstacles, then Jesus and Christian can be helpful allies in this battle against the Truth (God).*
On the other hand, asking for the Holy Spirit for help can introduce yet another challenge for non-Christian readers. Speaking for myself, I miss the rituals I used to practice my religious upbringings. The Course *seems to be directed more toward a Western audience than other cultures. Its language, cultural expressions, and poetic style speak to a reader comfortable within Western Culture. Can you please explain this in plain language."* - J

'This is a manual for a special curriculum, intended for teachers of a special form of the universal course. There are many thousands of other forms, all with the same outcome.' (M-1.4)

Even though *A Course in Miracle's* message is universal it points out in the quote above that it is only one of many thousands of forms that teach this message. When you want inner peace the means for your attaining it will come into your awareness. The *Course* has come into your awareness. Perhaps it has done so because despite your background and culture it is the way for you. Perhaps it has come into your awareness to show you that it is not the way for you. Sometimes we learn our way through contrast.

The *Course* is clearly intended for a western Christian audience, or at least for those familiar with western Christian thinking. (I, too, am not and have never been Christian. But I am certainly western and familiar with Christian ideas). However, it is important to note that it undoes traditional western Christian thinking. It does this by redefining familiar everyday and religious terms. For example, *Father* in the *Course* means *whole* and *son* means *part of the whole. Creation* does not refer to the universe of form being brought into being but to God's limitless extension of God. Some see it as the "correction" for the fearful thinking of traditional Christianity. And when you actually strip it down to its essentials the *Course's* ontology is actually closer to eastern religious thought. For example, *God* in the *Course* is not an authoritarian being but formless, limitless being. God is an experience of bliss. So just as you struggle with the *Course* because you are not a western Christian I can assure you that many western Christian's also struggle with it!

Keep in mind that the *Course* is intended for study not for just a quick read-through. It does what it teaches. It uses what you (or someone used to western Christian thinking) are familiar with to undo (forgive) your belief and attachment to it.

The *Course's* form does not "inevitably" breed separation unless you read it with the personal thought system (ego). With the personal thought system everything "inevitably" breeds separation! When you don't want what the *Course* teaches the personal thought system will happily supply you with all of the obstacles that it can find. But if you do want it you will be willing to overlook the form of the *Course* to learn its universal message.

Like all form spiritual teachings are neutral in themselves. Books are just collections of words. Words are symbols and symbols can mean what you want them to mean. This is why there are so many interpretations of every spiritual teaching. Read them with the personal thought system and they reinforce guilt and fear. But read anything with the Holy Spirit (the Truth in your mind) and It will use it to lead you back to peace. There is no one perfect form of teaching, but the Perfect Teacher is always within you. For It to come into your awareness all that you have to do is be willing for It to do so.

35. Ask: Why am I bothered when I am not liked? (July 15, 2011)

"I've recently joined a community action group and met some new people. To make a long story short, I got the impression that one of the young women really does not like me. I know it shouldn't bother me, but it does. Obviously, there's something in my mind that still believes strongly in the idea of being liked. How can I heal this tendency?" – SD

When you want something from others you make them your god. You tell yourself that they are the source of your well-being. If you get from them what you want (in this case, being liked) you are at peace. If you do not get from them what you want you are shattered. *A Course in Miracles* shows us that this is how the personal thought system thinks. "You are my source…"

This woman may or may not like you. You don't really know what is going on in her mind. But it does not matter. You see what seems like her dislike of you and that is very real to you because it reinforces thoughts that are already in your mind. If she seemed to like you (as many there probably did) you wouldn't even notice.

Of course, all personal selves are sometimes likeable and sometimes unlikeable. And the designations "likeable" and "unlikeable" are arbitrary anyway. What one finds likeable another may find unlikeable. And what one finds likeable they sometimes find unlikeable. And so forth. The problem for you is that it matters to you that the personal self with which you identify is sometimes unlikable. There are so many specifics that could be going on here. For example, do you have a reason for not liking yourself that overrides all that you do like about yourself? Did you come from a gregarious family in which it was a "sin" to be unlikeable? Do you equate not being liked with being abandoned? Do you equate not being likeable with not being lovable? Do you feel that if you are not a "good person" and liked by all God will not love you? Is it simply that you want to give others power over you because you are too afraid to claim your own power? Do you prefer to be a victim? There are many possible unconscious thoughts behind your need to be liked.

To find out what is going on in your mind bring this issue to the Holy Spirit. When you are truly willing to look at it simply ask the Holy Spirit to help you to uncover the thoughts that lead you to be bothered when you are not liked. Then let this go and leave your mind open. You will become aware of the answer when you are ready to hear it.

36. Ask: What is one's relationship to a profound spiritual experience? (July 22, 2011)

"…In '84 I had an experience that has become central to my understanding of oneness. …I awoke… to discover that my body was visibly radiant with a golden energy, the heart being the locus. My initial concern was replaced with awe and a feeling of joyful exultation. I moved my attention from my body to discover that everything without exception (animate and inanimate)

was radiant with this golden energy. I went outside...all was on fire with this golden light that, far from being a soft ephemeral glow, crackled with the intensity of a million volts. Emotionally I was overtaken with an awesome feeling of love and connectedness. After I came to normal consciousness, basking in the afterglow of this amazing experience, this instructive phrase was 'given' to me (by the Holy Spirit?): **Rest/abide as That I AM in, as, and through all arising.** *To this day, for me, this is the epitome of spiritual wisdom and a touchstone for truth.*
...Now, for the question: What do you make of this? Is the Golden Fire/Light I witnessed God, The Eternal, Pure Consciousness, Oneness, All That Is, etc.? Or is the Fire/Light a primordial creation of Mind, (son of God?), forming the energetic matrix within which form appears to manifest?

I guess, really my heart's question boils down to: What is the right relationship to an experience of this sort? Can, rightfully, anything at all be inferred or "known" by this? Is it merely another pointer, a metaphor, given by Spirit hinting at Truth?" – ES

It sounds like you had an experience that was similar to what Helen Schucman experienced in her holy relationship with Bill Thetford. In *A Course in Miracles* it refers to her seeing "Great Rays" instead of a body. You continued to see form as well as something that could be called "Great Rays", but the lesson is the same. There is another way of seeing.

A revelation is a direct experience of God, Which is formless and imageless. What you experienced was a miracle. It was a shift in perception away from separation toward Oneness. The visual image of light touching everything was your mind's metaphor for the Oneness that you were experiencing. Everything that you perceive is in your mind. God is everywhere because God is in your mind. You were also told this by, yes, the Holy Spirit.

One purpose of miracles is to demonstrate that the way that you perceive something is not fixed. It can be changed. You had a very dramatic experience of seeing the universe of form transformed, not from anything outside of you, but from within your own mind. But far, far more important than anything that you saw was what you experienced. Form and images will eventually fade from your mind, but your joyful experience of Oneness is eternal. So, as well as these other lessons, you learned that God is a real experience, not just a nice idea.

37. Ask: Is getting still and present the answer? (July 29, 2011)

"...I would like to know more about acting/behaving in this world. Even when I am able to become still, to get present, to let spirit show me the truth (and/or the right thing to do or say), I still operate within this dream. I still have physical and emotional struggles, I still have friends and family in crisis, and that's just what's right in front of me ... there's a "world" out there full of suffering. I "know" that this is ego perception, that it's not real, even if I haven't awakened from the dream. But since I haven't ...I guess I don't get present too often. Is that "the answer"? That all we can do is get still, listen to spirit for guidance, and practice true forgiveness? Is that what's meant by 'you need do nothing?'" - NK

Yes, "I need do nothing" is about practicing what *A Course in Miracles* calls the *holy instant*. This means bringing your mind into the present, turning it within, and opening it to God. In the holy instant you realize that you are already home in God so you "need do nothing" for salvation. Truth (God) is untouched by anything that seems to happen in the universe of form.

The more that you practice the holy instant the more that you experience God as reality and the universe of form fades into the background of your attention.

The personal self, including its body, is just an idea. You are the mind that thinks about it. As mind you are formless being. So when you identify with a personal self you make a mistake in identification. You are in conflict because of this and you search for peace through the personal self's "life". You believe that the world around the body causes your feelings of conflict. So you feel that you have to control or manipulate the world because your state of mind goes up and down with whether or not things in the world go the way that the personal thought system in your mind (ego) wants them to go.

But when you are aware that you are mind then you attend only to your state of mind. You maintain your peace by communing with Truth every day and returning your mind to Truth throughout the day. When you are not at peace you look for your obstacles to peace, which you understand are thoughts in your mind. You bring them to Truth (Holy Spirit) to undo them. You understand that the personal self is not you but is only an effect of your mind. You merely observe it and its world from the peaceful center of your mind. You let its "life" unfold without judgment. And as an expression or your peaceful mind the personal self's life unfolds harmoniously. When there is a decision to be made about the personal self you rest in Truth knowing that the answer will come when you need it. You simply know how to direct the personal self for its well-being.

Since behavior follows thought the behavior of the personal self in your awareness follows the thought system that you choose. As an effect of your mind, though, behavior is meaningless to inner peace. Inner peace comes only from an awareness of Truth. And behavior can look the same whether you are resting in Truth or identifying with a personal self. This is why if you want inner peace it makes no sense to attend to behavior. If you want inner peace then, yes, you want to attend only to the still, quiet Truth in your mind.

38. Ask: How do you know when boundaries come from love or fear? (August 5, 2011)

"I have been studying spiritual paths for several years now and there is one question that nags me most often. How do I distinguish between setting healthy boundaries for what I think I need and setting boundaries out of fear instead of love? I understand when it comes to things like not accepting physical abuse. My struggle comes from less obvious situations. For example, my ex, after 2 years of dating, decided she wanted to be able to date other people. I knew that what I wanted was a monogamous commitment from a partner, but I attempted to stay in the relationship because I loved her and I thought not being willing to open the relationship to include others was fear based. Eventually, I decided that, fear based or not, it wasn't what I wanted and lovingly exited the relationship. I still don't know, however, if this was loving or fear based boundary setting. Any insights you have would be greatly appreciated." - VLB

A fear-based decision for the personal self means one that comes from the personal thought system (ego). Fear indicates that you feel guilty. Guilt manifests as anger, defensiveness, and blame. When you come from fear there is a lot of hand-wringing, drama, and finger-pointing. Sometimes the finger is pointing outward (projection) and sometimes it is inward. Either way you believe that guilt is real.

A love-based decision for the personal self is one that comes from your True thought system (Christ/Holy Spirit). So it begins with your recognition that you are whole. You understand that you do not need something or someone outside of you to make you whole. You accept all personal selves without judgment. You are aware that personal values are not "bad" or "wrong" just because they are different. This does not mean, however, that you want to be around others if they are dysfunctional or that you have to change your values to fit theirs. You set healthy boundaries so that others' dysfunction does not disrupt your life and you let others go with love when your values do not mesh.

In the example that you gave it sounds like you came from love not from fear. You even went so far as to stretch your own boundaries in a relationship to see if they would change. In the process you found that they did not. You truly do value what you thought you valued. So you loved both yourself and the other by letting her go.

39. What is God's name? (August 12, 2011)

*"Lesson # 183 of the workbook for students for ACIM call upon God's Name, and to repeat HIS Name while sitting silently. My question to you is this: DO I NEED TO HAVE A NAME OF GOD TO DO THIS LESSON? Being raised in the Eastern culture, I know that Muslims call God's Name by **Allah**, Hindus call God's Name by **Bagwan** and in the West, I've heard some Christians call God's Name by **Jehovah**…I often call God's Name by **Love** because it has all the attributes of what **God Is**…Can you please share your thoughts about calling upon God's Name?"* – JJ

No, you do not have to have a name for God to do Lesson 183 because God does not have a name. The word *God* is the label given in *A Course in Miracles* to the experience of formless being. This experience is boundless love and peace and joy. What this lesson means to bring into focus for you is that God's being is your being. So you can use the word *God* for this lesson or you can use any other word that evokes the experience of God, as the word *love* does for you. Just be sure that you understand that what you are calling upon is the Truth in you, not some separate being with power over you.

40. Ask: Is prayer for physical things based on fear? (August 19, 2011)

"Is prayer for physical things based on fear? I'm a fifty year old man with a very struggling business. I have been studying the Course *for about nineteen months now with regular meditations. I'm in debt that I accumulated over the years and they have gone to such an extent that I am now receiving threats. I normally pray for love and peace but deep down there is strong yearnings to pray for money and good fortune for my business so that I can pay these people, get my business in shape and focus on my spiritual path. Is prayer for money intervention in order to pay my debts based on fear?"* - HPWS

Fear certainly leads you to feel that you need to pray for anything. And your strong desire to pray for money and good fortune reveals that you still believe that your fear is caused by the personal self's lack of money. The flip-side of this is that you feel that the personal self having enough money will release you from fear. It's true that if the personal self had enough money to pay its debts you would no longer be able to project the source of your fear onto a lack of money. But this would only undo your fear in this very specific context. Fear would still manifest for you in other ways.

A Course in Miracles teaches that true prayer is not petitioning a separate power for what you think you need but opening your mind to God to become aware that you have no needs. In Truth you are whole and complete. The story of lack that you see before you is only a false idea in your mind. So you also do not have to pray for love and peace. You only have to become aware that you already have love and peace and your sense of lack will dissolve.

Since what shows up for you in the universe of form is an effect of your mind, as you center your mind in Truth (God) and you grow in the awareness that you have everything in Truth this will be reflected in the universe of form. The answers that you need for the personal self's seeming-problems will come to you, either directly in your mind or through others. The irony is that this will happen when it no longer matters to you what is or is not showing up in the universe of form. When you are aware that you have everything within you, you recognize that the universe of form is only a meaningless effect.

So if you want inner peace you only have to invite Truth into your awareness. Use this situation to do just that. When fear comes over you, turn inward and remember your experiences of Truth. Remind yourself that only they are true, not what is showing up in the universe of form. Rest in this awareness. Ask the Teacher of Truth (Holy Spirit) for a new way of looking at the debt situation. Keep your mind open because sometimes the answer can surprise you. If your mind wanders back to worrying remind yourself that you have already asked for help. It is always given. You will hear the answer when you are ready to hear it.

41. Ask: What about making plans for uncertainties? (August 26, 2011)

"I wonder about insurances. Oddly, I have homeowner's and car insurance because they are required and they don't seem to concern me. I recently changed professions and now am without health insurance. I want to be open to guidance but find I am unsure. I know ACIM talks about not making plans for uncertainties. What are your thoughts regarding this?" – PB

You are unsure what to do because you are concerned with acting in a way that is "right" or "good" or in line with Truth. This is a common mistake for new students of *A Course in Miracles* because you are used to thinking that the personal self is you and that the goal is for you to "fix" the personal self to be "right" in the eyes of a separate, authoritarian god.

But that god does not exist. It is only a projection of guilt. As the *Course* uses the word, *God* is the one Being that is, not something separate with authority over you. And the goal for you is not to be "right" but to return to your natural state of peace. The reason that you experience conflict is not because of "wrong" behavior, but because you are not aware that you are the one Being that is. You can only be at peace by being aware of God within your mind.

Your belief in the personal self and its story are obstacles to your awareness of God. So you do no have to make the personal self "right" or "good", but you do want to let it go. In practice this means coming into the present and turning your mind inward to God again and again throughout the day as you let the body's story unfold without judgment.

The body is only an idea in your mind. Its behavior follows from your thoughts. When your mind is centered in Truth (God) you are at peace. This shows up as you knowing how to direct the body for its well-being. This is what the *Course* means when it says that you don't need to occupy your mind with plans for the body's uncertain future.

If you do have a question about taking care of the body simply take it to the Holy Spirit. It is the Teacher of Truth in your mind and you can lay any question, spiritual or practical, at Its feet. You will always receive an answer. You may not hear the answer immediately, but you will when you are ready for it. If you feel that you have not received an answer and that you must take action, then do so and you will be guided.

42. Ask: What are others? (September 2, 2011)

"...I am a married man with a very good female friend who I feel very close to. She is also a student of ACIM and we frequently discuss it. I find myself wondering...what is she really? Is she really just a vain imagining of my real self? Perhaps a reflection or projection of what my ego self believes itself to be?" – MW

Who anyone is to you depends on whether you choose to identify with a personal self or with Truth.

Truth (God) is formless being. The experience of Truth is boundless love and peace and joy. It is an experience of wholeness. When you are identified with a personal self you are out of touch with your natural state of being. So you feel conflict and lack. You seek to supply this lack through the personal self and you see relationships as the way to do this. The personal thought system (ego) teaches you that others are your source. It projects the cause of your unhappiness onto them. It also tells you that in others you will find the peace and happiness that you seek. This causes the stress that you see in abundance in personal relationships. Others are not the cause of your unhappiness. Your lack of awareness of Truth is. And you will never find in others the love and peace and happiness that you already have but are denying in yourself.

But when your mind is centered in Truth you are in touch with the love and peace and happiness that are your natural state of being. You live in this awareness of wholeness rather than through the personal self. You recognize that the universe of form is only a story unfolding from your mind. Others are then to you manifestations of your wholeness. They come into the personal self's story to supply whatever the personal self needs, spiritually, emotionally, and/or practically. You feel gratitude for them.

In either case you may be attached to those to whom the personal self is close. When you are coming from the personal thought system (ego) your attachment is heavy. You are dependent on others to make you feel whole and happy. You are desperate to hold onto them and you may become manipulative to do so. If they must fall away from your life you are devastated.

But when you are relating to others from an awareness of Truth your attachment is light. You feel no need to change others to be something to make you happy and whole. You are happy to have them in your awareness, and if they must fall away you feel momentary regret and sadness, but not devastation. Your sense of wholeness and peace is unchanged by anything that happens in the personal story.

If you find yourself relating to others through the personal thought system and experiencing conflict, lack, and desperation you can always make the other choice. Instead of looking to them for wholeness and happiness, you can turn inward and get in touch with the Wholeness and Happiness that are your natural state of being. This will transform the personal self's relationships from manifestations of a conflicted mind to manifestations of a mind at peace.

43. Ask: Who in their right mind would believe pain is an illusion? (September 16, 2011)

"I have been a student of ACIM *(off & on) for 5 yrs +…but still encounter basic problems that are becoming increasingly insurmountable:*
*1. The assertion that our physical existence is "a fantasy" or "an illusion"…Who in their right mind would believe this…?What about the **physical pain** we experience through the course of our lives?… I'm talking about e.g., Suddam Hussein's "go thru the wood chopper" pain, or anything remotely equivalent. Is this pain not transparently REAL to its recipients?… Without a reconciliation to what we intuitively experience and thus accept as truthful* ACIM's *assertions become sheer sophistry.*
2. It is even more troubling that we are told by ACIM *that GOD is in essence oblivious to our physical pain…but then HE…has thus dispatched the Holy Spirit to sort it all out, and lead us to the ATONEMENT. What could be more convoluted than this?*
3. Additionally, the fact remains even if we have the power deep within us to become (in effect) immune to physical pain, given attainment of proper Right Mindedness, it is axiomatic that the reality or experience of this pain is very much with us prior to our attaining this state, and that GOD despite his omniscience accommodates this.
I would appreciate your help with this because I am otherwise "blown away" by the truth and potential offered by ACIM.*"* – RM

1. Your questions indicate that so far your experience with *A Course in Miracles* has been largely intellectual. You cannot see from within the personal thought system (ego) that the universe of form, including physical pain in any degree, is not real. This is because the personal thought system is itself part of the universe of form. When you are aware of Truth and coming from the thought system of Truth in your mind (Holy Spirit) the unreality of the personal thought system and its universe of form is manifestly apparent.

The *Course* does not ask you to accept what it says in blind faith. It asks you to invite Truth (God) into your awareness so that you can see that It is the Truth. It sounds like you are at the point in your path to peace where you need to put aside intellectual reasoning and open yourself to actually experiencing miracles. These are shifts in your mind toward an awareness of Truth (they may or may not manifest in the universe of form). These experiences will give you a deeper reading of the *Course* and a whole new way of looking at the universe of form.

It is also important to note that the *Course* states that the universe of form is an illusion because this is a fact, not to condemn you for not yet being aware of this. Its whole lesson plan meets you where you are in your experience that the world is real. It is not asking you to deny your experiences but to invite Truth (Holy Spirit) into them so that they can be used to lead you back to peace. It is the personal thought system that takes the fact that the universe of form is an illusion to increase guilt and fear in your mind. It does this by telling you that you "should" deny what you are experiencing or that you are "wrong" or "bad" or "failing" for having these experiences. These thoughts are obstacles to you seeing the gentle process of re-awakening to Truth that the Course offers.

2. What the *Course* says it that God does not know of pain but sees that you believe in pain so has sent the Holy Spirit to you to help you undo this belief. ("The Atonement" in the *Course* means "correction"). There is no contradiction or convolution in this. It is, however, insulting to the personal thought system (ego) that God is completely unaware of it and its effects.

The *Course* does not teach that you have the power to make yourself immune to pain. It tells you that in Truth within you there is no such thing as pain. To be aware of this it to be in your "right mind". In other words, it is not asking you to perfect the personal experience and make it Truth-like. That is the personal thought system's attempt to "spiritualize" the personal experience. If you want peace the goal is not to fix the personal experience but to let it go. This is an important distinction because otherwise you may feel that you fail if the personal experience does not change. It will never change. It is what it is, and that is the opposite of Truth in every way. But you have the Truth within you and It is an experience of unchanging wholeness, love, peace, and joy. If you want to be at peace all that you need to do is be willing to let go of the personal experience and open yourself to experience Truth instead.

44. Ask: What is the experience of the "period of disorientation"? (September 23, 2011)

"On page 368 of The Message of A Course in Miracles *(Chapter 16; VI The Bridge to the Real World) it says "In your transition there will be a period of confusion and disorientation but do not fear this because it only means that you have been willing to let go of your hold on the distorted frame of reference which seemed to hold your 'reality' together." What is the experience of this "period of confusion and disorientation"? How do you recognize it?"* – WW

The transition mentioned here is how your whole awareness of Truth (God) unfolds. You feel discomfort the moment that you have an experience (miracle) that shows you that the universe of form, which you thought was reality, is not Reality. A single or even a few experiences are not enough to shift your mind entirely to an awareness that formless being is Reality. You must experience this awareness again and again to undo your fixed sense that the universe of form reality. Each time you feel disoriented and confused because you become uncertain of what is real and what is not real. As uncomfortable as this is it is a good sign because it means that you are on your way to accepting Reality.

You recognize the experience because you feel exactly as it says: disoriented and confused. You don't know what anything means or how to look at anything. You feel like you don't know who you are. You feel unmoored. In a sense, this is the whole overarching experience of being a student of the *Course*! But what I have experienced and what I have observed as a mentor is that this experience of disorientation is not constant. It happens each time that one has an experience of Truth that shifts them to an awareness that the experience they have of a universe of form is not real. Each time there is a brief, uncomfortable period of confusion and disorientation, which is then followed by a longer, quieter period of integrating what was learned. Then another experience comes and it all begins again!

Of course, after a while you recognize the process and you know what to expect, so it is not so uncomfortable. You ride out the disorientation because you know it will pass. In fact, you experience less disorientation as the Truth becomes True for you and your belief that the universe of form is reality gives way.

45. Ask: How as a child was I responsible for the outer picture of an inner condition? (September 23, 2011)

"I am studying a course that asks me to look back at my life. I suffered a lot of child abuse which resulted in no self esteem and a complete inability to function in the world. I am now 65 years

old. How do I use ACIM *when it says that what you experience is a picture of an inner condition? I was just a child. How could I project this into the world or the people that were responsible for me growing up? I just can't see that I was responsible but I am willing to accept it if that is the way* ACIM *explains it…"* – DH

Here is the quote from *A Course in Miracles* to which you refer:

"Perception seems to teach you what you see. Yet it but witnesses to what you taught. It is the outward picture of a wish; an image that you wanted to be true." (T-24.VII.8)

If you read the quote above in context (read the paragraphs around it) you will find that it is not referring to the specifics of an individual life but to the "son of God's" choice to make a universe of form that is the opposite of God in every way. When the *Course* speaks to you about the making of the universe of form it is speaking to "you" as the mind that is split between Truth (God) and not-Truth (ego), not to "you" as a personal self.

Personal selves are projections of the split mind. The circumstance into which each seems to be "born" is a random expression of the wish mentioned in the quote above. So the story of a young boy in your "memory" is an "outward picture" of the split mind's wish for not-Truth, not of the young boy's personal wishes.

When you choose peace you choose to remember that you are the split mind rather than a projection (personal self) of that mind. You choose to take responsibility for how your thoughts about a neutral universe of form determine your experience of conflict or peace. You are doing this now by looking at the personal thought system's story for you. Remember, if you are in pain now the source of pain is in your mind now. In other words, the source of your pain is not in an actual past but in your thoughts about a personal past that are in your mind now.

46. Ask: Can sex be a means of holy communication? (October 7, 2011)

"I have been attempting to understand how sex might connect us to divinity. I've read the ACIM *urtext. I've read your piece, 'Sex and the Course Student.'*

Remember that the Holy Spirit interprets the body only as a means of communication. *(T-8.VII.2).*

If this is the case, then can sex not be a means of …holy communication? A man I know, who says he is a teacher of the Course, *has decided that his assignment from God is to meet as many souls as possible for holy encounters involving "transcendent sex." He says his encounters have nothing to do with sex and the body but, rather, love and spirit. Is this really possible? Or is it a misunderstanding of the message of the* Course? *Is there such a thing as a misuse of the* Course?

I've had a few beautiful sexual experiences, and it seems the pleasure that spreads across my body brings me "higher," but I wonder if that's just my ego tricking me?…this man says that he believes Jesus was being cautious with His statements about sex. Also, he says the HS is doing Its miracle work through him." – Anonymous

First, let me address your question about the possibility of *A Course in Miracles* being misused. Like all form, the *Course* is itself neutral. It is simply a collection of words, and words are symbols of whatever you want them to represent. If you want to stay in conflict they will represent the ideas in your mind promoted by the personal thought system (ego). If you want peace you will open your mind to the Teacher of Truth (Holy Spirit) in you as you read it. They will then be used to lead you back to peace. I have yet to meet a student of the *Course* who did not initially misuse the *Course* at least to some extent, often for many, many years. This is because we all bring with us the guilty, fearful filter of the personal thought system and we have to learn to put it aside and open our minds only to the Teacher of Truth. You can be sure that if you read it and you feel an increase in guilt and/or fear you are reading it with the personal thought system. When you read it with the Teacher of Truth you will feel liberated and at peace, even though the personal thought system might not like what you read.

Be aware that when you read the urtext of the *Course* that some of what was in it that was taken out before the book was published (including passages about sex) was intended specifically for Helen Schucman and/or Bill Thetford. Reading what is specifically intended for someone at a specific time in their understanding of Truth can be confusing when it is read by others. This was why Helen and Ken Wapnick were guided to take out those passages when they were organizing it for publication. As it is, the *Course* is still pretty specific to Helen and Bill's relationship, but what was left in can be easily generalized by the rest of us.

With regard to sex the *Course* states specifically in the first paragraph of part II of Chapter 1 that physical relationships cannot achieve the experience of Oneness that you really want and can find only in God. The *Course* also teaches that only minds can truly commune. When speaking of the body as a communication device it makes it clear that the communication is the point, not the device. The point of all physical pleasure, as well as pain, is to distract your mind with a body, not to transcend an awareness of a body. This is why pain and pleasure are really the same.

You do not need any device to communicate with God. You only need to turn your mind inward, away from the universe of form, including bodies. The same goes for truly communing with others. True communion can never happen between bodies or personal, or separate, minds. But when I turn inward to God and you turn inward to God we go to the exact same Place. So only by turning inward to God can you truly commune with anyone. The only value the body has in this process is what is occurring now—this mind is communicating through this body via a computer (another communication device) to your mind, reminding you to turn inward to Truth if you want peace.

The "high" that you may feel from sex is caused by endorphins and is not the joy you feel when you are aware of Truth (God). It is no different than taking drugs to feel euphoric. Both induce a temporary state. True joy is not euphoria and, though it may pass in your awareness, when you experience it you know that it is true and eternal.

A miracle is a shift in your awareness toward Truth. This occurs in your mind. It may or may not result in action taken in the world. You cannot work a miracle on another. Another can only experience a miracle if they accept the experience of it within their own minds.

Do not take from any of this the idea that sex is "wrong" or "bad". As I said in the article you mentioned (http://acimmentor.blogspot.com/2007/04/sex-and-course-student.html) in Truth sex is nothing.

47. Ask: If I am a dream figure then who is the dreamer of this dream? (October 14, 2011)

"If I am the dream figure, then who is the dreamer of this dream? And how do I as the dream figure get in contact with the dreamer? Is Jesus in ACIM *addressing the dreamer of the dream? How do I change this dream into the 'happy dream'* ACIM *speaks of?"* - GP

You are the dreamer of the dream dreaming that you are a figure in your dream. *A Course in Miracles* addresses you as the dreamer.

The "dreamer of the dream" in the *Course* refers to the split mind, which it calls the "son of God" (lower case "s" on son). It is split between God (What it is) and not-God (the idea of the opposite-of-God). This split mind makes the universe of form and projects its mind into many seemingly-individual minds. So each seemingly-individual mind seems to be a dream figure but is really one form of the one split mind.

You begin your study of the *Course* almost wholly identified with a figure in the dream, or a personal self (ego). You think that the personal "life" and its world are happening to you and that you are largely powerless. You are not aware that you are mind and these are only ideas in your mind. But the universe of form that the split mind projects, and in which you seem to find yourself, has no meaning in itself. All of the meaning that you see you project from a personal thought system. This is true for every personal self. In this way each personal self makes up the world in which they seem to live. In other words, you don't really live in a universe of form but in your thoughts about a universe of form. This is your "world".

There is a process to realizing that you are the dreamer of the dream. You will not recognize that you are the dreamer of the dream while still thinking of yourself as a figure in the dream. So the first part of the process is getting in touch with the Truth, or God, within you (Christ, Holy Spirit). Only from this awareness can you detach from the personal identity. When you have a sufficient awareness of Truth you can observe the personal thought system. Because you can observe it you realize that it is not you. It is just an idea in your mind.

Once you are aware of Truth you also begin the process of letting go of guilt. The personal thought system's justification for guilt is the idea that you have undone Truth. Obviously, if you are in touch with Truth you have not undone it, so the justification for guilt starts to crumble. Eventually your awareness of Truth chips away enough guilt for you to observe without judgment how with the personal thought system you make a world for the personal self by projecting meaning onto the universe of form. These projections of meaning always somehow tie into the personal story that you have for the personal self with which you identify. The more you observe your mind and detach from the personal thought system the more you become aware that all minds work the same. The Truth in every mind is identical and not-Truth in every mind is the same in content, though different in form. Boundaries between minds collapse for you. You realize that there is only one "dreamer of the dream" that just takes many forms. You stop thinking in terms of "my" mind, "their" mind, and "your" mind and you think simply in terms of "mind". You accept, without guilt or judgment, that if it is in your awareness it is in your mind. You are the dreamer of the dream.

You do not have to make any of this happen. It is the natural result of inviting Truth into your awareness and choosing to undo your obstacles (guilt, fear) to being aware of Truth. You only have to be willing; Truth does the rest. In time you accept that only the Truth is True. You recognize that the dream is meaningless and you let it unfold without judgment or attachment.

The dream does not really change but you become a happy dreamer because you recognize that it is a dream and not reality.

48. Ask: About "teachers of God"... (October 21, 2011)

"From the point of view of A Course in Miracles, *only one teacher of God is needed to save the world. According to the* Course, *all the rest would be the ego's arrogant specialness.* ACIM *also talks about The Hundredth Monkey Theory of Salvation which states that a certain number of people are needed to tip the scales to favor of salvation, and as a corollary, that there is some sort of divine plan to have this done by certain special people... Speaking for myself, nothing wrong with this The Hundredth Monkey Theory, except that I happen to believe in the concept of the critical-masses of people needed to tip the scale of salvation of the world.*
Perhaps, that is why, I believe that part three of A Course in Miracles *is devoted to these God's teachers who are destined to tip the scale in favor of salvation of the world. I read somewhere that Helen, the scribe of the Course, mentioned about the "Celestial Speed Up" process. The manual for Teachers was written for these God's Teachers. Can you please explain your views on this subject?"* – JJ

There is only one split mind thinking about a world so there is only one mind that needs to let go of this thought. This one split mind takes many forms, but they are all the same in content, so they are all the same. This is why it takes only one mind to "save the world". When any seemingly-individual mind remembers Truth it is the one split mind remembering Truth. This is why your "sole responsibility is to accept the Atonement for yourself." (Remember, "atonement" in the *Course* means "correction").

It is important to clarify what the *Course* means by the word "world". Just as with so many other words, the *Course* does not use the word "world" in the conventional sense. It is not speaking of the universe of form, but of your thoughts about (perception of) a universe of form. This is what makes up the "world" for each seemingly-individual mind and why each personal self really does live in their own world. So by "saving the world" the *Course* is not speaking of changing the universe of form to somehow reflect Truth but "saving" your mind by correcting how it thinks about a universe of form.

The "Hundredth Monkey Theory" is never mentioned in the *Course*. With a little cursory googling I found that this theory is an observed phenomenon among monkeys where when a certain behavior is accepted by a certain number (critical mass) of monkeys in a group the behavior spreads spontaneously to other related groups of monkeys. This is not at all what the *Course* teaches. The *Course* is concerned with mind, not behavior. This circles back to what was stated in the first paragraph.

The "teachers of God" that the *Course* refers to are not special people but anyone whose mind is open to God. And you choose to open your mind to God because God is Truth and you can only be at peace being aware of Truth. If you have any other motivation, like "you have to do your part to save the world", be aware of the guilt lurking behind this thought. This implies that the universe of form is real and has an effect on God, so it implies that guilt and "sin" are real. Or it is the personal self seeking to glorify itself, so again implying that it is real and reinforcing guilt in your mind.

If you truly want Truth and peace, rather than just a better personal life, then do not be too attached to the story of "salvation" laid out in the *Course*. Like any spiritual teaching the

Course can be read superficially as only a means to a better personal experience. But if you want something more then you must be willing to put aside the personal story and allow the Teacher of Truth (Holy Spirit) in your mind to reveal to you the deeper message of the *Course*. Then the story of salvation in the *Course* will be a temporary bridge that meets you where you are when you first read the *Course*: almost wholly identifying with a personal self that longs for a purpose and a context for its "life". But you will eventually cross this bridge and leave it behind.

49. Ask: What is the difference between God's Love and personal love? (October 28, 2011)

"What are the differences in the love for God and the love for another 'special relationship' man / woman /child. I know one difference would be conditional love for another body and unconditional love between God and myself. But is it the same kind of love? My ACIM group says they are different and it is too bad they use the same word. I think the love between myself and my spouse is the same as, albeit, a small representation of God's love for me." – RQ

The most obvious difference between the Love of God and personal love is that God's Love simply is and personal love is always directed toward an object (person, animal, or thing).

God's Love is God's Being, which means It is your True Being. The experience of It is radiating joy and peace, without beginning or ending. It is an experience of wholeness that has no correlation in the personal experience.

God's Love is introduced to you as "God loves you" when you are identifying with a personal self not because God's Love is really directed toward the personal self that you think of as you but because you still think in terms of God as a separate being rather than as your Being. It is stated this way to reassure you that your perception of yourself as guilty and unworthy of God's Love is a fallacy. This motivates you to open yourself to the experience of God, which is the experience of Love, or joyous wholeness and peace. The more you experience God the more the boundary of a separate self falls away and you realize that God is the One Being that is. God is your Being, so you are Love.

My dictionaries refer to (personal) "love" as deep devotion or affection or regard for another or others; a fond attachment or kind feeling toward another or others. While God's Love is unconditional because It simply is, you can see by these definitions that personal love is always conditional. Personal love forms only under certain conditions, like an unconscious resemblance to another "loved" one, familiarity, similarity, needs being met, etc. Even a "kind feeling" is only present in the personal self when the personal self is in a good mood!

When you are in touch with God's Love within you, you exist in a state of Love, or wholeness. This Love is not inspired by anyone outside of you, nor do you direct It toward an object. It simply is. It manifests as a radiating "kind feeling" everywhere, without boundaries or conditions, but from you, not from the personal self, which always has boundaries and conditions. Your awareness of God's Love within you also manifests as loving personal relationships showing up for the personal self in the forms that it needs them.

You know that you are in touch with God's Love within you when your attachments to others are light and joyous. You see your relationships with others as the manifestation of God's Love within you, rather than as the source of love for you. So you are free to allow others to be themselves, without needing to manipulate or to change them so that you can be happy and whole. If others must move on you let them go with perhaps temporary regret but not with crushing loss. You may miss them, but you know that you will not be lost without them, because Love is always with you.

50. Ask: Where does the spirit world come into the teachings of ACIM? (November 4, 2011)

"I am working through ACIM and have not found any other teaching that has felt so right as ACIM... Where does the spirit world come into the teachings of ACIM? Is there a spirit world or is this also created by ourselves within the dream? Is it really past relatives that people try to connect to?...The spirit world seems to be the only thing created that we believe is beyond our world and seems to be the place we all end up after this dream has what we see as ended..." - AR

You are correct that *A Course in Miracles* never refers to a "spirit world". It is indeed just a concept of the personal thought system (ego). Like the idea of "reincarnation" it is meant to give to the personal self an aspect of Truth (God): eternality. It is the personal thought system's attempt to have you believe that the personal self, or at least some aspect of it called a "spirit", is real. Actually, all sense of individuality falls away in the awareness of Truth. There is only one Spirit (God, Truth).

Yes, some people try to connect to relatives who have passed away. Remember, all personal selves are only ideas. This is why when the body onto which you projected a personal self is no longer around it still remains in your mind. So sometimes when one feels they have something unfinished with one who is no longer around they do have an experience of a visitation from a "spirit" of the late loved one, often in a dream. This is really just their mind's way of manifesting the choice to heal the relationship.

Also, the Teacher of Truth (Holy Spirit) in your mind will use whatever symbols are meaningful for you to reach you when you have asked for help. Some minds have a hard time with the idea that the Truth is in them. This can be resistance to this idea out of a sense of unworthiness or simply because they find the idea too abstract. They need an image onto which to focus, like an "ascended master" or even a loved one who brings a "message" from "beyond". These are just temporary means that the Truth in you may use to reach you until you are ready to accept the Truth directly.

51. Ask: How do I find peace in a relationship where I fear to be myself? (November 11, 2011)

"I have a relationship with someone that seems to trigger a fear to be myself. I haven't felt this way with anyone in a long time. I have been asking to see only the face of Christ in her and have had many experiences of just that. I love her unconditionally and am not threatened by anything she seems to do. Yet, I still withhold my true thoughts from her because I am still afraid of what I have perceived about her, which is that she is degrading and not connected to humility in a way that I can relate to. I just feel so separated from her and can't seem to find a way to connect and disarm myself and her. I want to very deeply, but every time I seem to be making headway, I realize that she and I are talking different languages and we both haven't got a clue what the other is going through or saying.

I do not leave the relationship because it seems to me that since I feel such conflict in the relationship that I have not learned what I need to learn. I am willing to stay and walk through the circle of fear to get to the other side. I do see the Holy Spirit in her and am not fooled by our ego's dance together. I just wonder if there is more. The conflict and miscommunication that is always between us seems so unneeded and a waste of my attention.
I know that she is just an outside picture of my inward condition, but what now? OK so I'm in conflict. My ego and the Holy Spirit cannot communicate with each other. So What? I know that." – EP

If you want inner peace, then the first thing you want to determine when you experience conflict is what is fact and what is projection of meaning coming from the personal thought system's (ego's) story for you. For example, you say that this woman with whom you are involved is "degrading". Is it a fact that she says things meaning to degrade you or others or are you interpreting her words through your personal expectations based on past experience? You can usually determine fact from projection by your own emotional response. When it is fact you observe it without strong emotional charge and without taking it personally ("Wow, that was not a very nice thing to say. I wonder why she feels she has to put me down?"). You are able to deal with the person in a charge-neutral way. ("I was expressing my feelings and not attacking you."). When it is projection there is a strong emotional charge and you take it personally ("She's attacking me! Here I go again with another person treating me bad…"). You are defensive and you attack back. You and the other end up in a vicious cycle of fear and attack.

If you find that you are observing fact then it seems clear that you are with someone who feels a need to put others down to feel good about herself. Your options are to accept her as she is and learn to not take her lack of self-respect personally or to leave and find healthier friends. If you find that you are projecting, then you do indeed have something through which to work. You can observe, with the Teacher of Truth (Holy Spirit) in your mind, the "story" that you tell yourself about this woman and how it ties into your personal victim-story. Then you can choose to let it go in the recognition that this story is not Truth.

It may turn out that it is a fact that she means to put you down and that you are also projecting. When you notice a negative pattern in your relationships one or both of these are happening: You are interpreting others' actions through the lens of your victim-story or you are attracted to people who will help you to perpetuate your victim-story.

There are a couple of contradictions in what you wrote. You say that you are not threatened by anything this woman does, but you are afraid to be honest with her because you feel that she degrades you. So you do feel threatened by her. You also say that you are not fooled by the ego's dance between you, but you are distracted by the conflict, which means you must believe in it. Being aware of Truth does not mean that you have to force yourself to stay in a conflicted relationship. Sometimes the lesson is, "This is not the relationship for me." If you stay because you think you "should" then you are using the relationship to martyr yourself.

When you are aware of the Truth (God) within you, you feel whole and complete. This sets you free in your relationships because you don't need anything from others. You can be yourself and you are comfortable allowing others to be themselves. But this does not mean that you want to be around everyone. There are only three motivations for staying around disrespectful personalities. One is practical, like a co-worker or relative you cannot avoid all of the time. You make the conscious choice to put up with them because the benefits of doing so (like having a job or maintaining peace in the family during the holidays) offset the temporary discomfort their behavior causes you. You set appropriate boundaries to limit their disrespectful behavior toward you and/or your contact with them. Another is because you feel you need something from them that you think you lack, like love. So in essence, you are disrespecting yourself through your relationship with them. And the only other reason to stay around others who do not treat you with respect is because you want to play the martyr.

52. Ask: Are we told what our task is? (November 25, 2011)

"I am a beginner; still, things have changed so radically for me, and so quickly. I am now at odds about how to earn my living. Are we told what our task is? It must be a manifestation of His Will, but how do we find out? Is it one with "the light of the world"? Will it be unveiled to us?"
– L

A Course in Miracles states that, if you want inner peace, your one responsibility is to "accept the Atonement for yourself". The "Atonement" in the *Course* means correction of your perception that you are separate from God (Truth). This is accomplished through your becoming aware of God within you and your forgiving, or releasing, the thoughts that are obstacles to your staying aware of God within you.

So your "task" does not involve what the personal self does in the universe of form but what you do with your mind. And you become aware of God again in the course of an ordinary, everyday life because it is there that you run into the obstacles (guilt, fear, attachment) to being aware of God that you need to release.

Your growing awareness of God and forgiving is a process. It begins by you inviting the Holy Spirit (the Teacher of Truth in your mind) into your life where you are now. You do not have to change or to give up anything that you do not want to. The Holy Spirit meets you where you are, becoming your Constant Companion if you are willing. If you want inner peace you want to open up every aspect of your life to the Holy Spirit. In time, as your awareness of and trust in the Holy Spirit grows, you will find it natural to step back and let It lead the way. This practice will eventually lead you to experiencing the line between you and the Holy Spirit blurring. You will no longer experience the Holy Spirit as Other, but simply as the Truth in you. You will be living in "the Atonement".

Your values will change along the way and so you will find yourself motivated to make changes in the personal self's life that support your new values. This will happen more than once, and will reflect in the universe of form your change of mind. This might be what you are experiencing now. There can be long periods of feeling disoriented about the personal self's life and this is exactly the type of thing that you want to share with the Holy Spirit. You want to share both your disorientation and your practical questions. The Holy Spirit will use everything that you give to It to make you aware that It is always with you and undo your sense of separation from God.

53. Ask: How can I find my life-partner? (December 2, 2011)

"...How can a single person connect to their life partner? I have been single for several years and... I have learned I want a life partner more than a soul mate, I think I am looking for someone who can stand to be with me and I with them for more than 10 minutes at a time; someone to share the dream together while in the dream world." - JP

It is good for your peace of mind that you are being honest with yourself about what you want. So many *A Course in Miracles* students make the mistake of repressing personal desires in the guilty belief that they are "wrong". In Truth (God) personal desires are not "wrong" or "right"; they are nothing. But while you are aware of a world they can be either obstacles to or means for peace. The personal thought system (ego) uses them as ends in themselves, so they become obstacles to peace for you. But the Teacher of Truth (Holy Spirit) within you uses personal desires as means for peace if you share them with It. So the first step is for you to be honest with yourself so you can be honest with the Teacher of Truth: "I want someone to share my life with. I'm open and willing to follow Your guidance so this can be used for peace."

Of course, you have to do more than say this. You have to be truly open and willing. Remember, if you want peace the Teacher of Truth must be your primary relationship. All personal relationships will then be a loving manifestation of your one relationship with Love.

After sharing this goal with the Teacher of Truth go about your life and pursue your natural goals and interests. This is how you meet people with whom you share common values. Let your friends and family know that you are looking for someone with whom to share your life so they can look for you as well. And you can also try dating websites. If you are interested in a serious relationship then try one of those sites that are geared toward matching you with someone with the same values and relationship goals. In other words, take the same actions anyone would when looking for a life-partner while staying honest with yourself and being open to the Teacher of Truth.

Keep in mind that just because you want a life-partner it does not mean that you are ready for a life-partner right now. Given to the Teacher of Truth a life-partnership is an intense, accelerated class for attaining inner peace. (Just as, given to the personal thought system, it is an intense class for maintaining conflict in your mind!).You may have lessons to learn before you are ready for that level of commitment to peace. So you may date for a while before you find the one who is also ready to join you in that intense classroom. All relationships, though, will be useful lessons if you share them with the Teacher of Truth.

You can be certain that if there is something that you really want the Teacher of Truth will guide you through the lessons and growth that you need until you are ready to accept that for which you asked.

54. Ask: Do two people have to consciously decide to have a Holy relationship? (December 9, 2012)

) "*I have a close female friend my ego brings to mind a hundred times a day (thoughts of intimacy between us). The ego wishes to be closer to her but, even though we have not talked about it, it seems to me that we have both turned off the possibility of the experience of sexual intimacy. Me because I have made the decision to be faithful to my wife and her because she simply would not be an adulteress.*

We are both dedicated ACIM students who share a mutual goal of diminishing the ego and being more of what we truly are. While picking up a book for her one day I found Robert Perry's pamphlet on Holy Relationships. This is the first time I remember that subject coming into my awareness. I felt after reading it that at some level beyond conscious thought we have already made the decision to be in a Holy Relationship and it is just now coming to mind. Do two people have to consciously decide to have a Holy Relationship? Is there any value (to the degree that it would help us awaken) in speak to her of my ego thoughts in an effort to go beyond the ego together? I already do my best to see her as sinless no matter what and as what I think of as the "One Mind working together" creating experience for spiritual growth…" – MW

It is fascinating what the personal thought system (ego) will block out. You say you are a dedicated *A Course in Miracles* student yet you were unaware of the Holy relationship until you read another pamphlet about it. The entire *Course* is about a Holy relationship! It was written directly to two people (Helen Schucman and Bill Thetford) in one and once it formally introduces the Holy relationship in Chapter 17 it never lets up on the subject. The Holy relationship is the *Course's* primary teaching tool.

I have experienced the Holy relationship in two ways. The first was what I call a *mystical* Holy relationship where I experienced another literally as my Self. I was not consciously aware of making the choice for this, but I must've been open to it on some level for it to come into my awareness. The first lesson in it for me was that everything that the *Course* teaches about what is real and what is not real is true. Then, when the other moved away and my experience of Oneness did not diminish when I thought of her, I learned that the Holy relationship is really with the Truth (God) within me. My relationship with this other was only the "doorway" to my awareness of Truth. So I learned to make my relationship with the Teacher of Truth (Holy Spirit) my primary relationship and all of my personal relationships then became manifestations of this.

My other experience of the Holy relationship is what I call the *practical* Holy relationship. This is what I experience today with my wife, Courtney. She is not a student of the *Course*, but she is on her own spiritual path (12-step/Christian). The decision for a Holy relationship was conscious on our part, though she did not label it as such in the beginning. This type of Holy relationship is where the real day-to-day lessons lie and where I wanted my first Holy relationship to go. It occurs when you practice what I just mentioned: putting your awareness of Truth first. You can experience Holiness without another being aware of It, but for a relationship to be Holy in the sense that the *Course* teaches you both need to be aware of Truth. Then you can each and together choose to put aside the personal thought system's (ego's) projections and choose to come from Truth in the relationship instead. This is what makes the relationship Holy.

For a relationship to be Holy it requires that you be completely open and honest first with yourself, then with the Teacher of Truth, and then, if you are guided, with the other. So how much you share with this other woman about your feelings for her is something that you want to discuss with the Teacher of Truth within you. Your relationship is under Its guidance now.

I recommend you re-read Chapter 17, perhaps with this woman. Also, be aware that a Holy relationship is a very intense classroom and that the personal thought system will be very, very threatened. In the beginning its attacks will be relentless, as you are experiencing with these fantasies. If you understand that this is what is occurring then you can support each other through this. (You can read about this phase in *The Healed Relationship* in Chapter 17). This can be an opportunity for you to learn to hear the personal thought system without actually listening to it. You can let its fantasies run in the background as you go about your day. Eventually, without your attention, they will fade away. Then the personal thought system will find a new way to distract you! But everything that comes up will be a useful lesson, if you give it to the Teacher of Truth.

55. Ask: How do I approach "private thoughts"? (December 16, 2011)

"...I haven't been doing "the Course*" for very long, but I do seem to get caught up in "my thoughts". At the beginning of doing the* Course, *are we just to be concentrating on releasing fearful, anxious, jealous, so called "lower" states of mind? Sometimes, when I am daydreaming about my new bedroom furniture (for example), I become aware that I am thinking "private thoughts" and not thinking with the Holy Spirit. This is causing me a good bit of hyper vigilance, which does not make for a peaceful day!!*

...practically, when the Course *says we want neither the "good nor the bad" thoughts, that confuses me. How do you suggest approaching these so-called "good thoughts'? Or, am I jumping way ahead of myself to a goal that is not within reach for me at this time?"* – SL

You do not have to force your mind to stay focused on Truth (God) all day long. This is not realistic, and frankly there are times when you need to be focused on what the body is doing (when it is running a chain-saw, for example). If you want inner peace, you simply want to return your mind to Truth again and again throughout the day.

For example, when you find your mind running off with a meaningless distraction, like fantasizing about your new bedroom furniture, just let those thoughts go, come into the present, turn your mind inward, and take a moment to commune with Truth. Remind yourself that the Truth is What is True. Feel yourself relax. Then go about your day, taking these moments when you remember to.

The thoughts in the Workbook are important for new students, but what you are going to take away from the Workbook is the practice that it instills in you after a year. These are the habits of communing with Truth daily, watching how your thoughts contribute to your experience of peace or conflict, and taking moments throughout the day to remember Truth.

The more you open yourself to and experience Truth the quieter your mind will become. This quiet is the peace that you crave. You will then recognize that all of the personal thought system's (ego's) thoughts, whether it judges them as "good" or "bad", are obstacles to peace. They are just meaningless babble that obscures the peace that is in your mind now.

56. Ask: What is your advice for handling distractions during meditation? (December 23, 2011)

"I've been a student of ACIM *for nine years. I very recently was led to your plain language versions and feel my progress had been sped up immeasurably. However my meditation honeymoon period seems to be over. The first 2 weeks after reading "The Four Habits for Inner Peace" I easily fell into a wonderful mindless state and barely noticed the hour that seemed to just fly by. Now, most mornings...all manner of things begin to happen...barking..., the phone rings, a leaf blower...a car alarm suddenly ignites...I get a coughing or yawning fit, short unexplainable stabs of pain manifest in parts of my body etc. It's comical!*

Sometimes I get frustrated and give up and feel guilty, thinking my progress has been arrested. Sometimes I just smile and wait a bit till everything calms down and continue, able to ignore the illusory external chaos. My questions concerning this are...

What is your advice when all of these distractions manifest. Should I stop and wait until later? If I don't meditate that day is my progress hampered? Do you meditate every single day without fail?" – SB

The goal of meditation is not to be perfect about it but to grow your awareness of Truth so that you will be at peace. There is no reason for guilt if you do not meditate or you do not meditate perfectly. Who are you meditating for? You can only be doing it for you. There is no authoritative god to disappoint because you are not meditating perfectly. And you can be aware of Truth anytime. This is a matter of willingness, not of effort. So your progress is not impeded if occasionally you do not meditate or do not meditate well.

The Teacher of Truth in you (Holy Spirit) never inspires guilt, so when guilt shows up like this know that it comes from the personal thought system (ego). Don't let this guilt pass without finding the thoughts behind it. You believe those thoughts; that's why you accept the guilt. And they are obstacles to peace so you want to bring them to the light and release them.

The vast majority of days I meditate at least once out of a strong desire to do so. Communing with Truth (God) is the purpose of my life, so it is the purpose of every day for me. I turn inward to Truth several times a day. On those rare days that I do skip a formal meditation it is either because my day has been so meditative that it is simply not necessary or I am so strongly in the personal thought system that I know to not bother. The latter case is extremely rare because I've found that I like to make the attempt even if I think I'm not going to successfully quiet my mind and experience Truth.

Meditation can be used to process, to bring something to the Teacher of Truth in your mind, and/or to commune with Truth. The latter is the ultimate goal and you can really do it any time. Throughout the day take moments to remember Truth and sometimes it will be in one of those moments that you feel the connection, rather than during a formal meditation.

What you described is pretty typical: sometimes you will let distractions pass; other times you will allow yourself to be distracted. But the latter does not matter. Truth is not changed because you are distracted. This is of what you can remind yourself at the time. Later, when you feel more open to Truth, try meditating again.

57. Ask: When is personal love and obstacle to True Love? (December 30, 2011)

"I had written and received the most wonderful response from you in regard to feeling deep love and joy when interacting with my family which consists of my husband of almost 20 years and our two pugs. We are at our happiest when we are all together. I felt guilty because I felt I was "loving" myself deeper into the dream and your advice was that my family is a manifestation of the love I feel within and that I should gratefully continue appreciating and loving them. I felt complete release from guilt but it has returned. There are moments of joy we share that just seem so full and wonderful and I can't help but think I'm ignoring the text and strengthening the illusion.

This passage, from The Message of ACIM, *specifically illustrates my fear:*

"Do not make any illusion your friend, because if you do, it will take the place of the Holy Spirit, Which God has made your only Friend in Truth."

How do I process the love I feel without going in the opposite direction of the one I spend most of my day striving for? Are they my illusions? Am I theirs? Is my "love" for them shutting the Holy Spirit out?" – SB

Inner peace is the result of being aware of the Truth (God) within you, and of nothing else. What that quote means is that you do not want to make anything in the universe of form rise to the level of Truth for you or it will become an obstacle to peace for you. Something rises to the level of Truth for you when you think that it is the source of your peace and happiness. If you have given your husband and dogs the role of being the source of your happiness and you find that you cannot be aware of Truth because of your feelings for them, then your feelings for them are obstacles to peace for you. But if you find that you can enjoy them and you can still be aware of Truth, then the love in your relationships with them manifests the Love within you.

Your line *"There are moments of joy we share that just seem so full and wonderful and I can't help but think I'm ignoring the text and strengthening the illusion"* is very telling. It shows that you expect that being aware of Truth will lead to personal lack and unhappiness, and since you are experiencing fullness and joy you figure you must be doing something wrong. This is what the personal thought system (ego) teaches to scare you away from Truth! It teaches that Truth will lead you to an empty personal life. But in fact when you are aware of Truth this awareness manifests as a healthy, bountiful, loving personal life.

Remember, you are mind. The personal life is an effect of, or an idea in, your mind. The personal self's unfolding story reflects your choice of thought system (Truth/Holy Spirit or not-Truth/ego). When you seek through the personal life for lasting love and peace and happiness you never find them because the universe of form is only an empty effect. But when you are aware of Truth you are aware of eternal Happiness and Love. Your mind now causes the effect of a personal self whose needs are met, who has meaningful employment, and is in relationships that are happy and loving.

58. Ask: How do you help someone change a hurtful interpretation? (January 6, 2012)

"I have been trying to help someone and have been trying to have them, when they see something disturbing, to tell the Holy Spirit that you are willing to see this differently. Last week she saw a beggar yelling at his dog. She has a particular problem with suffering dogs of the world. I tried to explain how we perceive and then interpret what we perceive. She wrote back "what about when you see something hurtful or sad when it is obvious and not an interpretation." She got me there. The problem is it all results in her giving large amounts of money and it completely ruins her day and results in a deep depression that can last a week or most likely longer. During this time she can do nothing. I think you get the picture. How can I answer her comments?..." – DH

If you want inner peace then you want to sort out fact from interpretation (projection of meaning). You never respond to facts, but to your interpretations. Your interpretations always tie in some way to your own story for the personal self with which you identify. Usually, it is some form of "victim" story. Or it may tie into a role that you play and that you value. The value in your seeing this is in seeing how your thoughts make up the world in which you seem to find yourself. You don't really live in the world of form; you live in your thoughts about it. When you accept this then you are empowered to change your mind and therefore your experience from conflict to peace.

In this situation a person yelled at their dog. "Hurtful" and "sad" are your friend's interpretations (if she used those words to refer to this particular situation). These thoughts are to what she is responding and they lead to her depression. She thinks her thoughts are facts. No doubt she identifies with the vulnerability of dogs, which are at the mercy of humans, just as she feels she is at the mercy of the world at large.

There are many ways in which to interpret anything in the universe of form because it is neutral. But *A Course in Miracles* simplifies things greatly by teaching that what isn't love is a call for love. The experience of love or the call for love is always in the mind of the perceiver. But in the beginning most see these calls "out there" in the images that they perceive because they believe that their experience comes from the images and not from their own mind. This is a beginning, however, in that choosing to see a call for love at least replaces their initial interpretation and teaches them that they can choose to see things differently. This opens the process for them to eventually accept that their experience of love or a call for love can come only from their own mind.

Generally in a situation where another feels attacked I help them to understand that their perceived attacker was coming from their own pain. They were calling for love. Their attack was not personal. But what makes your friend's situation so difficult is that she takes personally situations that do not even involve her. Someone yells at a dog and now she is hurt and saddened, not just in passing, but for many days. She has made herself a victim of the beggar when the beggar was not even addressing her.

One obsesses on the perceived pain of others to avoid dealing with their own pain. Your friend is not yet ready to ask the Holy Spirit for another way to look at things. She would have to be willing to look inward to become aware of the Holy Spirit. And she is not going to be willing to do that until she is willing to look at her own perceived problems. At this stage traditional psychotherapy is probably called for. You can encourage her to get help, which is her choice to make. And in the meantime you can be her friend simply by listening and understanding. Sometimes, "That sounds very painful; I'm sorry you're hurting" is all the love that someone is ready to hear.

59. Ask: How do I use guidance to awaken rather than to dream a better dream? (January 13, 2012)

"...When I hear people talk about guidance it seems to be involved in a lot of different aspects and areas - I'm not sure if that makes sense - but I guess the question is about how to get in touch with guidance and what real guidance is being used for - how to use it to awaken rather than in a way that the personal mind might use it to keep you in the dream and "fixing" up the dream? I'm not really clear how to ask about this because I think it's probably quite an in-depth topic in the sense of really receiving guidance and how guidance can be distorted and misused and also guidance for more personal activities or how the body is utilized and more deeper clearing of the mind and really joining with the presence of God and releasing identity with the personal." – AL

Inner peace results when you are aware of Truth. So when you decide that you want inner peace you are ready to grow your awareness of Truth. This is where the Teacher of Truth (Holy Spirit) comes in. The Teacher of Truth is the thought system in your mind that represents the Truth in you. It is your guide to growing your awareness of Truth. It is the bridge in your mind between Truth and your belief that you are in a universe of form. It will be in your mind until you completely release the personal thought system..Then you will no longer need another thought system to counteract it because you will no longer believe in form. You will *be* Truth.

When you choose inner peace you decide to shift your relationship to the universe of form. With the personal thought system the universe of form is seen as the source of peace and happiness. But the Teacher of Truth uses your awareness of a universe of form as a means to make you aware that lasting peace and happiness are already within you. Every personal goal and relationship and situation becomes a classroom where you learn to observe your own mind and release the personal thought system's judgments and attachments, which are obstacles to peace.

You are not going to trust the Teacher of Truth right off. Until you experience It you won't have an honest basis to even believe that It is real. But if you take a chance and open yourself to the Teacher of Truth, It will meet you where you are. This means that while the world is so real to you It will help you with goals and decisions and problems in the world. In time, as you experience It more and more, your trust will grow. You will experience (words, formless ideas, intuitions) the Teacher of Truth more clearly and if you truly want peace, you will allow It to redirect you to observing your thoughts and how they cause your sense of conflict or peace. Even when you are fully aware that the world is an idea in your mind there will still be practical decisions to make and you will always be able to give these to the Teacher of Truth so that you do not have to be burdened with them.

The Teacher of Truth is always with you, and has always been with you, even when you weren't aware of It. You are in charge of your relationship with It. You will accept as much peace as you want, so you decide how much guidance you want. You can decide to simply make a better life for the personal self and call on the Teacher of Truth only in relation to that goal. But if you want total peace then you will pass through that stage and naturally reach the stage where you allow the Teacher of Truth to lead the way instead. Then It will lead you to releasing the personal identity, so It will lead you to total peace.

60. Ask: What does "I am under no laws but God's" mean? (January 20, 2012)

"I don't understand what the Workbook says about 'I am under no laws but God's', particularly when it comes to economic laws. A part of me wants not to worry about money but another part says I have to. This quote from the Course *makes me feel free, but I wonder if it will make me irresponsible as well."* – SD

The personal thought system (ego) teaches that if you follow certain rules in the world you will be happy, peaceful, complete, etc. What *A Course in Miracles* is saying is that your peace and happiness are not determined by anything in the universe of form but by your awareness of God. God is the eternal Truth in you.

What you are seeing here is that the personal thought system (ego) equates worrying with responsibility. But in what way is worrying responsible? It is a waste of time and energy and it certainly does not lead to inner peace. The personal thought system values worrying because it distracts you from Truth (God). That's its only use for anything in the universe of form.

When you are centered in Truth you will know what you have to do to take care of the personal self. If you are not yet able to center yourself in Truth use the personal self's concerns to become aware of the Teacher of Truth (Holy Spirit) within you by bringing personal concerns (like money issues) to It. It will always answer you. This is how you will learn that It is always here with you. And it is this awareness that will bring you peace.

61. Ask: How do I use ACIM when others won't forgive me? (January 27, 2012)

"My adult children have refused to speak to me for years. I have explained my past actions and I have apologized but this has not brought about a change in my relationship with them. How can I use what ACIM *teaches to change my thinking about this?"* – Anonymous

By taking responsibility and apologizing you have taken steps to undo the guilt in your mind that the personal thought system (ego) may have been using as an obstacle to peace. This clears the way to peace for you. But whether or not your children want peace is up to them. Every mind has peace in it, but most are not willing to work through their obstacles to peace. Most continue to seek peace through grudges and victimhood rather than through an awareness of Truth and the releasing of the personal story.

Frankly, even if your children came around and forgave you the personal thought system in your mind would find something else lacking in the personal life about which to gripe. It can never be lastingly happy, because it is a thought system of lack. This is why personal peace is not true inner peace. And this is why the only way to peace is to release the personal thought system, not to try to fix it or to make it happy. If you want inner peace, no matter what is happening in the personal self's life, you must grow your awareness of the Truth within you.

If you find that you cannot let your children go and this continues to be an obstacle to peace for you, then you need to look into your own mind for the thoughts, beliefs, and attachments that are obstacles to peace. You will want to invite the Holy Spirit into this process.

62. Ask: How does one turn their thoughts over to the Holy Spirit? (February 3, 2012)

"Throughout the Course *Text and lessons there is the directive to turn our ego thoughts over to the Holy Spirit. I have a very difficult situation which is making me very unhappy. I know it is the result of my need for a special relationship. I know on some level I am resisting changing my thoughts and the root of this is probably feeling the need to be loved and this most likely goes back to feeling I lost God's love. The difficulty I am having is "turning it to the Holy Spirit" How does one do that? I am practically begging and I am still feeling like this person owes me more demonstrations of love. This is not the first time I have asked the Holy Spirit to take some ego thought away but I rarely feel peace. I feel like the ego has a strangle hold on me and I cannot just think these things away..."* – MM

The Holy Spirit (Teacher of Truth) is the thought system that represents Truth in your mind. When you "turn" a situation "over" to It you are saying that you want to come at the situation from that thought system instead of the personal thought system (ego). You have to be willing to let go of the way that you look at the situation now. You have to be willing to look at it in a new way.

It sounds like you have done this. You have become aware that your need for love from this person represents your deeper feeling that you do not have True Love (God's Love) within you. Sometimes when we ask the Holy Spirit for help we are given a thought that brings immediate relief. Sometimes we become aware of a false belief that is going to take some time to work out.

In your case you continue to look for demonstrations of love from this person even though you know that they cannot supply the True Love that you feel you lack within yourself.

Even if they behaved as you wanted it would not be enough and you would continue to feel that they or someone else was not supplying what you need. You understand this intellectually but your experience has not yet shifted for you to be truly aware of this. So your focus now needs to be on building your awareness of Love within you. You can do this by inviting Love into your awareness through formal meditation daily and by turning inward to Love throughout the day and reminding yourself that you have all that you need within yourself. And when you find yourself feeling needy or empty or demanding of others remind yourself that they cannot supply the Love that you seek. Then turn inward to find True Love where It really is.

Growing your awareness of Love within is a process, so be patient and gentle with yourself. In time you will feel whole within yourself and no longer feel a need to demand anything from others. You will simply enjoy them as they are.

63. Ask: Are we being thought? (February 10, 2012)

"Are we being thought? Is the one split mind, that fragments into 7 billion and then other species' minds, thinking our life situations that come to us and then our decision maker has only 2 choices which teacher to listen to, the holy spirit or ego, we really don't have any other active ability to attract what we want in life just the way we interpret it, is this correct?" – JB

No, you are not being thought. You are the one mind doing the thinking. But when you identify with a personal self (ego) you think that you are the thought in some other Mind. Maybe you label that Mind, God; maybe you never bother to label it. You may not even think of yourself as in mind but in a real universe of form. But it is the equivalent to a personal self having a dream while sleeping and thinking that they are a figure in the dream rather than the dreamer of the dream.

This is the split in the mind. It seems like there is "you" and a universe outside of you with many billions of minds. Or that there is your mind and a mind outside your mind in which you reside. But there is really just one mind thinking it all. You will not come to this awareness through the personal thought system, however. But you will become aware of this as you grow aware of Truth.

The personal thought system interprets this awareness with fear. This is why you will not look at this idea while you are listening to the personal thought system. It equates responsibility with blame. Look at what you have wrought! This whole tragic, painful, limited universe of form that is the opposite of God in every way! But that is because it wants to make the universe of form real to you. As you grow aware of Truth formlessness becomes the real experience for you and you recognize that form is just an empty, meaningless idea. You do not have to give it any thought. And you certainly do not have to feel guilty about it.

On a personal level you do attract whatever shows up in the personal self's life. But whatever it is it is always meaningless and open to interpretation. That is why, if you want inner peace, it makes no sense at all to be concerned with what is or is not showing up in the universe of form. It has no meaning in itself. And if you give it meaning you make it real to you and teach yourself that you are what you are not. This keeps you in conflict.

For a while, the world will still be very real to you and you will not be able to avoid interpreting it. The personal thought system offers an interpretation that emphasizes the details and reinforces your sense of lack and limitation. The Holy Spirit offers an interpretation that looks at the larger unfolding and reinforces your awareness that all must be unfolding perfectly because you are aware of Truth. These are the choices in interpretation that lead to your sense of conflict or peace. And, in time, you will not need any interpretation because you will not be giving form much thought at all.

64. Ask: How can I better hear the Holy Spirit? (February 17, 2012)

"...I am constantly praying, asking, seeking and knocking on the door to be opened so that the Holy Spirit speaks to me more frequently and at greater volume than my ego mind. I think that "undoing" the ego mind is not so much a "goal." To me it seems that communicating and communing with the Holy Spirit will *inherently* undo the ego. Yet in spite of prayers and many efforts, I find "that still small voice" almost inaudible against the din of my ego habits. I have been a long time (30+ years) seeker and Course student for about 8 years. Please help suggest ways to more frequently hear the voice of the Holy Spirit." – AR

You state an obstacle to hearing better the Holy Spirit (Teacher of Truth in your mind) when you say that you think that communing with the Holy Spirit alone will undo the ego (personal though system). Your obstacles to hearing the Holy Spirit are the guilty and fearful thoughts of the ego that you believe and you can remove these obstacles only by looking at them directly and undoing them. Because they are belief's they are not undone by your simply ignoring or denying them.

What this means in practice is that when the ego seems to be so loud that you cannot feel God or hear the Holy Spirit you look at what the ego is saying. On the surface it may simply be throwing up distractions but you are accepting the distractions because you believe something fearful that it is saying beneath the distractions. You want to be willing and open to looking at these thoughts. If you cannot access them then ask the Holy Spirit to help you uncover them. They will always be some form of guilt and fear.

Also, keep in mind that you do not always experience the Holy Spirit through a Voice in your mind. You also experience the Holy Spirit through formless ideas, insights, intuitions, and ideas and answers coming to you from "outside" of you (others, TV, books, movies, etc.). Sometimes one's expectations of how they will experience the Holy Spirit are obstacles to their seeing that they already do experience It.

65. Ask: In Truth will I still be aware of myself as an individual? (February 24, 2012)

"...Once the ego has been conquered and one is in the state of permanent peace, does the awareness (I am) still perceive individualistically - i.e. this is me (peace) I exist in the sea of peace and I will always be aware of myself as an individual piece of stillness, in this bodied life and beyond, or is it a case of I dissolve into peace (stillness) where we exist as one but not aware of myself sort of like an infant's unknowing 'awareness.'" – PS

Your sense of existence is eternal but your sense of individuality is temporary. In other words, the "I am" that you experience deep within is an experience of the eternal but your projection of your sense of existence onto limited form ceases in time.

So in essence neither one of the scenarios you suggest is accurate. In Truth you do not experience yourself as one among many nor as one within something greater. You experience One without limits. And your individuality does not dissolve into a vast Oneness, either. The part of your mind that is eternal is eternal now. It is whole and complete. It is completely untouched and uninterrupted by the idea of time and all that it seems to contain. Your experience of individuality never becomes part of the Oneness. It is the false idea that falls away.

A Course in Miracles stresses the Holy Instant because you do not need time to experience eternity. You do not have to wait to attain something in the future or for the passing of the body to experience Truth. You can turn within to Truth (God) right now. Truth is your Being; your sense of existence, of "I am". And you know when you experience Truth that It is all that is real and eternal. Then when you return from eternity to an awareness of time, time never has the same hold on you again. Truth and peace have come into your awareness.

66. Ask: Was the MFT dictated by a different Spirit of the God Head? (March 2, 2012)

"I have been studying the Course *for years, and have been through the Manual for Teachers more than a few times. This time I realize that the prose is so much easier to read and understand than in the Text. It ran through my mind that perhaps there was a different Spirit of the God Head that dictated this part of the* Course. *What do you think?"* – GF

There is only one Spirit, or Truth, Which is called "God" in *A Course in Miracles*. The part of your seemingly-individual mind that is one with God is called "Christ" in the *Course* and the teaching aspect of the Christ Mind is called the "Holy Spirit". Because there is only one Truth It is universal, so Christ is the same in every mind. There are no individual spirits.

It was the Christ Mind that dictated the entire *Course* and its two supplements to Helen Schucman. (She called Christ in her mind "Jesus"). The fact that the Workbook and the Manual for Teachers are easier to read than the Text attests to Helen's growing comfort as a scribe. The Text, too, gets easier after the first few chapters.

Also, the Workbook and MFT are practical, so more straightforward than the Text, which is theoretical. Many find that the practical approach of those books makes the message of the *Course* more accessible in them.

Notice that you have read the MFT more than a few times and you only now realize how much easier it is to read than the Text. This shows your growing acceptance of the message of the *Course*. Helen Schucman was the first student of the *Course* and she was just like those who followed. Her mind, like ours, was filled with guilt and fear. She began incredibly resistant to its message, though willing to take it down, just as we are willing to keep reading despite our fears. The more guilt and fear we work through the easier we find it is to read and understand the *Course*.

67. Ask: Is feeling "elevated" from the world part of the process? (March 9, 2012)

"I have been doing the Course *since three years ago, and I deeply felt I resonated with its message of Love as the only Truth...After some months of doing it, my life started to change, I felt the calling to change my way of living, to leave behind my career as a lawyer, and I started to get very in touch with "spirituality"...I have made many of the mistakes you point out in your blog...for a long time I resisted the world, tried to force the experience of the* Course, *and went into spiritual sacrifice, I went deeply in trying to understand my ego and others' egos...I felt depressed, and kind of elevated from this world... instead of feeling joyfully and lovingly here on earth...I am not sure if what I lived was necessary, but I know that today that I want to choose*

differently...I am starting to choose what feels light, joyful, and free instead of dense and heavy...But I feel I need a guidance on this matter, because there are times when I feel I am working on something deep, (for instance a deep attachment), where I feel led to be inwards, away, passive, I feel kind of apathetic to the world, and elevated, but I feel in peace...This peace however is not alive and joyfully on earth...Is this part of the healing process? Should I be patient when I feel in that mood, or should I not give it much space...I am kind of sorting out if it comes from a healing of the Holy Spirit, or if it comes from a part of me that doesn't want to live in joy and stay focused in the 'healing'"... - NA

What you described that you initially experienced was what I call the "honeymoon" phase. You accepted the goal of inner peace, but then felt closer to it than you really were. You still had to work through your obstacles to fully experiencing peace, which takes many years. You then entered a phase of trying to force yourself to be further along than you are, of sacrificing, etc. and this is also very typical. In the beginning you are used to listening to the personal thought system (ego) and it tries to take over your spiritual process.

As you grow aware of Truth you will feel detached from the world. You will feel love and peace and joy within yourself and not from the world or about the world. You will become aware that you are leaving the idea of the world behind. But this will not cause you to feel depressed. If you feel depressed from your experiences of feeling detached or "elevated" from the world it is because the personal thought system interprets these experiences as loss and you still agree with it. It will take some time for you to fully accept that leaving the idea of the world behind is not loss. The more that you experience Truth the less that you will feel that letting go of the world is loss. You will recognize that your attachment to the world is an obstacle to peace.

Sometimes when you feel peace it will be a neutral, quiet experience rather than something that is vibrantly joyful. But if this turns into depression then you want to look with the Holy Spirit (Teacher of Truth) at the thoughts and beliefs that lead to the depression.

Everything that you experience as you grow your awareness of Truth is necessary. It wouldn't come up if it was not there within you to be embraced or released.

68. Ask: Am I missing something in the forgiveness process? (March 17, 2012)

"I have a boss who has been undergoing treatment for Bipolar Disorder for over 30 years, and I have all of the typical litany of "I love my job, but I hate my boss because.......…" issues that many of us have throughout our lives, which could let my ego be obsessed with anger and revenge thoughts, if I let it. He has several other health issues, which I honestly believe I could help in healing if it were not for the fact that when I look within, and am vigilant of my thoughts, I know that I am not truly forgiving him, but hold some sort of deep seated pleasure at his "justifiable punishment." Yes, I realize that if anyone deserves forgiveness "in the world," it is someone whose inherited and biological issues are the total cause of his hurtful actions. Yes, I realize that we are all worthy, and during or immediately after meditation, I feel I have turned it over to Spirit for healing, but either I am not truly handing it over, or I am not yet seeing the personal healing that might be occurring. Perhaps I am already having the healing lesson experiences and improved thoughts that I am looking for, but if so, it is happening at a slow rate. I have been working on this issue for several months. Odd, that I know, if he apologized, I truly would let it go, but I am aware that I have not completely let it go, as yet, on my own. Should I just be

patient and continue to "practice forgiveness" or do you think there is a specific piece of the forgiveness process that I might be missing?" - JL

True forgiveness means releasing whatever is appearing in the universe of form in the recognition that only God (the eternal Truth within you) is real. So ultimately true forgiveness means recognizing that there is nothing to forgive. This is a realization that comes to you as you grow your awareness of God.

What happens in the universe of form is neutral – it has no meaning in itself. What disturbs your peace is never what is occurring in form but the meaning that you give to what occurs in form. So if you want peace what you want to forgive (release) are your thoughts about your boss' behavior. You want to sort out what is fact (he did such and such) from the projection of meaning (this was wrong, bad, I'm his victim, etc.) from the ego (personal thought system). Then you can just observe his behavior without judgment and without taking it personally. This sets your mind free to rest in the awareness within that only God is real.

You have written some thoughts that you will want to correct if you want peace:

You write that the ego could be obsessed with anger and revenge if you let it. The ego is always obsessed with anger and revenge and it will not change. The goal is not to change the ego but to change your mind by choosing to not listen to the ego's thought system in your mind. It is not you. You do not want to repress its thoughts, which are a means for holding onto them. You want to let them come up so that you can correct them for yourself and let them go (forgive).

It is clear that your repressing the ego's angry thoughts is not working for you because you "hold some deep seated pleasure at his 'justifiable punishment'". Seeing (and wanting) your boss' health issues as "punishment" is also typical of the ego. His illnesses are simply part of the personal experience for him. They have no meaning in themselves. The ego's interpretations are not "wrong" or "bad"; they just give meaning to what has no meaning.

You cannot heal another. When one heals it is because they have accepted healing within their own mind, even if it seems to come from outside agents. And you cannot look to the universe of form for "proof" of healing, either. The proof of whether or not your mind is healed is whether or not you are in touch with the peace that is always within your mind. If you are then it will not matter to you what is or is not showing up in the universe of form.

You write that you would let your boss' behavior go if he apologized but that would not be true forgiveness. That would be the ego feeling validated for seeing itself as a victim of this man, so being "magnanimous" and "forgiving" him. This is the ego's version of forgiveness, but it would not release you from identifying with an ego, which is the result of true forgiveness.

69. Ask: Is it attacking my brother to ask for child support? (March 23, 2012)

"I have a 14 teen year old daughter and her father feels that he shouldn't have to pay child support. I want to file for child support because I really do need his help. But when I bring it up to him he attacks me with his thoughts and then I feel guilty that I am attacking Christ. Is it attack towards my brother to file for child support? I find my mind justifying my reasons and I get confused. I really want to release all attack thoughts because they bring nothing but hell to my dream. Sometimes I am confused about what is attack." – YH

You "attack" yourself whenever you choose the personal thought system (ego) because it is not you. This is the same as attacking Christ, because Christ is the label given to the universal, eternal Truth in you. So everything that proceeds from your choice for the personal self then perpetuates your attack on yourself. This is not "bad" or "wrong". Christ is not changed in any way by this. It is simply a mistake that brings you pain. So correction, not guilt, is justified. And the correction is to turn to Christ in your mind instead.

Another is not Christ in their person, though Christ is in their mind whether or not they are aware of It. Filing papers to get your child's father to contribute money to help you raise her is not an attack on Christ or even on him. It's simply a legal means of asking him to take responsibility for what you feel is his responsibility. His attacking comes from the fear that he experiences identifying with a personal self. You are not responsible for undoing this; he is.

70. Ask: Can other parts of the sonship influence us while we're dreaming? (March 30, 2012)

"... is my illusion being impacted by a collective illusion? ... if the Voice identified as Jesus broke into Helen's dream, can other spirits or parts of the sonship also influence us while we're dreaming: i.e. so called ascended masters or channeled souls, aliens, demons etc.?..." - P

There is only one mind that seems split between Truth (God) and not-Truth. *A Course in Miracles* calls this the "son of God". This is the one mind that is "dreaming" of the universe of form, time, and all of the stories in time. And each seemingly-individual mind projected into the dream also projects its own meaning onto the universe of form. So there is an overarching, or collective, dream in which cause and effect applies. This "story" is neutral in that it has no meaning in itself. And then there is also your individual dream, which is your projection of meaning onto the universe of form.

For example, if the company that you work for goes out of business then this has an impact on what you see as your individual story. But how you experience this occurrence is determined by the meaning that you project onto it. (Or you could choose to not project any meaning onto it at all).

There are only two voices in your mind: the Teacher of Truth (Holy Spirit) and the personal thought system (ego). For some, the Teacher of Truth is represented to them in a specific form, like Jesus or another "ascended master". For others, they recognize the Voice of Truth as the Truth in their mind reaching them and they do not assign It any specific form.

Any other voice in your mind is not-Truth (ego). It's part of the dream whether or not it seems to be the personal thought system in your mind or another voice in your mind that you "channel". Whether you hear Truth or not-Truth you are influenced by either only by your own choice.

You may "hear" the Teacher of Truth as words in your mind, as unformed ideas, or as intuitions. You know when you are hearing Truth when you feel set free. The Truth is quiet and emotionally neutral, though It inspires joy in you. Not-Truth may communicate with you in the same ways, as well as with its tell-tale clamor. But it is never emotionally neutral and you never feel set free, joyous, or at peace when you hear it.

71. Ask: How did you deal with anxiety and panic? (April 6, 2012)

"...I was interested when reading your personal story, that you experienced anxiety and panic attacks... there is a lot of talk about 'energy therapy' that releases the 'trapped' energy in the subconscious mind. I use it sometimes and it does help to bring me back to a rational state of mind where I can then more clearly ask the Holy Spirit for guidance. Do you have an opinion on this? If you don't mind sharing, how did you approach dealing with your anxiety and panic attacks? Were you using the course at the time? You spoke about "processing" time with the Holy Spirit. How did you go about doing that and were you able to remove subconscious blocks and beliefs by doing that alone? Sometimes, when doing the exercises, I feel a literal 'block' almost like a brick wall that makes it very difficult to absorb new thoughts and truths." – SL

Yes, I used to experience anxiety and panic attacks. They began before I was a student of *A Course in Miracles* and continued for many years after I began the *Course*. I got past them not by focusing on them but by growing my awareness of Truth (God). In time, as Truth became a real experience for me and not just a nice idea, they fell away naturally.

If energy therapy works for you that is great! Use whatever works. You make the choice for healing and the means for healing manifests in the universe of form in a way that works for you.

When I refer to "processing" in my writing I am talking about letting the thoughts that fill your mind just go on by. For example, if you meditate at the end of the day your mind is likely to be filled with thoughts about what happened that day. Just let those thoughts run their course without embracing them or fighting them. You will find a need to let your mind process not just at the end of a busy day but often after an intense movie or TV program or when you are in the midst of any emotional experience. When the processing is done you will find it easier to quiet your mind and open it to Truth.

Apart from processing and communing with Truth I also look with the Holy Spirit at mistaken beliefs that are obstacles to peace. If a false belief is not conscious, but I know that it is there because of the guilt, fear, and/or anger I feel, I ask the Holy Spirit to help me find it. Then, with the Holy Spirit, I look at the belief from an awareness of Truth and undo it. This practice and my experiences of Truth combine to help me undo my blocks to peace.

Don't worry about doing the Workbook perfectly or understanding every lesson. You are not going to be ready for every idea in it. For one year just do a lesson a day as best you can that day. You are only meant to practice the lessons for one year, but you will want to go back and read the Workbook through as you would the Text. And just as with the Text, you will understand more each time you read it.

72. Ask: How can I be more diligent with the lessons? (April 13, 2012)

"Every year I go gung ho and start off doing a lesson each day using index cards to write the day's lesson down and in a couple of months I falter and stop completely. Why is that? How can I make myself more diligent so that I do at least one lesson per day?" – DH

If you have been unable to complete the lessons in the Workbook then you need to ask yourself what form of resistance is coming up around the time that you falter and stop. Some students think that they have to do the lessons perfectly each day and when they don't they give up, feeling like a failure. Others bump into ideas that they find hard to accept and give up. When you find yourself resistant go back and read the introduction to the Workbook. It gives you instructions for doing the lessons and it makes it quite clear that you do not have to accept the ideas in them. Simply do not actively resist them. Each day just do the best that you can with that day's lesson, then move on to the next lesson the next day. Only do one lesson per day.

You can find the lessons on cards at www.acim.org so that you do not have to write them down to carry with you each day.

If you have completed the lessons once then you do not have to do them again. As it says in the introduction to the Workbook, the mind training period the lessons cover is one year. After that you may want to read and study the Workbook as you would the Text and the Manual for Teachers, but you do not need to put the lessons into practice again. In fact, doing so will hold you back. At the end of the Workbook you are left with the Holy Spirit, Who guides your mind training from then on.

73. Ask: How can I let go of the wheel when I'm going 60mph on the freeway? (April 20, 2012)

"...But facing what I feel are the 'facts' of the state I find I'm in, I can't do this when I'm driving my car and in heavy traffic on the freeway going 60 mph to simply say : 'This is all not reality, it's not, in Truth, happening and is an illusion' With that I, simply let go of the wheel. Intentional or not the physical world is what it is for me. Telling the Holy Spirit that I don't know how to resolve this and turn it over to my Teacher I confidently fear such a physical act will harm me and many bodies. Forgive my mistaken thinking. I'm not intending to be argumentative but am truthfully wrangling with what's real, what's illusion and live in it without making things worse. In what I read currently I can't be in both 'worlds' and expect the Holy Spirit to fix this..." - LM

Only the ego (personal thought system) would think it was necessary for you to let go of a steering wheel while going at 60mph on the freeway. To do what? Prove your trust in the Holy Spirit (Teacher of Truth)? The Holy Spirit will never test you. If you think that you are being tested or that you must prove something then you are listening to the ego.

There is a misconception at the heart of your question and it is that turning your mind over to the Holy Spirit means that the body stops acting. The difference between driving while consumed with ego thoughts and driving while centered in God (Truth) is that in the former you are in conflict and in the latter you are at peace. But the body is still doing the same thing: driving.

The body's life in the world looks the same whether your mind is centered in Truth or it is centered in ego. It has a job, family, friends, hobbies, interests, etc. It eats, its sleeps, it watches TV, it goes on vacation, it brushes its teeth, etc. You know if you have peace by how you feel within, not by how the body's life in the world looks.

There is no value in looking around at the universe of form and saying, "This is not real; it's an illusion." It is the ego that instructs this. It wants to keep your attention on form, even if it's to futilely try to convince yourself that it is not real. You come to an awareness that illusion is illusion by turning away from it and turning inward to Truth instead. In time, as Truth becomes a real experience for you and not just a nice idea, it will be obvious to you that illusion is illusion. You do not have to lie to yourself or force this awareness. If you experience the world as very real, this is where the Holy Spirit will meet you. Invite It in to be your partner in everything and in time your awareness of It will be more real to you than form. You can only do this by being completely honest with yourself, and therefore with the Holy Spirit, about what you are experiencing.

Your mind cannot be in both ego and in Truth at the same time because your mind always commits completely. But you will vacillate between the two for a long time. The Holy Spirit cannot fix this, because the choice of which is more valuable to you is yours to make. But the Holy Spirit is always ready to come into your awareness when you are willing to have It in your awareness.

74. Ask: How does the Course fit in with the fear eating at me? (April 27, 2012)

"I have been studying the Course *for 3 years now…My life in the world is stressful, I have enough money to sustain myself for a few more months, and then…… Being 70 makes it difficult. I am distracted by the pressures of survival… I love the* Course, *it does and has sustained me. Just wonder where it fits with the fear that is eating me."* - CG

It sounds like *A Course in Miracles* is a bunch of nice ideas for you but that you are not really experiencing Truth (God) within you enough to trust It yet. Trust that you will be guided as to how to take care of the personal self will only come when Truth is a real experience for you. So your first object is to develop your awareness of Truth. Your situation is a perfect opportunity to do so. Ask the Teacher of Truth (Holy Spirit) for guidance about money and any other issue bothering you. You will always be answered. You may not accept the answer the moment you ask, but it will come to you when you are open and willing to hear it.

Fear will come and go as you grow your awareness of the Truth and learn that your trust in It is justified. But now that you've chosen peace everything, including fear, has the new purpose of being an opportunity to bring Truth to your mind. The more you call on the Teacher of Truth and accept It into your awareness the faster your trust in It will grow. Make the Teacher of Truth your Constant Companion and in time fear will fall away.

If you find it hard to call on the Teacher of Truth or to hear It then you want to look at the thoughts in your mind that are blocking your awareness of Truth. These will be some form of guilt or unworthiness. You need to bring these thoughts to the light so that you can undo them with the Teacher of Truth. This may seem circular – you have to call on What you fear to help you undo your fear of It – and this is why growing trust in Truth is so slow going at the beginning. But it does grow over time and you will find peace.

75. Ask: What makes the Course different from other specific answers? (May 11, 2012)

"…Considering the topic of the latest newsletter (revisited on May 4, 2012, http://acimmentor.blogspot.com/2007/06/one-limit-to-holy-spirits-guidance.html) about specific questions being answered by Holy Spirit, and that those 'answers' aren't for anyone else, it's more about the fact that communion with HS is happening for that person regardless of answers: What makes the Course in Miracles *text any different? Were they answers to Helen's request for better ways to relate that were relevant to her and not necessarily to anyone else? Why are people gathering and sometimes almost forming a religion over answers that came just for Helen? Shouldn't we just be celebrating that she had a huge*

communication with Holy Spirit rather than trying to live by answers meant just for her and just for that specific time in her life?" – BJ

A Course in Miracles is different because Helen Shucman kept out anything that was very specific to her from publication. She had dialogues with Jesus that were apart from her scribing of the *Course*. And she and Ken Wapnick were guided to take out some personal passages before publication. (These can be read in the urtext). Also, the *Course* was not a specific answer to a specific question. Helen and Bill Thetford were looking together for "a better way" to relate to each other and their colleagues at work. They were not consciously asking to become aware of Truth. But Helen was subsequently asked by the Holy Spirit, through a series of dreams, if she would be a "receiver". She agreed. So this was a case of the Holy Spirit seeing an opening, not of Helen asking for a specific answer.

But it is important to know that the form of the *Course* was shaped by the context of Helen and Bill's lives, minds, interests, and situation. Otherwise much of it can be (and is!) misread, as happens with all spiritual teachings taken out of context. Remember, the *Course* is just one form of a universal curriculum. The universal curriculum is the way to inner peace through an awareness of Truth. The many forms this lesson plan takes are always shaped by (and sometimes limited by) the mind(s) scribing, channeling, or collaborating with the Holy Spirit to write them or to speak them.

For example, Helen and Bill's decision to find a better way to relate with others did provide the context for this form of the Holy Spirit's lesson plan for peace. The *Course* teaches how to use relationships in the world to become aware of the Truth within. This is why the *Course* can seem to have two different levels. On the surface, it seems like it offers a better way to live with others in the world. And you can choose to limit yourself to learning only that. But it also contains a deeper message, if you want it, which leads you inward to true, lasting inner peace.

Helen was a child-psychologist and Bill was a psychiatrist, so the *Course's* approach is very psychological. There are a few passages that use teaching children as examples, clearly speaking to Helen's experience. It speaks in terms of "healing" the mind and "teaching". Mental health professionals are types of "teachers" in what is generally regarded as a "healing" profession. So the *Course* speaks their language and to their identities.

Helen was not Christian, but was drawn very much to Christianity. So the language of the *Course* is Christian, though it redefines traditional Christian symbols, words, and concepts in loving ways that undo their frightening connotations.

Helen's love of iambic pentameter shapes much of the writing style of the *Course*.

Helen also felt a need for a greater purpose, which is also stated directly in the *Course* ("you asked for a purpose..."). So the *Course* gave her a story for her part in "saving" the "sonship". This story, though first for Helen, can also be used by students who feel a need for a purpose as they release any sense of purpose the ego gave them. It's a temporary but necessary bridge that falls away when one becomes fulfilled by their awareness of God.

There are occasionally in the early chapters of the Text sections, and even paragraphs, which suddenly veer slightly off-topic. These read as answers to questions provoked in Helen's mind while scribing. So in a sense they were specific to what Helen was thinking at the moment. But these are passages that contain ideas that are useful in general.

There are also passages that say something like, "you are now experiencing", which are clearly directed toward what Helen was experiencing at the moment she scribed those passages.

They wouldn't have applied even to her specifically later on, as she advanced. Most of these, however, are things that are generally experienced by most students at some point in their study.

In the Workbook there is a lesson that says that if you are doing it right you should be seeing light around objects. This was clearly directed to the way Helen's mind worked. Others may have a different experience, but it would be something that makes one aware of a different way of perceiving. (Frankly, nothing changed for me when I did that lesson!).

The Holy Relationship that Helen and Bill experienced is not common to most students. They were both at the exact same teaching/learning level. They were experiencing the same thing at the same time. As it says in the Manual for Teachers, these relationships are rare. The vast majority of students are either more or less advanced in their awareness of Truth than those around them, even if they know other *Course* students. But we can all learn the general lesson of Helen and Bill's relationship, which is to look past the projections of the ego and to turn inward to remember God (Truth) instead.

The explanation of metaphysics (the relationship between mind and the universe of form) in the *Course* deals primarily with physical illness. It revisits again and again the idea that the mind, not the body, is the source of illness in the body. This indicates that this was a recurring issue for Helen. If she had ongoing fears about other forms of lack instead the *Course* would have discussed metaphysics in those terms.

So when you read the *Course* you want to keep in mind that it was written first to Helen and Bill. But its usefulness did not end with them. All spiritual teachings require lengthy and deep study with the Holy Spirit. This is because of the limitations and imperfections of the minds through which they come into the world. But also because of the limitations and imperfections of your mind. Only the Holy Spirit in your mind is Perfect, so only It, not words on a page, should be your Guide.

76. ACIM and Body Disorders (May 18, 2012)

As a student of and mentor for other students of *A Course in Miracles* I have both experienced and seen how the ego's (personal thought system's) inherent guilt and fear distort its teaching. Some of the ego's greatest distortions are around the *Course's* teachings on metaphysics, or the relationship between mind and the universe of form. Guilt is provoked in particular around its discussion of the body and the manifestation of disorders (illness, injury, misalignments, etc.) in the body. What is stated in the *Course* as fact is viewed through the ego as condemnation or admonition.

Like most students of the *Course* I used to feel guilty when I got sick. I felt that I was failing. But this did not stop me from doing what I needed to do to take care of the body and relieve myself of pain or discomfort. So I have been shocked to learn that many students of the *Course* actually deny themselves relief from suffering, sometimes even refusing to seek treatment for life-threatening conditions. They do this because they interpret getting treatment for the body as "wrong" or "bad". They feel that they "should" heal the body by employing the mind for this purpose. Some spend a lot of time, even years, seeking in their minds for the thoughts that they believe are manifested as disorder in the body. The *Course* never prescribes any of these courses of action or inaction. All of this is done because the student believes the ego's guilty interpretation of the ideas in the *Course*.

So here I have culled quotes from the *Course* which show what it really teaches. I have summarized each collection of quotes at the end of each answer. Hopefully this will help you undo and/or avoid some of the guilt that the ego inspires regarding disorders in the body.

For simplicity and clarity I use here quotes from *The Plain Language A Course in Miracles* [Text: *The Message of A Course in Miracles (MACIM);* Workbook: *Practicing A Course in Miracles (PACIM); * Manual for Teachers: *The Way of A Course in Miracles (WACIM)*]. If you prefer to read the quotes from the original the designation after each quote also matches the original. (For example, MACIM-1.1.1 refers to the Text, chapter 1, part 1, paragraph 1).

At the very end I share my own experience with the body and the Holy Spirit.

<u>What is the purpose of the body?</u>

God did not make the body, which is destructible and therefore not Eternal. (MACIM-6.5a.2)

The body is the personal mind's idol. It is your belief in separation from God made into form and then projected outside your mind. This makes it seem like there is a wall of flesh around your mind, limiting it to a tiny spot of space and time, obligated to die, and given an instant to sigh and grieve and die in honor of separation. (MACIM-20.6.11)

The body is the symbol of the personal self, as the personal self is the symbol of your separation from God. Both are nothing more than your attempts to limit your Communication with God to make Oneness impossible. (MACIM-15.9.2)

The personal self uses the body to attack your mind because it realizes that you can end it and the body merely by recognizing that they are not real. It tries to persuade you that the body is more real than the mind and that the mind serves the personal self. (MACIM-6.4.5)

The personal mind regards the body as its home and all appetites and needs, whether they are physical or emotional, originate in the personal mind and are the means of "getting" something to confirm the personal self's existence to itself. (MACIM-4.2.7)

Your perception of yourself as separate from God - a personal self in a body within a world - is a distortion of your mind; a fantasy. Your reactions and actions in the world that you perceive stem from your unawareness that it is a fantasy. This fantasy, which includes the fantasies that you have in the world and recognize as such, are attempts to satisfy the false needs that have arisen from your sense of separation from God. (MACIM-1.7.3)

But:

The body does not contain you who are Life and it neither lives nor dies. (MACIM-6.5a.1)

The body can no more die than it can feel. Of itself it is neither corruptible, nor incorruptible. It does nothing and it is nothing. (MACIM-19.4c.1.3)

The body is simply a part of your experience in your perception of a world. It is almost impossible for you to deny that you experience a body and doing so you will also deny the power of your mind, which made it. (MACIM-2.4.3)

The belief that you are a body is a mistake that calls for correction. (PACIM-91.6)

The body was not made by Love but Love does not condemn it. It can use the body Lovingly, respecting what you have made and using it to save you from your illusions. (MACIM-18.6.4)

So:

The body has no purpose of its own but only the purpose that you give to it. Whatever goal you assign to the body, the body will seem to be a means of attaining that goal. (MACIM-19.4b.1.2)

The body is neutral and it can be used by your mind to extend God's Love or to perpetuate your sense of separation from God. (MACIM-1.5.1)

It is the purpose of the body itself to tempt you to forget your Identity in God. But the Holy Spirit has another use for the illusions that you have made, so It sees another purpose for them. (PACIM-64.2)

For a while you must extend God's Love through a body because you are not yet aware enough of your Oneness with God to see beyond it. The only real use the body has is as a learning device through which you learn to remember that you are One with God. (MACIM-1.7.2)

Your mind can bring the body into alignment with it by recognizing that the body is not the learner and by looking past it to Spirit. (MACIM-2.5.6)

In the service of uniting your mind with the Holy Spirit the body becomes a beautiful lesson in communion until you are again aware of your Communion with God. This is how God makes you aware of your Unlimited Mind, Which you want to limit to a body. The Holy Spirit knows the only reality of anything in the world that you perceive is the service that it renders God on behalf of your Function of extending Oneness. (MACIM-8.7.3)

The personal self's temple thus becomes the Holy Spirit's temple and only in this way is the body a temple to God. The Holy Spirit abides in the body by directing the use to which it is put. (MACIM-8.7.9)

If you give the body to the Holy Spirit to use as a means of uniting your mind you will see the physical world is nothing. (MACIM-8.7.4)

Summary:

God did not make the body. It was made by the split mind to be the personal mind's symbol of separation from God. Your belief in it as you is the personal mind's purpose for the body. Since you are mind and the personal mind is a thought system in your mind it perpetuates itself by teaching you that the body is more real than the mind. And that the mind's purpose is to serve a body.

The ego teaches you to use the body to fulfill the sense of lack that you feel for separating from God. Doing this reaffirms the ego and the body as your identity.

But the body is neutral. It is really nothing but an empty idea with no meaning in itself. It is simply something that you are temporarily experiencing. You do not need to deny it. In fact, denying that you experience a body denigrates the power of your mind, because this experience is made by your belief. And this belief is not a sin; only a mistake that requires correction if you want peace. The Holy Spirit respects what you have made and, because it is neutral, can use it to teach you that you are formless Mind instead. Using the body for this purpose gives it the only real value that it has.

Where do disorders in the body come from?

All forms of illness are the result of your identifying with a personal self in a body. (MACIM-1.1.8)

Sickness is of your mind, not of the body. All forms of sickness signal that your mind is split and that you do not accept One Purpose. (MACIM-8.9.8)

The body's suffering is a mask your mind wears to hide that it is really your mind that suffers. You identify with a body to deny that you are your own enemy, that you attack yourself, and that you want to die. (PACIM-76.5)

The guilt in your mind keeps your mind split as your guilt is projected onto the body. The body suffers and dies because it is attacked to keep your mind split so you don't remember your Identity. (MACIM-18.6.3)

Sickness is anger that you take out on the body so that it will suffer pain. (MACIM-28.6.5)

You choose suffering because you believe that it gives you something of value. You think it is a small price to pay for something of greater worth. Sickness is a decision that you make; it is your choice for weakness, in your mistaken conviction that weakness is strength. (WACIM-5.1a.1)

Your guilt is the cause of all of your suffering. Illness is your attack on the body, which you identify with in the personal mind, in an attempt to lessen God's punishment of you for separating from God. It is a form of magical solution for guilt. (MACIM-5.5.5)

Whenever you consent to suffer pain, to be deprived, unfairly treated, or in need of anything, you project responsibility for your attack on yourself onto another in the world that you perceive. You hold a picture of your crucifixion before their eyes so that they may see their sins are written in Heaven in your blood, damning them to hell. (MACIM-27.1.3)

The personal mind has a profound investment in the body's sickness because if it is sick it proves that you are vulnerable and cannot be of God. (MACIM-8.8.3)

The personal mind uses the body's sickness as an argument that you need its guidance and it dictates endless prescriptions for avoiding catastrophe. (MACIM-8.8.6)

Summary:

Your identification with a body results in a mind that seems split between God (Truth) and not-God (personal mind). This is a disorder of your mind that manifests as disorder in the body. Projecting disorder onto the body hides from you the awareness that it is really your mind which is disordered.

Disorders show up in the body as manifestations of guilt and anger in your mind. Disorders also show up because in your identification with a personal mind you believe that they give you something of value. Your split mind seems to be an attack on God and results in guilt. To mitigate the punishment you expect from God you punish yourself in your identification with a body *for* your identification with a body. You believe both that this takes care of your guilt and that it takes God's power away and makes you stronger than God. You also use sickness to project your guilt onto others and make them feel guilty.

The personal mind also uses sickness to "prove" to you that you are not of God and that you need it to guide you.

How is the body healed?

The body cannot heal because it cannot make itself sick. The body does not need healing because its health or sickness depends entirely on how your mind perceives it and the purpose for which your mind wants to use it. (MACIM-19.1.3)

The body is not the source of its own health, then, but its condition is the result of how you interpret its function. (MACIM-8.8.1)

When you can accept that only the mind is real you will no longer confuse yourself with a body and manifest sickness. (MACIM-2.4.2)

The thoughts that result from your identification with a body instead of with your Mind are the thoughts that need healing, and the body will respond with health when those thoughts have been corrected and replaced with the Truth. (PACIM-135.10)

Healing is accomplished the moment that you no longer see any value in pain. (WACIM-5.1a.1)

The basis for healing, then, is your accepting that sickness is a decision of your mind, which then uses a body for its purposes. This is true for healing in all forms. Decide that this is so, and you will heal. (WACIM-5.1b.2)

When the personal mind tempts you to sickness do not ask the Holy Spirit to heal the body, which is not the source of sickness. Ask instead that the Holy Spirit show you the correct perception of the body because sickness is caused by your distorted perception of the body's purpose. Only perception can be sick or mistaken. (MACIM-8.9.1)

But all healing must come about because you recognize that your mind is not within a body and your mind's healing and Innocence are apart from a body. (MACIM-28.2.2)

You only need to perceive the body as apart from you and it will be a healthy, useful instrument through which your Mind can operate until its use is done. You will have no use for it when it has finished serving your Mind. (PACIM-135.8)

When you join the Mind in Which all healing rests the body is healed because you came without it. (MACIM-19.1.2)

Health is the result of a united purpose. If the body is brought under the Purpose of your Mind it becomes whole because your Mind's Purpose is One. (MACIM-8.7.13)

One Purpose, then, is the Holy Spirit's way of healing you. Healing only has meaning at the level of your mind and re-establishing Meaning in the chaotic thought system that you made is the only way to heal your mind. (MACIM-8.9.9)

But:

Healing always stands aside when it is perceived as a threat, but the instant that it is welcome, it is here. (WACIM-6.2)

While you believe that a body can get you what you want the body will appear to you to be a symbol that separation from God is real. (MACIM-4a.1.8)

While you believe that the body can give you pleasure you will also believe that it can bring you pain. (MACIM-4a.1.8)

Sickness is a decision that you make; it is your choice for weakness, in your mistaken conviction that weakness is strength. When this occurs, you see True Strength as a threat and health as a danger. (WACIM-5.1a.1)

The compromise that you try to make to keep both Truth and illusion as your goal is the belief that the body, not the mind, must be healed. This divided goal gives both the body and the mind equal reality to you. (MACIM-19.1.6)

You think Peace will replace the body and leave you homeless so you deny Peace a home within you. Giving up the body is the "sacrifice" that you think is too great for you to make and that you think is too much for the Holy Spirit to ask of you. (MACIM-4a.1b.2)

Healing represents God's total opposition to the personal self in a direct form that you are forced to recognize. It stands for All that you want to hide from yourself to protect your personal 'life'. Because, if you are healed, then you are responsible for your thoughts, and you believe that God will kill you to prove to you how weak and pitiful you are. You feel that if you choose death yourself, then your weakness becomes your strength. Through death, you give yourself what you think that God wants to give to you, so you think that you have entirely taken God's Power for your own. (WACIM-5.1a.2)

If you ask the Holy Spirit for something that you want but that you fear then your attainment of it would not really be what you want. Sometimes you don't achieve specific forms of healing even when you have changed your mind enough to call on the Holy Spirit. For example, you may ask for physical healing because you are afraid of physical pain and discomfort. But in your identification with a personal self, physical healing that comes from the Holy Spirit may be more threatening to you than the physical discomfort that you are experiencing. In this case you are not really asking for release from fear, which is true healing, but from release from the symptoms of fear that you have chosen. (MACIM-9.2.2)

And:

Your recognition that you are mind and not a body can be used for either true healing or for magical thinking. (MACIM-7.5.3)

True healing recognizes that the Oneness that you teach yourself is everywhere; magical thinking wants you to see your mind as a healer with special gifts that can be offered to those who do not have this gift. As a magical healer you could think this gift comes from God but if you think that God's Gifts are for you alone then you limit your awareness of God to a personal self and you do not know that God is Everywhere. (MACIM-7.5.4)

The body is healed by miracles because they show you that the mind made sickness and employed the body to be victim, or effect, of what it made. But this in only half of the lesson. The miracle is useless if you learn only that the body can be healed, for this is not the lesson it was sent to teach. The lesson is always that the mind was sick that thought that the body could be sick. Projecting the mind's guilt onto the body caused nothing and had no real effects. (MACIM-28.2.11)

Summary:

The body is only an idea in your mind. So the body never really needs to be healed. Disorders in the body indicate that your *mind* needs to be healed.

Since identifying with a body is the disorder of your mind that manifests in the body then the body will manifest its neutral state of health when you no longer identify with it. So you do not need to ask the Holy Spirit to heal the body. What you want to ask for instead is the Holy Spirit's help in recognizing that the body is not you. The Holy Spirit does this by using the body's life in the world for the purpose of returning your mind to its correct identification with Mind. This heals your mind and therefore the body.

But while you still want to identify with a body you will feel that giving it up is too great a sacrifice to make. The guilt and fear this causes you will continue to manifest in the body. You will fear the awareness that the body's healing is a choice you make because you will associate this awareness with acknowledging your guilt. You will think this awareness will bring God's punishment down on you. And you will associate sickness and death with strength because you will think that by making yourself sick and die you are taking God's power away. From this point of view health will seem like weakness to you.

The awareness that the mind can heal the body can be used by either the personal mind or the Holy Spirit. The personal mind is happy to use this awareness to make itself a special "healer". And it uses this awareness to perpetuate the idea that the mind's purpose is to serve the body. These may sometimes result in healing a specific form of disorder but it will not truly heal your mind. The body will therefore continue to manifest the disorder of the mind that comes from believing that the body is real.

How should I respond to disorders in the body?

You never have to consider the form of sickness that appears to you. If you do, you are forgetting that all forms have the same purpose, so they are not different. (WACIM-5.1c.3)

The Holy Spirit recognizes sickness is an error and It does not bother to analyze its form because it is meaningless. (MACIM-8.8.6)

You can give the personal self and the body to the Holy Spirit so that you can be free of concern for them and the Holy Spirit can teach you of their unreality. The Holy Spirit understands your temptation to believe in them as real and in order to heal your mind It needs you to teach yourself through the Holy Spirit that they are not. (MACIM-4.1.13)

As you let the Holy Spirit teach you how to use the body only as a means for communication and as you renounce the personal mind's use of the body as a means for separation and attack you will learn that you have no need of a body at all. In the Holy Instant there are no bodies and you experience only your attraction to God. Your attraction to God is Limitless and you join with God wholly in an Instant because you place no limits on your Oneness with God. (MACIM-15.9.7)

The body is not guilty or innocent. Since it is nothing, the body cannot be invested with attributes of your Christ Mind or of the personal mind. Either view of the body is an error because both give attributes of the mind where they cannot be. For you to remember Truth you must undo both views of the body. (MACIM-20.7.4)

Certainly, it does not appear as though sickness is a decision of your mind, and you probably don't believe that you want to be sick. Maybe you can accept this idea in theory, but you rarely, and inconsistently, apply it to all specific forms of sickness, in your perception of yourself and of others. But this is not the level at which you call for healing. You must overlook the personal mind and the body, and see only Christ, Which corrects all mistakes, and heals all of your perception. Healing is the result of your recognizing that it is your mind that needs healing. This recognition must be applied to your entire mind; in this recognition, all of your illusions will be undone. (WACIM-22.4)

But:

Any *way in which you handle sickness is meaningless because it is nothing.* (MACIM-8.8.6)

Magical thinking teaches you that the body makes its own illness; using physical remedies to heal it reinforces this mistake. But it is not evil to use them. Sometimes your belief in the illness is too strong for you to let in the awareness that healing is the result of correcting your perception of separation from God. When this is the case it is better for you to temporarily believe in the physical remedies. When you are sick you are already in a fearful state and if you confuse God's Love with fear then the experience of the miracle will only increase your fear. (MACIM-2.4.3)

So the 'physician' is always your mind, and the outcome is what you decide that it will be. You may see others as attending to the body, but they are only giving form to your choice. You choose to perceive them to give tangible form to your desire, and this is all that they do. You don't actually need them, because you could rise up without their aid and say, 'I have no use for this'. Any form of sickness will be cured at once if you mean these words. (WACIM-5.1b.2)

Your belief in physical remedies is magical thinking but you should not use the mind to heal the body if you are afraid to do so. Fear and egocentricity go together and fear makes you vulnerable to perceiving physical healing as coming from the power of the personal mind rather than from the recognition that you are One with God. When you are afraid it is actually better for you to accept physical remedies for healing the body because you will not make the mistake of thinking they come from your personal power. As long as you are afraid you should not attempt to accept the experience of the miracle for physical healing. (MACIM-2.5.1)

One of the most difficult temptations for you to overcome is to doubt a healing because of the appearance of continuing symptoms. This is a mistake in the form of a lack of trust in the Holy Spirit, and it is an attack on yourself. Usually, it seems to you to be the opposite; it does not appear reasonable to you that continued concern is an attack, because it appears as 'love'. But Love without trust is impossible, and doubt and trust cannot coexist. (WACIM-7.4)

Summary:

All forms of disorder in the body are manifestations of the disorder in your mind. So the specific form of a disorder is never relevant. Disorders simply signify that you still identify with a body. This is an error of the mind that calls for correction, not analysis of the disorder.

You can give the care of the body over to the Holy Spirit's guidance. It will not reinforce the error in your mind but help you to remember that you are Mind. This is accomplished through the practice of the Holy Instant. In the Holy Instant you set aside concern about the body and its life in the world and commune with God instead.

To let go of the body means to not give it any meaning (good/bad, right/wrong, etc.). The goal is not to change your view of the body to Truth-like. Healing does not occur at the level of the mind where you are concerned with the body. Healing occurs when you transcend thoughts about the body and turn your mind inward to Truth in your mind instead. Your identification with the body must be completely undone for your mind to be completely healed.

It does not matter how you choose to handle body disorders because neither the disorder nor the treatment are real. Even though physical remedies do not actually heal the body they are not "evil". You should use them until your mind is healed and the body is healed as a result. Otherwise you will only reinforce fear in your mind.

Until your healed mind manifests a healed body your choice for healing will be given tangible form through practitioners of whichever healing art in which you believe. Until then you will be afraid of God and your attempts to heal the body with the mind will reinforce the personal mind. You are likely then to confuse the source of healing with the personal mind.

If you ask the Holy Spirit for true healing (mind) you can trust that it has occurred. If you doubt that healing has occurred because you still perceive physical symptoms then you lack trust in the Holy Spirit. This indicates that your mind still needs healing.

My experience with the Holy Spirit:

As I shared in the introduction, like many students I initially read the *Course* through guilt and fear. I would feel guilty when I got sick or injured. I would take medicine or get treatment, but this only made me feel guiltier. Because of the guilt I felt I did not retain those passages that said that until I no longer had any fear of God I should use the remedies the world offers. I did not remember that it said that my choice for healing would manifest in the world through "attendants" to the body. And I never noticed that it said whatever I do to heal the body is meaningless (so no need for guilt).

I thought I was making progress when I decided that I would look for the specific thoughts that led to specific disorders. I thought I was taking responsibility. But the *Course* does not say to do this. It teaches that specifics are irrelevant. My overall identification with a personal self is the disorder of my mind that needs to be healed. So of course my approach at "taking responsibility" only led to increased guilt in my mind. It kept me focused on the problem rather than on the solution.

I was trying to deal with guilt on my own because I was too afraid to call on the Holy Spirit. I unconsciously expected to be shown how guilty I was. I expected to be condemned. But eventually, through other experiences with the Holy Spirit, my trust in It developed to where I knew It would show me the way out of guilt, not condemn me. When I was sick or hurt and called on It I was not condemned. I was told to take care of myself. I was guided in what to do. And I was taught to look at disorder in the body the same way I looked at conflict in my mind: As a reminder to turn inward to Truth.

I realized that I had been making body disorders "special". But they have no more meaning than the verbal attacks of the personal thought system in my mind. Or than disorder that shows up in other ways, like my car breaking down. The personal experience is really all one disordered experience. No part of it is different from any other part of it. That's why I have to let go of the whole thing, not just pieces of it.

I've learned to let go of the personal experience not by denying it or fighting against it but by turning away from it, inward to Truth. As my awareness of Truth has grown peace has come to the forefront of my experience. The personal life goes on, in the background of my awareness. I used to look to it for wholeness; now it manifests my wholeness. If thoughts about the personal life come forward and threaten my peace I see that as a reminder to bring my mind back to peace. This is true for all of it, even physical symptoms. I have learned that I can be at peace no matter what is happening in the personal self's life, even in its body. Peace is a state of *mind.*

I used to make the mistake of trying to fix the personal thought system. But since peace has come despite the personal thought system I've learned that true peace is not personal. The personal self will never be at peace. Its life will never be perfect. The body will manifest disorder as long as I still want it in any way. But since I have peace, none of this matters. What more could I want? I can attend to the inherently disordered personal self or I can attend to the peace in my mind. Whichever I choose grows in my awareness.

77. Ask: Can you talk about co-dependency and intimacy in relationships? (May 25, 2012)

"Can you discuss in one of your articles co-dependency in relationships? And also, the basis for intimacy from a spiritual perspective." -LB

"Co-dependency" is a term that describes a lack of healthy boundaries in a relationship. It is the personal thought system's (ego's) dysfunctional response to your longing for the Unity (Wholeness) that you experience in Truth (God). It begins by you seeing you and another as incomplete. So you blur the line between where your personal self ends and another's personal self begins to "join" and try to be whole. In practice this means you take responsibility for the thoughts, feelings, situation, and/or actions of another. Or you ask another to take responsibility for your thoughts, feelings, situation, and/or actions. This is unhealthy because it means you enable another to remain immature, dysfunctional, or in an active disease, like addiction or mental illness. Or someone else enables you to remain immature, dysfunctional, or in an active disease.

The result of co-dependency is a conflicted relationship. The one who takes more responsibility than is really theirs feels burdened and victimized, even when the other has not asked them to take responsibility for them. And if the other does give up responsibility they feel manipulated, controlled, and victimized even though they have chosen this.

A co-dependent relationship is a relationship based on the idea that sacrifice is love. At least one person in the relationship feels that he or she gives more than the other. Usually, both feel this way. If you think that this describes most human relationships then you are correct! The belief that love means sacrifice is why the world equates relationships with resentment and pain and feeling "trapped". And it is why Truth (Love) is feared.

A healthy, loving relationship is not stressful. It is affirming and supportive. So when you feel stress in any relationship, ask yourself where you are taking responsibility for the other. If you are not taking responsibility for them, ask yourself where you are asking the other to take responsibility for you. *When you experience stress in a relationship the problem is always within you.* This is why all relationships are really relationships with yourself.

When you are aware of the Truth within you, you feel whole and complete within yourself. So you don't feel a need to drop your identity boundaries to become whole by "joining" with another. You are also aware that the Truth is in others just as It is in you. So you know that others are whole, too, even when they are not aware of it. In practice this means that you maintain the boundaries of personal identities because you realize that enabling others to remain in their dysfunction is not the way to love them. You love them by recognizing their wholeness and giving them an opportunity to grow into this awareness themselves. If they choose to grow, they will be grateful for your boundaries. If they do not choose to grow, they may resent your boundaries. But they are responsible for this choice, not you. When you have healthy boundaries you do not have unhealthy people close to you. This leaves room for healthy, loving people to be close to you.

To be "intimate" with another means to feel emotionally close to another. So the source of true intimacy is open and honest communication. Of course first you must be honest with yourself before you can be honest with another. So intimacy with another first requires self-awareness and self-acceptance. You must be intimate with yourself before you can be intimate with another.

The source of intimacy is the same whether one is spiritually aware or not. But an awareness of Truth facilitates intimacy because it frees you from the insecurity that makes intimacy impossible. If you fear that if someone really knows you that they will reject you, or if you fear that if another knows your vulnerabilities that they will use them to attack you, then you will not feel that you can be open and honest with them.

An awareness of Truth leads to you feeling secure within yourself. So you are set free to be honest with another because you are not dependent on them to feel loved and whole. You look at relationships as manifestations of the Love within you, rather than as your source for love. And you accept that any conflict that comes up in a relationship is an opportunity for you to undo an obstacle you have to being aware of Love within you.

78. Ask: Should I give up striving? (June 15, 2012)

"I just came across this passage… 26. VI.1. 'Anything in this world that you believe is good and valuable and worth striving for can hurt you, and will do so'…I did some research in blogs and explanations and found that the emphasis is on the 'striving.' What is your take and valuable insight on this passage?" – KM

I agree with the emphasis on the word "striving". It is your belief in yourself as a personal self (ego) that hurts you. And striving for anything in the world is an expression of the belief that you have to make and maintain a personal identity to exist.

Follow-up question: *So stop trying to prove myself?*

The phrase that you quoted from *A Course in Miracles* is stating a fact, not suggesting a course of action. The need to prove yourself will fall away naturally as your identification with a personal self falls away. This is not something that you can force. You can't pretend to not identify with a personal self when you do. That leads to repressing, not releasing, the personal identity. And repression is just another way to hold onto it.

Grow your awareness of Truth and the process of releasing the personal identity will unfold naturally. You can grow your awareness of Truth by sharing your goals in the world with the Holy Spirit. It will transform your goals from ends in themselves to means to remember Truth by using every situation as a classroom.

79. Ask: I feel like I'm never going to "get it"... (July 13, 2012)

"...I read the lessons for the day. It's breathtaking, yet I feel so far from experiencing what the Course *talks about. I feel pain in the body, emotional distress, and obsess about people places and things. When I notice this going on— how much of my mental, emotional and physical space it all takes up I feel like I'm just never going to "get it" or be able to keep my mind focused on "God" or not be affected or afflicted by all the things people suffer. I can't really say I've ever experienced a moment's respite from these afflictive thoughts of what happened in the past, what will happen in the future, what I did wrong, what they said, what they meant bla bla bla!...I'm wondering what your days are like? Is your mind clear? What does it all feel like? Or are you just telling yourself certain things? I feel like I have no new thoughts, just recycling the same ol' same ol'."* - MCD

Don't aim for a perfectly quiet mind. Instead, simply open yourself to the Eternal Quiet (God; Truth) beyond all of the thoughts in your mind. Grow your awareness of This through meditation. Bring your mind into the present and turn inward. Become aware of your thoughts and then go past them. You will find yourself dipping into the Quiet and then back into the thoughts; into the Quiet and back into the thoughts. Just let the thoughts go and listen past them for the Quiet. The Quiet will grow stronger in your awareness. Devote a few minutes of each day to opening to the Quiet.

During the day don't try to force your mind to stay in the Quiet. Just take moments when you can throughout the day to bring your mind into the present, turn inward, and remember God. You can do this with your eyes opened or closed; when you are alone or with others.

Once you become aware of God within you, you will be ready to deal with the personal thought system. You need to question and correct these thoughts to undo the hold that they seem to have over you. They represent false beliefs that are obstacles to peace. Do not argue with the personal thought system. It is what it is: the idea of the opposite of Truth (God). It is not going to change. But with the Teacher of Truth (Holy Spirit) in your mind you can correct its thoughts for yourself.

Yes, this takes effort. At first, it seems like a lot of effort because you are not used to attending to your mind. You are used to letting it just run on and run you. You are going to have to slow down your mind, which often means slow down your outer life. But you are worth the effort this will take and if you believe this you will find the willingness to work through your obstacles to peace.

As long as you identify with a personal self you are going to be affected and afflicted by the limitations, lack, and loss of the personal experience. But you can use these experiences to transcend the personal experience by looking at them as reminders to turn within to Truth.

My mind used to be like yours. But now it is much, much quieter and it is very clear. My days are simple and quiet. Peace is always in my awareness now. The personal thought system is also still in my awareness but it shrinks as my awareness of peace continues to grow.

80. Ask: Why don't I hear God's messages of love? (July 27, 2012)

"I was just re-listening to lesson 155…'And now He asks but that you think of Him a while each day, that He may speak to you and tell you of His Love, reminding you how great His trust; how limitless His Love.' I was wondering why I don't hear those messages of love, why I think I need and want the love of a 'man' (in this case, a particular one) more than the 'love of God'. 'Death' sometimes seems as if it will be the only release from all this emotional agony! Sigh…" – MCD

You read *A Course in Miracles* so you do hear God's messages of Love. The *Course* is a love letter from the Truth (God) in you asking you to remember What you really are. Remember this as you learn how to hear the Teacher of Truth (Holy Spirit) within your mind. You are not comfortless.

The *Course* was scribed by one (Helen Schucman) who was obviously hearing the Teacher of Truth within her mind at the time. Not everyone who picks up the *Course* is already hearing the Teacher of Truth within. So if you do not hear the It invite It into your awareness. Just ask the Teacher of Truth to come into your conscious mind and keep your mind open. It will come into your awareness in a form that you will understand. You do not always hear the Teacher of Truth as words. Sometimes it is as intuition or unformed thoughts and insights. Sometimes you may feel the Truth as peace descending on you for no seeming reason. And most students feel Something with them when they study the *Course*. In the beginning, that is often the only time one feels the Teacher of Truth. But it is a beginning and it teaches you to what experience to be open.

You are looking for love from another because you do not yet trust that Love is within you always. As you grow aware of God (Truth) within you, you will find yourself seeking less and less outside yourself to feel love, peace, or happiness. When that happens you will no longer look to your relationships with others to supply you with love. You will recognize your loving relationships as manifestations of the Love that is always within you. So make growing your awareness of God within you your priority. Use the pain of your present state as a reminder to turn inward to God.

You are in pain because you think that the personal self (ego) and its story are your reality. This is a mistake in thinking (mind) and the death of the body would not undo it. In fact it would do nothing.

"When your body and your ego and your dreams are gone, you will know that you will last forever. Perhaps you think this is accomplished through death, but nothing is accomplished through death, because death is nothing. Everything is accomplished through life, and life is of the mind and in the mind. The body neither lives nor dies, because it cannot contain you who are life. If we share the same mind, you can overcome death because I did. Death is an attempt to

resolve conflict by not deciding at all. Like any other impossible solution the ego attempts, it will not work. " (T-6.V.A.1)

You overcome the painful, limited personal experience not by running away into death but by letting it go. On some level you have already accepted this because you became a student of *A Course in Miracles.* You have chosen the true way out of pain, so use it. It is going to be painful for a while because you will encounter the obstacles to peace (false beliefs) in your mind. But painful situations are now opportunities for you to look at these obstacles and undo them. And the more you undo the less you have to undo.

81. Ask: Why express gratitude for things in an illusion? (August 3, 2012)

"*...The self-help industry stresses a gratitude practice. If nothing exists and everything is an illusion, why express gratitude for the things in the illusion? Does it play a role in awakening from the dream?*" – CL

Self-help practices are centered on the personal self but do play a limited role in growing your awareness of Truth. Practicing gratitude is important not for the specifics of the gratitude practiced but for the mind training involved. It is especially helpful for those who have a tendency to dwell on lack. The real lesson is not that you need to be grateful for what shows up for the personal self but that your thoughts are your choice and are not happening to you against your will.

You will notice that much of *A Course in Miracles* focuses on replacing dark thoughts with lighter thoughts about a world that it teaches is not real. This teaches you that you have control over your thoughts and therefore over your experience of peace or conflict. Eventually you will realize that since you can change your experience of the world by changing your mind about it then it must not have any meaning in itself. You will recognize that the universe of form is a neutral projection onto which you have projected meaning. This is when you will begin to understand that there is really nothing there. And you will realize that you do not have to think about it at all. This awareness is not something that you can force but that you will develop naturally as you take more responsibility for your thoughts.

So exercises like practicing gratitude have value for spiritual awakening in the short term but they will fall away naturally when you no longer need them.

82. Ask: How do I find peace when a family member is suffering? (August 17, 2012)

"*I find it very hard to find peace when a family member is suffering. My son who has terrible allergies suffers with chronic itching and pain. Doctors are not able to help him as of yet. I know that all illness comes from the mind. My son is an atheist and does not believe as I do. How do I find peace when I know someone I love is suffering? And, is it possible to heal him without him knowing how he was healed.*" – SM

Until the Truth (God) is real to you it will be very hard for you to watch loved ones suffer because you will think that you are looking at reality. So until Truth is real and true for you use those appearances in form that disturb your peace to remind you to turn your mind inward to Truth. Simply quiet your mind and invite Truth into your awareness. You can do this in a moment or as a longer meditation when you have the time. This is how you can use what is not true to grow your awareness of Truth.

Your willingness to be aware of Truth is all that is needed for It to grow in your awareness. And the effect of inviting Truth into your awareness is comfort and peace and answers at the level of form that you can understand at the time.

In time your awareness of Truth will grow to the point where you know that It *is* Truth. Then when your peace is disturbed by an appearance you will turn your mind away from what is occurring in the universe of form and remind yourself that only the Truth is True. This will re-center your mind in Truth and shift you back into peace. This is how to use what is not true to remind you of Truth again and again.

The Truth in your mind is the same Truth in your son's mind. That is all that is real in either of you. And It is whole (healed) forever. Everything else falls away. By focusing on the Truth in his mind rather than on a passing appearance you reinforce the Truth in both of your minds. You reinforce the awareness that in Truth he is already healed (whole). But the body in his mind will only be healed when he wants it to be healed. This will show up either as doctors, practitioners, medicines, treatments, etc. that work (common) or through spontaneous healing (rare). He will make this decision, consciously or unconsciously, when the value of the body being healed outweighs the value of it being itchy and painful. So the body's healing is wholly up to him. And your part is simply to know the Truth for him until he is ready to accept It for himself.

83. Ask: Do you think it is possible to not be reincarnated? (August 24, 2012)

"I don't want to be reincarnated. I know that I am 'Home' already, and if I fully believed that would cease to appear to exist here in form. When I die, or transition, from this 'world', I don't want to come back (be reincarnated). I don't want to experience a life time of searching for the Truth and finally finding it after years of believing the insanity and experiencing the pain of this life. I want to go 'Home' - all the way Home. When I think of reincarnating I feel a kind of despair (which I know exists only because I believe it). Do you think it's possible not to have to 'come back'?" - KS

You will be happy to know that there is no such thing as reincarnation. As it says in *A Course in Miracles*:

'In the ultimate sense, reincarnation is impossible. There is no past or future, and the idea of birth into a body has no meaning either once or many times. Reincarnation cannot, then, be true in any real sense. Our only question should be, "Is the concept helpful?"' (M-24.1)

I suggest you re-read question 24 in the Manual for Teachers. Reincarnation is only a concept, not reality. When one has not yet experienced the eternal (timeless) Truth within they are only aware of the personal thought system (ego) in their mind. So the only way that they can understand that they do not die is to believe that some aspect of the personal identity goes on when the body dies. For those individuals reincarnation may be a comforting concept for a time. The concept becomes an obstacle to peace, however, if they are not willing to let it go and let Truth into their awareness *now*.

And once you do experience Truth you understand that you are already "Home", as you say. The rest is an illusion and will fall away. What does it matter if you still perceive it? It is nothing! Remember this and don't give it power over you. Only the Truth is true. Be present to the eternal Truth within and simply observe without judgment the story of time passing before you. This is the way to be Home now.

84. Ask: Can you explain Lesson 253? (September 14, 2012)

"I have a real problem understanding the phrasing of Lesson 253—'My Self is ruler of the universe'. Maybe it's the language; but even instinctively I am confused. 'You are the Self Whom You created Son.' Can you explain that a little more clearly? It sends my mind into a spin..." – MD-T

Maybe you would understand it better replacing the word "Self" with the word "Being": "My Being is ruler of the universe" and "You are the Being Whom You created Son." When the word "self" is capitalized in *A Course in Miracles* it is referring to the one, limitless Being (God) that is rather than to the limited personal self, or ego, with which you are used to identifying. The lesson reminds you that God is your True Being, not a power over you. There is no power over you.

Perhaps some of your confusion comes from the use of the word "create", which we typically use to mean "to bring into being". In the *Course* the word "create" means "to extend". So God "creates" by extending God. As God's "Creation", in Truth your mind is an extension of God. And, in Truth, you can only "create", or extend, God. So your "creations" are extensions of God.

As is typical of the *Course* it is here taking a concept – "creation" – that usually reinforces the idea that you are separate from God (Creator and Its creation) and using it in a way to instead remind you that, in Truth, you and God are one Being.

85. Ask: How do I balance spiritual practice with the other parts of my life? (September 28, 2012)

"My goal is to fully awaken to the truth and reality of who I AM. I have confusion in balancing my time and energy spent in meditating, reading and being alone in the peace of the Spirit with work and enjoying outside life activities. I have an enjoyable job but would like more income to have more choices. I have good ideas for added income but do not want to be distracted from my Spiritual journey or peace within but want to live life to its fullest." – EB

Your statement that you "want to live life to its fullest" indicates that you have conflicting goals. You do want Truth (God) but you also still want to have a full personal life. But you cannot be invested in a personal life and transcend it (be aware of Truth) at the same time. This conflict is why you are confused and having a hard time finding balance.

However, you do not have to deny or fight against your personal goals and desires. They are only obstacles to your being aware of Truth when you see them as ends in themselves. You can instead turn them into the means to becoming aware of Truth. This is in fact the "shortcut" to peace that *A Course in Miracles* teaches.

Your goal of being aware of Truth means that you must look at every situation as an opportunity to remember Truth. In addition to meditation and study, share your work, relationships, interests, goals, plans, ideas, desires - everything - with the Teacher of Truth (Holy Spirit) within you. Make It your partner in everything that you do and your guide in pursuing everything that you want. You do not have to worry about being distracted from Truth when you use every situation as a means to grow aware of Truth.

In time, your awareness of and trust in the Teacher of Truth will grow to the point where you find yourself naturally putting aside personal goals and desires. Then you will happily follow only the Teacher of Truth because you will truly have only one Goal.

86. Ask: At what point do you point out your brother's error? (October 5, 2012)

"...Forgiveness says to look past what appears to be our brother's error because it is really our own error projected upon his body. It never happened because it is all imagination, all a dream in our mind...at what point do you point out your brother's error as 'his' error? At what point do we point out his error and have him suffer the consequences of his error. Such as filing charges against him and thus having him pay a fine or go to jail...At what point does the 'seriousness' of the offense make it necessary to point out the error and take steps to diminish the possibility of it happening again? What, if any, is the difference between the more serious offense and the tiny, minor offense?...My ego wants to point out every error, no matter how minor, and take actions to see that the brother doesn't do it again to me or any other brother." – RB

The errors to which *A Course in Miracles* refers are errors of mind not errors of behavior. You do not have to point out to others when they are coming from ego (the personal thought system). If you are bothered that another is coming from ego it is the ego in your own mind that is bothered. It believes that it is "wrong" or "bad" to come from ego and projects away its own guilt by seeing the other as "wrong" or "bad" to come from ego. So what you need to forgive is not the other for coming from ego but the ego in your own mind that is bothered by seeing itself reflected in another.

This is quite apart from you pointing out when another's behavior is inappropriate or harmful. You do not do others a favor by enabling them to continue in unhealthy behaviors. In fact, by pointing out their inappropriate behavior to them (even up to having them arrested when it is called for) you give them an opportunity to take responsibility for their own thoughts and beliefs (the cause of their behavior) and grow. They may not want or appreciate this and may in fact be resentful. But what they do with this opportunity is their choice.

What you want to sort out before you take action to stop another in their harmful behavior is fact from projection. What happens in the universe of form has no meaning in itself. It is neutral. Any meaning (right/wrong, good/bad, a perpetuation of your personal story) that you see comes from you. If you observe another's behavior, even when it is directed toward you, without taking it personally, you are not projecting. You are merely observing a fact. But if you feel defensive, angry, upset, offended, etc. then you are making their behavior personal through your projections of meaning. Once you have cleared up your own projections you will have a clearer view of the situation. And you will then act, if necessary, from detachment rather than from emotions that may only make the situation worse.

87. Ask: Is it enough to intellectually master the ideas in the Course? (October 26, 2012)

"I have read that if one undertakes the Course *as an exercise in academic learning, as a study of ideas to be mastered, you will fail...I'm in a study group where I think this is exactly what we are doing."* – MW

A Course in Miracles intends for its ideas to be used, not just thought about:

"This is not a course in the play of ideas, but in their practical application." (T-11.VIII.5)
"This course has explicitly stated that its goal for you is happiness and peace." (T-13.II.7)

But that can be quite apart from your goal for studying it. The measure of your success or failure in any endeavor is determined by your own goal for it. If your goal is to intellectually grasp the concepts in *A Course in Miracles* then study alone may be enough for you to reach your goal. But if your goal is lasting happiness and peace, which is the goal the *Course* intends for you, then you must put its ideas into practice to attain this goal.

Every student begins studying the *Course* as a merely intellectual exercise. This is because you are identified with ego (personal self) and you are afraid of what the *Course* teaches. It teaches that the way to peace is to become aware of your true identity in God (Truth) and to release your identification with ego. So it feels at first that you are being asked to give up the only identity that you think you know and this feels like death. Reading and thinking about this does not undo your mis-identification with ego so it feels safe to study the *Course* as long as you do not put its ideas into practice.

This stage seems to last 5-10 years, although I have met students who have stayed at this point for much longer. (I was there for 15 years myself). This is not wasted time. The loving message of the *Course* chips away at your misunderstanding and fear of God. And you can also take the first step in practically applying the ideas in the *Course* by inviting the Holy Spirit (Teacher of Truth) in your mind into your study. This is necessary to grow your awareness of God within and begin the shift in your identification away from ego.

You eventually reach a point in your studying where you realize that as much as you understand the *Course* you are still not at peace. This is when you find the willingness to put its ideas into practice in your everyday life. Putting the *Course's* ideas into practice means to come from the Holy Spirit within you. And this is how you learn that the Holy Spirit is you. This is when you begin to experience success in achieving your goal of lasting peace and happiness.

88. Ask: We made the universe of form...should I use meditation as prayer now? (November 2, 2012)

"My question is about prayer...The idea of Oneness is beginning to feel more natural as is accepting that we, not God, made the universe of form. I've been used to saying traditional prayers as well as praying for special intentions for myself and others. Given my emerging new thought system, that kind of prayer just doesn't feel right anymore. I still feel the need to pray, however. Should I use meditation as a form of prayer now?..." LD

Before I answer your question about prayer I want to address your statement that "we, not God, made the universe of form" because I hear this often from students of *A Course in Miracles* and there is great confusion about this idea.

The maker of the universe of form is what the *Course* calls the "son of God" in the original and what I called the "split mind" in *The Plain Language ACIM*. The split mind is the part of God's Mind that contains the idea of the opposite-of-God. So it is split between What is (God) and the idea of not-God. To fill the emptiness of the idea of not-God it projects a universe of form to make another "reality". Into this universe of form it projects billions of versions of its split mind in individual forms (bodies). This is what you think of as your individual mind, which is split between God and not-God (ego/personal mind).

So in your experience as an individual split mind you are not responsible for the making of the universe of form. You simply find yourself in it. But you are responsible for your projections of meaning onto form from not-God in your mind. These thoughts, or perceptions, make up the "world" that the *Course* teaches you must forgive (release) to be at peace. Each individual must forgive their own "world" (perceptions) because it is made up of projections from their own personal story.

I clarify this so that you do not struggle to understand how you make form. If you want inner peace all you need to attend to are your thoughts about form.

On to prayer: Prayer is traditionally a petitioning you make toward a power over you to fill the sense of lack inherent to identifying with a limited personal self. But there is no power over you. God is your Being, so It is your Power, and It is within you always. Your only lack is a lack of awareness that you already have everything within you in God. So instead of prayer what you need to fill any sense of lack is to become aware again of God within you. To do this, yes, you want to use formal meditation as a means to open yourself to and commune with God every day. You also want to take moments throughout the day to come into the present and turn your mind inward to feel God, to call on the Holy Spirit for guidance in everything, and to remember you are Love by extending Love in your awareness in place of personal projections. These will fill up any sense of lack you have and you will find that you do not need to "pray" for anything.

89. Ask: Don't I need an ego to live in the world? (November 9, 2012)

"Don't I need an ego to live in the world? If not how do I go to work, take care of my family, etc.?" - Anonymous

No, because the body, personality, and unfolding "life" of the personal self are neutral projections. They don't have any meaning in themselves. They manifest either the personal thought system (ego) or your True thought system (Holy Spirit). The choice of thought system is yours to make. Either way the personal self eats, sleeps, goes to work, raises kids, makes love, plays, relates to others, etc.

Your choice of thought system determines your internal experience of either conflict (personal) or peace (Truth). And because personal values, choices, and behaviors (effects) always follow from thoughts (their cause) the personal self's life unfolds harmoniously when you choose the thought system of peace.

This is how you can tell which thought system you are choosing: When you identify as a personal self your mind is not in its natural state. So you experience conflict and lack. You try to deal with your discomfort and unhappiness *through* the personal self. You direct it to find wholeness in relationships, a career, by acquiring various things, through a variety of activities and interests, etc. You have a strong need to control the personal self's thought system, body, relationships, and environment in an attempt to be happy, whole, and secure.

But when you rest in Truth instead you know that you are whole. So you do not have to seek for anything through the personal self. You let it go (forgive it), which means you let it be without judging its thoughts or actions. You live in the moment in an awareness of Truth and peace. You find that you simply know how to direct the personal self to get its needs met. You watch its story unfold, trusting that it is perfectly manifesting your awareness of Wholeness.

90. Ask: Since the world isn't real is there a basis for compassion? (November 16, 2012)

"Since the world is not real and all that we are experiencing is an illusion is there a basis for compassion?" - Anonymous

Actually, true compassion arises naturally and spontaneously *only* when you are aware that the world is not real and that the personal experience is an illusion. True compassion is an effect of true forgiveness.

The experience of Truth (God) is wholeness. It is boundless love, peace, and happiness. Any other experience is not-True (illusion). So all pain is caused by a lack of awareness that the Truth is in you and that you have everything in Truth.

The personal thought system's (ego's) version of compassion is to reinforce in your mind the idea that lack and pain are real. It has you join with another in their pain. You hurt with them and/or for them. This version of compassion carries a lot of weight and baggage with it. You experience suffering, sacrifice, and reinforced feelings of victimhood and powerlessness. To offset the pain of this a bit the personal thought system allows you to "feel good" that you are a "compassionate person" suffering with and/or sacrificing for another.

But when you are aware that the Truth (God) in your mind is all that is true you are also aware that the Truth is all that is true in every mind, whether others are aware of this for themselves or not. When another hurts you observe their pain but you know for them that the basis of their pain is not real. You know for them that they are whole in Truth. So you are detached from their pain but not from the Truth in their mind. You do not correct their perception of hurt but you meet them where *they* are, offering what *they* say they need. You say, "I am sorry that you are hurting" or "That sounds painful". You listen to them and you offer whatever support you can. You may be temporarily saddened by their story but you do not carry away this sadness with you.

True compassion begins first with yourself. The personal experience is one of limitation and inevitable loss. But the pain of the personal experience turns to suffering only when you resist it or indulge it. So you will naturally be compassionate (gentle, patient) with yourself when you are aware that the Truth in you is untouched by the personal experience (forgiveness). You will accept the personal experience as it is and no longer judge it, fight against it, or try to control it. You will allow the personal self to have its reactions of fear, anger, and grief. And then you will turn inward to remember that only the Truth is true.

When you have compassion for yourself it will naturally extend to others. You will remember from your own experience that in the absence of an awareness of Truth a person is going to act out in ineffective and dysfunctional ways to relieve their sense of lack, loss, conflict, guilt, and fear. So your compassion will extend not just to seeming-victims but to seemingvictimizers as well. Really, your compassion will extend to just about everyone you encounter because very few are willing to be aware of Truth so they live in pain. And since they are unwilling to be aware of Truth because of feelings of unworthiness, guilt, and fear you will feel compassion for their lack of willingness as well.

You cannot force true compassion. It is the natural effect of your awareness that only the Truth is true. So you do not need to work at being a "compassionate person". Instead, grow your awareness of the Truth within you and true compassion will occur without effort.

91. Ask: Does the universe we perceive exist only in the ego's mind? (November 23, 2012)

"In the lesson 'What is Creation?' the following passage answers the question:

"Creation is the sum of all God's Thoughts, in number infinite and everywhere without limit. Only Love creates and only like Itself."

I suddenly found today that I could not see how this fitted with the idea that all form (creation) is the sum of God's thoughts, if it is also illusory. Does the Universe we perceive exist only in the ego's mind - or is it the result of God's Thought?" – MD-T

A Course in Miracles redefines the word "Creation" to refer to the Extension of God's formless Being rather than to the universe of form, as the word is commonly used. When it speaks of "you" being God's "Creation" it is referring to your True Being in God, not to the forms (body/personality) with which you mistakenly identify. You experience God's boundless Creation – your True Being – not in form but within your mind.

You "create" like God when God's Being extends through your True Mind. This "creation" or extension is eternally ongoing and automatic whether or not you are aware of it. This re-definition undoes the usual concept of a "Creator" bringing into being a separate entity. So in the *Course* "Creation" is another way to say "Oneness". In God there is only God extending infinitely. God is One (the same throughout).

The universe of form does not exist at all. Being All, God's Mind must contain the thought of God's opposite. But being All God cannot have an actual opposite. The thought-of-the-opposite-of-God is only ever an impossible thought. It has no purpose or intention. It occurs because everything must occur to God's Mind. So while it is a thought that must be in God's Mind it is not "Creation" or Extension of God's Mind because it is unlike God. It has no reality.

A meaningless thought is dismissed as meaningless. That is God's point of view. But within the thought-of-the-opposite-of-God there is an emptiness which is filled by a universe of form, or the opposite-of-God made manifest. The part of God's mind where this thought seems to occur the *Course* calls the "son of God" (lower case "s" on "son"). It cannot leave God so it is split between God and not-God. This split mind projects billions of versions of itself into the universe of form (individual minds in bodies). For the seemingly-individual split mind the *Course* refers to the projection of not-God as "ego" and to the awareness of God as "Christ" (or "Son of God"; upper-case "s" on "son").

The universe of form is a meaningless projection. All the meaning that a seemingly-individual mind sees in it, it projects from its own personal (ego) story. These projections of meaning are what make the universe of form seem to really exist. Withdraw your projections of meaning and you find that form is empty, not in a way that depresses you, but in a way that liberates you.

You will never intellectually understand that the universe of form does not exist. You cannot understand that something does not exist when your mind seems to be in the midst of it. To learn this you must grow your awareness of the Truth (God) within you. As the Truth becomes true for you, you will find that you are able to let go of the personal story that you have for yourself. Then you will be able to withdraw the projections of meaning onto a meaningless universe of form that makes it seem real to you.

(This article is corrected below).

92. Ask: Where in the Course does it use the lower case "s" on "son"? (November 30, 2012)

Where in ACIM *does it use the lower case "s" on "son of God"?* - Anonymous

[This question refers to this paragraph from my last article*: "But within the thought-of-the-opposite-of-God there is an emptiness which is filled by a universe of form, or the opposite-of-God made manifest. The part of God's mind where this thought seems to occur the Course calls the "son of God" (lower case "s" on "son"). It cannot leave God so it is split between God and not-God. This split mind projects billions of versions of itself into the universe of form (individual minds in bodies). For the seemingly-individual split mind the Course refers to the projection of not-God as "ego" and to the awareness of God as "Christ" (or "Son of God"; upper-case "s" on "son").*].

Well, gosh, golly, darn…I could swear…But doing a search on my *A Course in Miracles* CD I cannot find an instance where the lower-case "s" is used for "son of God"! Oops! And not only did I read the *Course* several times over many years I translated the whole thing into plain, everyday language paragraph by paragraph! The mind is an interesting thing. Here's a good example of it seeing what it has come to understand through experience rather than what was there on the page.

I apologize for any confusion that this has caused.

93. Ask: Does someone who does not "awaken" still go back to God when they die? (November 30, 2012)

What happens to someone who dies before they "awaken" or are aware of Truth? Do they still go back to God? – Anonymous

No. But someone who has become aware of Truth (God) also does not return to Truth upon death. The self does not come from Truth and can never be a part of Truth. It is only a mistaken idea in your mind *now*.

The Truth is already in your mind, whole and complete. It has no beginning and no ending. It is ongoing and untouched by the story of a self that you have in your mind. You do not have to wait for the self to die to be aware of Truth. Right now you can put aside the idea of a self and be aware of Truth and be at peace. It is your belief in the self as reality that blocks your awareness of Truth *now*.

Only the Truth in any mind is real and eternal. Everything else passes away. Some selves will choose to be aware of Truth and be at peace. Others will not make this choice and will stay in conflict. But the Truth is untouched either way. It is only one's temporary (time-bound) experience of a self that is affected by this choice.

94. Ask: It makes me sad to think I will never see my loved ones again… (December 7, 2012)

If what you say about death is true it makes me sad to think that I will never see my loved ones again. This is how I have coped with their deaths… - Anonymous

What you are actually feeling is fear of lack of Love (God; Truth). True Love is your Being and is always within you. But because the personal thought system (ego) is the denial of your Being it teaches you to look outward for its version of "love" (attachment). One place it teaches you to look for love is in the specialness of others. When they pass away it tells you that you have lost love. To deal with your pain it then tells you that you can hope to find this love again after you "die". As usual, it does not address the actual source of your pain: your perception that Love is outside of you. It also does not address your pain *now*. Instead it tells you to hope to find relief for your current pain in a future that never arrives. Is it really comforting to think that Love comes and goes with passing forms? Does it really relieve your pain to think that Love is not here now but may be found in the future?

There is no lack or loss in the Truth within you. True Love does not come and go. Use painful personal experiences as reminders to turn inward and grow your awareness of Truth. Your awareness of Truth will bring you ongoing peace, even in the midst of the limitation, lack, and loss of the personal experience. You will accept that this is a passing experience; not Reality. True Love is with you always.

95. Ask: "My holiness" is not working… (December 14, 2012)

"I have a family member who's had a rough time of it for quite a while. He got married, quickly had 2 children, then the marriage went sour and now he is dealing with a narcissistic ex-wife who seems determined to make his life a misery and a job that takes up most of his time. I get upset about the situation he's in and sometimes cry over his situation. I think "There is nothing my holiness cannot do…" but it doesn't seem to work. Then I get angry that this whole story is appearing and become impatient that he's not changing. I'm furious with his ex-wife too." – SD

It is your belief that what is appearing is real and true that is making you unhappy. If you are willing to be aware of your Holiness, or the Truth (God) within you, then this awareness will lift you out of your fixed belief in the world as reality. But this is not going to change the world. It will change your relationship to the world.

The universe of form is the opposite of Truth in every way. It is an experience of lack, limitation, and loss. Everyone in it is in pain. This makes them resort to inappropriate and ineffective means to ease their pain. Some resort to attacking others in the hope that this will bring them relief. Of course, no form of external searching works. They are looking for the Wholeness that they can find only within.

Be grateful that you know where to find Wholeness and don't have to be in pain. When you see something in the world that makes you unhappy use it as a reminder to turn inward to Truth. As your awareness that only the Truth is true grows your experience of inner peace will transcend all appearances of dysfunction and disorder. This is how your Holiness takes care of every problem.

96. Ask: What happens to the spirits/souls of psychopaths? (December 21, 2012)

"In the tri-union of mind, body, spirit, what happens to the spirits/souls of psychopaths? Those defined as 'individuals who are often intelligent and highly charismatic, but display a chronic inability to feel guilt, remorse, or anxiety about any of their actions.'

My understanding is that a psychopath also cannot genuinely feel or display love, either. Yet, our essence is essentially the energy of love. Can you explain?" – DL

There are no souls or individual spirits. There is only one Truth (Spirit) and It is universal. It is the same in every seemingly-individual mind. It is all that is real and eternal in any mind. Everything else is false and falls away.

The body, the mind, and Spirit (Truth) do not form a union. Mind is the aspect of Truth through which Truth knows Itself. They are one and the same. The body and its thought system (ego/personal thought system) are ideas in the mind. They are a mistaken identity. They are an illusion. They are completely apart from Truth. Your seemingly-individual mind is split between this illusion of identity and Truth. Your mind is affected by which of these you choose to have in your awareness, but illusion and Truth never intersect within your mind. Your concept of a self (body/personal thought system) and its story never affects the Truth in your mind. And it never becomes Truth. This is true for every seemingly-individual mind. To understand this is to understand true forgiveness.

Human love and True Love are not the same. Humans are social animals and depend on each other for survival. Human "love" in all of its forms is attachment for survival of the species. Psychopaths are humans who are unable to experience this attachment and contribute in that way to survival of the species. They are also unable to experience social guilt. So some of them are actively destructive to their own species. But none of this has anything at all to do with Truth. It is just part of the story for a world that is meant as a substitute reality for Truth. In its entirety the world is only a mistaken concept of reality. It is not real. None of it ever attains Truth.

True Love is universal and apart from the world. It is not energy, which is form, so part of the illusion. True Love is formless, infinite, and eternal. It has no purpose but to be. It is everywhere, always. It is in every seemingly-individual mind, beyond the story of a self, however that shows up. A mind may or may not choose to be aware of Truth. But this has no effect on Truth, only on the mind making the choice.

97. Ask: Your recent articles about death have not been very comforting... (December 28, 2012)

"Some of your answers about death lately have not been particularly comforting...would you tell someone who just lost a loved one that they will never see them again?" - Anonymous

I can see where the personal thought system (ego) in your mind would not find what I wrote about death to be comforting. It would like to be real and eternal and I stripped that idea away. Stripping away the personal thought system's cherished wishes is what I do! I am a teacher of Truth, not a minister or therapist, so I do not teach to comfort personal selves. Instead, I teach minds the way to release themselves from guilt and fear so that they can be aware of Truth and be at peace. This indeed will make the personal thought system in your mind uncomfortable, but if you understand the forgiveness that I teach it will set *you* free.

"Undermining the ego's thought system must be perceived as painful, even though this is anything but true. Babies scream in rage if you take away a knife or scissors, although they may well harm themselves if you do not. In this sense you are still a baby. You have no sense of real self-preservation, and are likely to decide that you need precisely what would hurt you most. Yet whether or not you recognize it now, you have agreed to cooperate in the effort to become both harmless and helpful, attributes that must go together. Your attitudes even toward this are necessarily conflicted, because all attitudes are ego-based. This will not last. Be patient a while and remember that the outcome is as certain as God." (T-4.II.5)

The only way to inner peace is through an awareness of the Truth within you. Truth and the personal thought system (not-Truth) are diametrically opposed. If you choose inner peace you have to be willing to let go of the cherished wishes and beliefs of the personal thought system that you have taken on for yourself. They are your obstacles to peace. Within them lurk guilt and fear. Your level of discomfort in this process is in direct proportion to your identification as a personal self. But as your awareness of Truth grows you will detach from the personal thought system and its discomfort. You will recognize that it is not your own. This does take time and it is very hard in the beginning.

I teach from experience, not from theory. I do not teach to be popular, but to reinforce the Truth as I have experienced it in my own mind. I am certainly not the teacher for everyone. Whether or not I am the teacher for you depends on your goal for yourself. You have to decide whether you want to be set free from guilt and fear or if you want to be comfortable in your identification with a personal self. You cannot have it both ways. The former leads to lasting peace and happiness; the latter is never wholly possible. Whichever choice you make the Truth in you is unchanged.

No, I would not tell someone who just lost a loved one that they will never see them again. Even if they asked me a direct question about this how I answered them would depend on what I knew about their beliefs, how recent the loss was, etc. I am not cruel. And I also feel no need to force what I know onto others. Obviously, how I respond to paying clients and email questioners is very different from how I respond to others. I only share directly what I have learned with those who come to me asking.

I try to meet someone at their level of understanding, but this is difficult to know when answering emails. So I answer questions with what I know to be the truth. My answers are meant to strip away beliefs that are obstacles to peace. I expect that if someone asks me a question and/or reads my newsletter/blog that they want an honest answer. I expect that they want their false beliefs revealed so that they can undo them and be at peace. Why else would they write to me or read what I write? If my answer is beyond what the writer/reader can understand at the time I leave it to them to ask another question for clarification.

98. Ask: It seems to me that ACIM is saying that I don't really exist... (January 4, 2013)

"All of my life isn't real...it seems to me that A Course in Miracles *is saying that I don't really exist...yet here I am existing..."* - Anonymous

What *A Course in Miracles* says is that your experience of yourself as a personal self in a body in a world (ego) is not real existence. It is a false sense of reality (illusion).

Within you is the solid experience "I am" or "I exist". This is True Being (God). It is real, infinite, and eternal. You also have this other experience of a limited, time-bound personal self in a body in a world. These two experiences have become conflated in your mind so that you think that the experience of "I exist" refers to the personal self. This confusion is the source of all manifestations of pain. What the *Course* teaches is that your experience of Existence and your experience of a personal self are actually two disparate experiences. It teaches you how to sort them out so that you can release the false sense of limited identity and know true, infinite, and eternal Being again. This is the only way to lasting peace and happiness.

The chief tool the *Course* teaches to sort out these two experiences is the Holy Instant. In the Holy Instant you bring your mind into the present and turn it inward to commune with the simple quiet sense of "I exist" at its center. You drop for a while the personal story and all that comes with it. You rest in True Being. The more you practice this the more you recognize that only True Being is true. You accept that the personal experience is simply a passing idea.

Your experience of "I exist" is not the limited "I" of "I" alone, one among many. It is the one, universal, limitless "I". "I exist" is the same in every mind. It is where every mind is One. Everything else is different, separate, temporary, and passes away.

99. Ask: What about ghosts and near-death experiences? (January 11, 2013)

"You say there are no individual spirits but what about ghosts? What about people who say they've seen Jesus? Or people who have near-death experiences say that they see their loved ones..." - Anonymous

Just like material bodies, ghosts are projections of the split mind. Just like material bodies, any meaning you see in them you give to them. They are another form of not-Truth, or illusion.

Part of the confusion is that the word "spirit" is commonly used for both non-material form (ghosts) and Formlessness (Truth/God). And they are not the same. Part of the confusion is also that the personal thought system (ego) confuses anything "supernatural" or unseen by the body's eyes with Truth. This spiritualizes some forms so that you do not seek beyond form for Truth.

To help you sort out illusion from Truth remember that Truth is formless. So all form is not-Truth (illusion). Anything that can be perceived, measured, or has boundaries or limitations is form. Some form is material and can be seen with the body's eyes (material form themselves). Some forms, like ghosts, are not material but are still perceived by the body's senses. Other forms are not experienced through the body's senses, like energies or thoughts, but can be measured or have boundaries. If something can be experienced through form it is form.

Formlessness (Truth) is known, not perceived. It cannot be measured. It has no boundaries or limitations. It cannot be contained in words or thoughts or by any other form. This is why Truth is unlike any experience that you have in form. And this is why you can experience Truth within you but you cannot convey it to others. Limited form cannot capture Limitless Formlessness. Truth cannot be "proved" in or by form.

A near-death experience is a choice on the part of one who is ready to learn of Truth. Usually it is an unconscious choice. They are not yet ready to experience Truth directly so they need a bridge to Truth. So images of loved ones who have passed are used by the Holy Spirit (Teacher of Truth) in their mind to reach them and teach them of Truth. This is similar to the use of Jesus or other historical teachers of Truth to reach those who find the idea of "Holy Spirit" too abstract. The Teacher of Truth in your mind always meets you where you are, at your level of understanding, with what you can accept without too much fear. But all bridges to Truth are not Truth Itself. They are part of the illusion used by the Teacher of Truth to help you transcend the illusion.

100. Ask: Any thoughts to help us in these difficult economic times? (January 18, 2013)

"In this time of financial woes, hopefully many can benefit from some words for guidance on surviving the money crunch. Trying to see things from the perspective of abundance and not from lack does get difficult when in the physical world bills pile up, debts get larger and income starts to shrink. Please share some of the thoughts that can keep us in line with Truth in these difficult times…" – MLN

Do not define yourself by what does or does not appear in the universe of form. The self in the world is not you. What does or does not show up is not you. These are all just passing thoughts.

As with anything that disturbs your peace, use it as a reminder to turn inward and feel your wholeness in Truth (God). If you are not yet able to feel your wholeness in Truth, then use disturbing appearances to remind you to turn inward and *grow* your awareness of Truth. Sit quietly and let disturbing thoughts rise up. Do not embrace them; do not fight them. Observe them and let them go. Become aware of the whole, quiet, limitless Truth beyond them.

Since the world that you perceive is an idea in your mind you can trust that if you are in touch with your Wholeness It will manifest in form. If there is something that the personal self must do to make it happen, you will know how to direct it to act when the time is right. Keep your mind open to guidance.

If certain fearful thoughts of lack persist and you find that you cannot release them, then look with the Holy Spirit at the underlying belief that they represent. Perhaps you feel undeserving. Maybe you have an expectation of punishment (guilt). Maybe you just do not yet trust that your Wholeness is unfolding perfectly in form. Trust takes time to build so be patient with yourself. The more you use disturbing appearances to remind you to commune with Truth, the truer Truth will be for you, and the faster your trust in It will grow.

101. Ask: Which guilt is ACIM talking about? (January 25, 2013)

"When ACIM talks about guilt is it talking about guilt for things I've done or is it talking about guilt for separating from God or both?" - Anonymous

In a practical sense both, not because they are the same, but because the personal thought system (ego) blends them.

In the world there are laws and moral codes that are set up for the civilized functioning of society. These laws and codes vary from culture to culture and over time. When you are a child adults are supposed to teach you the laws and codes of your culture and instill in you a social conscience that is bothered when you violate them. When you do violate them you make amends or "pay your debt to society". In theory your conscience could be wiped clean. But the personal thought system in your mind will never allow you to have a clear conscience because it requires guilt to maintain itself in your mind.

Your mind's natural state is limitlessness. In your identification with a personal self it is limited. So you are uncomfortable. You feel that something is "wrong". All that is occurring is a mis-identification. It is only a mistake. And a mistake can be easily corrected. But to defend itself as your reality, the personal thought system needs you to believe that something real, not just a mistake, occurred. The personal thought system whispers in your subconscious that the feeling of "wrong" that you experience in your identification with it is "*you have done something wrong*". Since the personal experience is the opposite of Truth (God) in every way you are guilty of attacking, separating from, or killing Truth.

So unconscious guilt is the personal thought system's way of maintaining your belief in it. Your guilt is the "proof" that you have attacked Truth and that the personal self is real. You won't look inward, where you would find Truth, because you think that if you look within you will find out what a horrible "sinner" you really are. Further, you don't want to find Truth anyway because you think that It wants to get retribution on you for your attack on It.

So there is no personal thought system in your mind without guilt to defend it. And there is no guilt in your mind without the personal thought system to cause it. This is why you can only release your mind from guilt by releasing yourself from identifying with a personal thought system.

The idea that you have attacked Truth is not something that the personal thought system says to you directly. It is important to it that this idea stay buried in your subconscious so you won't question it and undo it. One of its ways of dealing with your discomfort is to have you project away guilt and see it in others instead of in yourself. Of course, this does not really release you from the belief that guilt is real. It's actually a way of keeping the belief in guilt in your subconscious. And if you see guilt as real anywhere, you believe that guilt is real in you.

But feelings of guilt are bound to rise to the surface anyway, especially since they are heavily reinforced by the world. So the personal thought system projects the source of guilt onto the personal self's mistakes, imperfections, and limitations. This blending of social conscience and the personal self's inevitable mistakes with the inherent guilt of the personal thought system serves three purposes: as something to which to point as the source of your guilt, as a way to spiritualize the personal self by giving its behavior spiritual significance, and to reinforce your fear of punishment from Truth.

So the way out of guilt is to question it when it comes up. Sort out what is social conscience and what is guilt. If you feel guilt, is it justified? Is Truth changed by the personal self's imperfections and mistakes? This is impossible. Remind yourself that only the Truth in you is true. It is eternal, unchanging, and unchangeable. The personal identity is just a passing, imperfect, mistaken thought. It does not affect the Truth in you in any way.

You will know that you are undoing (forgiving) the guilt in your mind when you find that you can accept your mistakes and the mistakes of others as simply part of the limited, imperfect, and passing human experience. When you behave imperfectly you apologize, make correction or amends, and you let go of the situation. And when others make an apology, correction, or amends you accept it and let go of the situation. In fact, you will realize that no apology, correction, or amends was really required because nothing real has occurred. The Truth is untouched by anything that seems to happen in the world. So guilt is not real.

102. Ask: If there is no duality how does that allow for relationships? (February 1, 2013)

"...The Course *speaks repeatedly about relationships, especially "The Holy Relationship". However, if those that we have had relationships in the illusion do not really exist, who do we have relationships with in Heaven? If, in Truth, there is no duality which means "all is one" - how does that allow for a relationship? Doesn't it take "two to tango"? Or, is it what I sometimes intuit, that when we see the Truth in another, we are really seeing a reflection of the Truth in us. And it is only in that state that we can truly "relate" to another? Could it be that when our Oneness is re-cognized, we do have relationships with all, knowing that the essence that flows through us is the same for all? Or am I trying to make a pseudo-illusion with this example?..."* – SL

Like all forms of forgiveness, the Holy Relationship manifests only at the level of perception, or illusion. It is a temporarily useful illusion that strengthens your awareness of Truth (God). It is a bridge to Truth. The only part of it that is eternal is the Love within it. Everything else is false and falls away.

You are correct: Heaven is Oneness, or One Being, and there are no "relationships" in It. And, yes, there is only One Truth and when you see It reflected in others you are experiencing what *A Course in Miracles* means by a "Holy Relationship". The more you are aware of the Truth in you the more you are aware of the universality of Truth. It is in every mind, whether or not others are aware of It. When you come from this awareness in your relationships with others you are choosing to make them Holy Relationships.

103. Ask: How do we best cultivate willingness? (February 8, 2013)

"How do we best cultivate 'willingness' or is it by grace that we come to this? After a trauma in my life, it took me 4 years of suffering all the while thinking I was 'willing'...while praying and saying 'words' of surrender ...to realize that I was really being resistant!" – L

A Course in Miracles points out that you do not have to look for Love because you already have It. You only have to look for your obstacles to Love so that you can remove them and be aware that you have Love. It is the same with willingness. You do not have to *cultivate* willingness. You only have to look for your obstacles to being willing and the willingness will be there.

Wanting, wishing, hoping, and intending are all passive states of desire. Willingness occurs when you allow the necessary shift or change to actually occur within you so that you will have the desired experience. Often, this shows up as taking action or a change in behavior. But if it is only an internal experience that you desire, then willingness leads to you having the experience.

For example, Janel dreams of being a doctor. When she becomes *willing* to be a doctor she will enroll in the appropriate classes to become one. She will take action.

John is tired of the consequences of his alcoholism. His life has become unmanageable. When he becomes *willing* to heal his life he will accept the means (rehab, 12-step program, therapy, etc.) to become and remain sober. His behavior will finally change.

Becky wants to hear the Holy Spirit. When she becomes *willing* to hear the Holy Spirit within her she will hear the Holy Spirit within her.

Willingness comes when you "hit bottom" or experience pain that threatens to be more than you can endure. Or it comes when you value the experience that you want more than you value whatever resisting it gives to you. So you can move toward willingness by looking for your obstacles to achieving what you desire. *Without judging yourself,* look honestly at what you value instead of the experience that you desire. Look at what you think you might lose if you get what you desire. Look at what you think you might lose as you work toward what you desire. Understand that some of your obstacles may take a while to undo. When they are removed, willingness will come. And if you are unable to find your obstacles, then accept that you are not yet *willing* to know what your obstacles are! You cannot force yourself to be willing.

104. Ask: I have never really had love... (February 15, 2013)

"I've never really had love... I've been the one out here who was born illegitimate, mom was a state child and abused. So when I was born I really wasn't shown love but lots of rejection. My own grown adult kids have shut the door in my face, I long to have my family but they threw me away. I wasn't abusive towards them...I have sought God all my life and at this point of age 62, I realize there is still hope, but I've found people can be nice, but it's all just words, nothing more and love always dies. It will eventually kill you..." DK

You are clearly not aware of it, but you have always had Love (God). You have Love right now. What you do not have is an *awareness* of Love. And that is easy to correct!

A Course in Miracles points out from the start a very observable fact: You feel Love not when others seem to love you but when you choose to come from the Love within you. By extending Love in your awareness you learn that you are (have) Love.

Love cannot go into you from others. Nor can it go out from you to others. If this were possible human relationships would be whole and satisfying. They would be Truth (God)! And you have learned that this is not so. Human relationships work when you are aware of the Love within you and you recognize them as an extension of the Love within you, not as the source of Love for you.

When you seek for Love (God) in the world you teach yourself that you lack Love. "Love" is the word we use for the experience of wholeness that is Truth (God). So when you feel lack, emptiness, lonely, etc., do not seek for Love from others but stop and rest in your awareness of Love within. Sit quietly and let the personal thought system's (ego's) thoughts come and go as you rest in the Quiet Love beyond them.

And when you are engaged with the world choose to come from Love so that you grow your awareness of the Love within you. The personal thought system always responds quickly and emotionally, with guilt, judgment, and fear. Allow it to do so, then step away from its responses and choose to come from Love instead. This will teach you that Love is within you and will never leave you.

If you have a feeling of sacrifice in your dealings with others then you are coming from lack (the personal thought system) and not from True Love. If you behave toward others in a way that you feel is "loving" but is designed to get love or something else from them, then you are coming from lack and not from True Love. When your mind is centered in Love you deal with others from an awareness of your Wholeness. So you do not seek Love from them. And you do not have any sense of loss or sacrifice. You extend Love because it is natural to do so. You also know that True Love is in their mind, even if they are unaware of this.

If you find that you cannot come from Love with others then you need to look for your obstacles to being aware of the Love within you. These will be feelings of guilt, fear, unworthiness, etc. Or you may be very attached to your personal story of lovelessness and rejection. You will need to work through these with the Holy Spirit. If you are not yet able to hear the Holy Spirit directly, then consider a therapist or some other form of counseling. You may need to hear the Holy Spirit through others first to help you reach a point where you feel worthy enough to hear the Holy Spirit within yourself.

105. Ask: What does ACIM say about manifesting? (February 22, 2013)

"Can you give me any insight on Manifestation which is the big thing now? Jesus is always the example of the great Manifester, but what does ACIM say about manifestation, and does the Enlightenment that ACIM allows to a lucky few come with Manifestation possibilities?" – DH

This quote best sums up what *A Course in Miracles* says about manifestating:

"You see what you expect, and you expect what you invite. Your perception is the result of your invitation, coming to you as you sent for it. Whose manifestations would you see? Of whose presence would you be convinced? For you will believe in what you manifest, and as you look out so will you see in. Two ways of looking at the world are in your mind, and your perception will reflect the guidance you have chosen." (T-12.VII.5)

Your choice of peace or conflict is made manifest to you immediately through your choice of thought system. Choose the personal thought system (ego) and you will believe in the world of lack and limitation and manifest conflict in your mind. Choose the Holy Spirit and It will teach you how to overlook the world and look on Truth instead. This will manifest peace in your mind.

The Enlightened Mind is in every mind. The *Course* calls this Mind within you "Christ". The story of Jesus is the story of one who manifested an awareness of Truth (God), or Christ Consciousness. Christ Consciousness is available to everyone right now, not just to "a lucky few". All you need to be aware of It is willingness to be aware of It. And your willingness manifests as you working through your obstacles (guilt, fear, unworthiness, etc.) to being aware of It.

When you are aware of the Truth within you It manifests in your experience as inner peace. You do not have to wait for complete Christ Consciousness to manifest peace. You will manifest peace along the way anytime you allow Truth into your awareness. For a long while peace will come and go for you as you grow your awareness of Truth. Then peace will come to stay even while you are still aware of the personal thought system and its world. Finally, when you have released the personal thought system altogether, you will manifest only peace. And then the personal thought system and its world will fall away from your mind completely.

106. Ask: How do I forgive a situation where a friend lied to me? (March 1, 2013)

"I have a friend who likes to say actions speak louder than words. And recently, I found out that she lied to me and it appears purposely deceitful...Initially, I felt sadness that a person who professed to love me would for lack of a better description lie to me. When I did tell her I knew about the whole event she acted like she wanted to counsel me on my sadness. This seemed to make me angry...All I ever ask for is the truth. As the truth stands on its own. I am having a challenge forgiving her in this moment. I am having feelings about the deliberate lie. I know this is a lesson for me and caring for myself. How do you see this?" – Anonymous

Your (former?) friend is correct: actions do speak louder than words. And she spoke loud and clear about herself to you with her behavior. Your choice now is to maintain the friendship as-is, maintain the friendship with new boundaries that address what you now know about her, or to end the friendship.

You don't really need to forgive her, but you want to forgive your thoughts about her. You discovered she told a lie. The lie is a fact. However it is not the source of your upset. You are upset because of the story you tell yourself about the lie and the liar. This will probably be some sort of victim-story that ties into your personal identity and personal story. It may have many angles or layers. This is what you need to look at with the Teacher of Truth (Holy Spirit) and release (forgive) if you want to be at peace.

107. Ask: What does it mean to look at things with the Holy Spirit? (March 8, 2013)

"What does it mean to look at things with Holy Spirit. What are we actually doing? You wrote an answer to a person who spoke about being lied to and you said to look at it with Holy Spirit. How does one do that? And when we invite Holy Spirit to look at things with us....what are we actually asking for and what is the experience?" – K

The Holy Spirit (Teacher of Truth) comes from God (Truth) in your mind. It is the thought system in your mind that is aware that only God (Truth) is real. It comes into your awareness to replace the ego (personal thought system) when you decide that you want to return your mind to an awareness of God. It knows that only God is real but it knows that you think that you are a personal self in a body in a world. So it meets you where you think you are, serving as a bridge over Which you can cross to full awareness that only God within you is real.

You call on the Holy Spirit when you are willing to put aside the ego's perception of a situation because you are aware that it causes you pain. You think about the situation as always, but with a mind willing to set aside judgment of yourself, others, and the situation. You are open to truly seeing your obstacles to peace. You are open to truly helpful answers from within, even if they are not what you expect.

A feeling of true openness and willingness will bring the Holy Spirit into your awareness. You don't need words, but you may use them to remind yourself to be open to the Holy Spirit. "I'm willing to look at this with You," might be words that accompany your releasing judgment and opening your mind to the Holy Spirit.

The Holy Spirit comes into your awareness when you are merely open to It rather than through your effort because It comes from What your mind is. It is a thought system that is natural to your mind. It has always been a part of your experience in your perception that you are a personal self in a world, just not one that you were used to identifying as the Holy Spirit. So it is not a foreign experience, just one that you have probably not sorted out from the many experiences of the ego thought system. You may hear It as a still, quiet Voice in your mind. You may receive unformed thoughts or intuitions that you recognize come from a deep, quiet place within you. You may receive answers or help from what seems like sources outside of you, but your recognition of them as the answers and the help that you asked for comes from the Holy Spirit within you.

You know when you experience the Holy Spirit when you feel set free from guilt, fear, or other limitations. You feel "lighter", both with regard to the darkness lifting from your mind and a weight lifting from your shoulders. The Holy Spirit's answers are often surprising, redirecting, reframing, or shifting the way that you look at a question or a situation.

Your awareness of the Holy Spirit will evolve over time. At first It may seem "other"; a Teacher, Guide, Advisor, etc. within your mind but not wholly a part of you. You can make It your Constant Companion, a Presence of Which you are always aware and that you can always call on for answers. It can serve as an inner Therapist with Which you discuss what you see as your problems and obstacles to peace. But as your awareness of It grows the line between you and It will fade and It will simply be the "higher" part of your mind. Where once answers seemed to come from an "Other" you will simply know.

108. Ask: Does the ego always respond emotionally and the Holy Spirit rationally? (March 15, 2013)

"Is it safe to say that the ego always responds emotionally and the Holy Spirit always responds rationally?" - Anonymous

The Holy Spirit (Teacher of Truth in your mind) does always respond rationally. But the ego (personal thought system in your mind) can be either emotional or rational. Its initial response to anything is emotional. This is how you can recognize it. But it may revert to rational thought quickly to repress or deny.

When you are rational you can tell which thought system you are using by the results. The Holy Spirit uses rational thought to set you free from limitations, guilt, and/or fear. You feel love and liberation when you come from the Holy Spirit in your mind. The personal thought system uses rational thought to deny or to repress guilt and fear. You continue to feel bound and fearful when you come from the ego.

For example, a new student of *A Course in Miracles* reads in it that the personal experience is not real. The ego in their mind tells them that this means that they do not have to deal with their personal issues. This is rational on the surface but not realistic so it is not loving and it is not going to set them free. For the new student who has not yet experienced God (Truth) to the extent that they know that only God is real it is only an idea that the personal experience is not real. It is not something that they know to be true. So this use of rationality does not lead to them releasing themselves from the personal experience. It leads to them denying their belief in and feelings about the personal experience. This reinforces their unconscious guilt and fear. This prevents the student from inviting the Holy Spirit into the experience. The student is not set free.

The Holy Spirit, however, would rationally, realistically, and lovingly point out to the student that the awareness that only God is real will come in time. They have only just embarked on the process that will lead them to this awareness. Hearing this would release the student from the pressure of feeling that they have to accept and understand what they do not yet have reason to accept and understand. It would set them free from guilt in this area.

The Holy Spirit is rational but also realistic, gentle, kind, and patient. It always meets you where you are to lead you to Truth. It does not demand that you understand what you do not yet have reason to understand. You know when you have been learning from the Holy Spirit when you find that you, too, have become rational, realistic, gentle, kind, and patient with yourself and with others.

109. Ask: Is there some way to speed up knowing that only God is real? (March 22, 2013)

"...I'd like to know more about the experience that only God is real. Are there any references to this experience in any of the 5 Course *books/supplements? Do we have any way to speed up experiencing only God as real? Does this experience grow and mature, is it permanent once experienced initially or does it come and go in our mind? Tell us what you can about this please."* - JK

There are many descriptions throughout the books of *A Course in Miracles* of the experience that you have when you know that only God (Truth) is real. Here's one that is characteristic of them:

"In Him you have no cares and no concerns, no burdens, no anxiety, no pain, no fear of future and no past regrets. In timelessness you rest, while time goes by without its touch upon you, for your rest can never change in any way at all." (W-109.5)

The means for "speeding up" your awareness that only God is real is what the *Course* calls the "holy instant". The holy instant is any moment that you choose to turn inward and touch God. This can be anything from just a few seconds that you take anytime during the day to a more formal meditation where you set aside a block of time to quiet your mind and commune with God. Chapter 15 in the Text discusses the holy instant in depth. The holy instant is such an essential practice that once it is introduced in the Text it is referred to again and again.

Your practice of the holy instant demonstrates your willingness to become aware that only God is real. One experience of God is not usually enough to shift you fully to the awareness that only God is real. And initially you are not going to have some sort of experience of God every time you invite it because you won't necessarily be truly open to it. But once it happens you will be motivated to open to it again. You will be able to use your memory of the experience in your practice of the holy instant to remind you that want the experience.

"The experience of an instant, however compelling it may be, is easily forgotten if you allow time to close over it. It must be kept shining and gracious in your awareness of time, but not concealed within it. The instant remains. But where are you? To give thanks to your brother is to appreciate the holy instant, and thus enable its results to be accepted and shared. To attack your brother is not to lose the instant, but to make it powerless in its effects." (T-17.V.12)

The holy relationship is how to extend the experience of the holy instant as you go about your day. A holy relationship is any relationship where you choose to come from your awareness of God rather than from the ego (personal thought system) as you relate to another. Once you have had some experience of God in a holy instant you can extend this awareness by choosing to put aside the ego's judgments and stories for yourself and others. You let the ego's judgments come up and then you let them go. You remind yourself that only the experience of God within you is real. You are already whole in God. You don't need others to make you whole. You don't need them to change to make you happy. You don't need to fix them because they, too, are already whole in God, even if they are not aware of this.

The effects of the holy instant are cumulative. You never lose what you experience in one even if you turn back to the ego afterward. As you have more and more experiences of God and extend these in your relationships with others it will sink in that only God is real. This will be so gradual and natural that you won't even know that it has occurred until you have experiences that show you that you have changed. You will find that you do not react to situations in the world as you once did. You have an awareness of Something within you that is solid and unchanging and more real to you than the world. In your awareness of It you feel whole and safe no matter what seems to be occurring in the world.

110. Ask: Can you explain the "fear of release"? (March 29, 2013)

"In the process of reading the ACIM *Text a second time, the following stumps me a second time:*

Chapter 2.V.1 'Before miracle workers are ready to undertake their function in this world, it is essential that they fully understand the fear of release. Otherwise they may unwittingly foster the belief that release is imprisonment, a belief that is already very prevalent.'..." - MS

The passage you quoted is where *A Course in Miracles* first discusses physical healing specifically, though what is teaches can be generalized to all forms of healing. Here is roughly the same passage from my book *The Message of A Course in Miracles: A Translation of the Text in Plain Language:*

"Before you can accept physical healing as an extension of God's Love it is important that you understand your fear of release from your identification with a personal self. If you do not understand this fear you will teach yourself that release from the personal self is loss…"

You can only be truly free in God (your True Being). But the ego (personal thought system in your mind) has projected its own attributes of arbitrariness, untrustworthiness, judgment, viciousness, etc. onto God. To understand your obstacle to accepting God you must understand that you fear God because you believe what the ego says about God. So you feel that letting go of the ego and accepting God is a "sacrifice" too great to make.

111. Ask: What is a day like for you, Liz? (April 5, 2013)

"…Liz, I would like to know what a current day is like in the mind of an Advanced Teacher of God. Specially, I'd like to know spiritually what a whole day is like for you from waking to

bedtime...some real life situations as to what you do in your mind relative to practicing ACIM *with everyday practical situations. What is your waking hour like in terms of meditation or prayer? How do you deal with life situations that arise during the day like finding out your water is off due to a pipe in the street bursting, like what words do you say to the Holy Spirit relative to frustration? You see someone on TV who is in your eyes stunningly beautiful. Do you laugh with the Holy Spirit knowing it's just an erroneous belief in the ego? What words to think in your mind and can you allow yourself to continue to watch without any serious investment as to that attractive person being 'salvation'? I think I'm struggling to understand the daily practical application as to exactly how an advanced teacher of God actually converses with Spirit..."* JK

Before I answer this I want to caution you that you should not try to make your mind as my mind is. You must let your awareness of God (Truth) grow naturally and let this have its natural effect on your mind. Be where you are now and learn the lessons that are in front of you today. The only way to move forward is to take the step in front of you, not to stretch to one somewhere down the road that you have not reached yet. You will only fall over and delay yourself.

I cannot speak to the day of an advanced teacher of God because I am not one. I am *advancing* but hardly advanced. I have spent the past few years coming to the understanding that the next step for me is true release of the ego (personal thought system). If I have even begun that I have only *barely* begun. I am at the *very* beginning of the end.

My mind is, however, very different from the way it was. It is much quieter. I am able to live in the present with Truth. I have Everything right here right now within me so I blissfully have no goals for myself in the world. Peace is always in my awareness to some degree. When I have been absorbed in something in the world I turn my mind back to peace very easily now. The line between me and the Holy Spirit (Teacher of Truth) has blurred. It is no longer "other". I do not "call on" It anymore. It is What my mind is when I release the ego. The world does not seem dense and real to me anymore. I am not really aware of this, however, until I speak with someone for whom the world is very dense and real. Then I remember how dark it used to be for me and I gratefully see how my mind has changed. My whole experience is lighter, both in terms of brightness and weight.

My life is like meditation in action because peace is always in my awareness to some degree. Just as in formal meditation, where I am in ego thoughts, then I dip into peace, then I'm back into ego, then back into peace, and on and on—I dip in and out of peace all day. Sometimes the peace dominates and it is in the forefront of my experience. Sometimes it is in the background and the ego's clamor dominates. But I always have some degree of peace. So I no longer need structure with regard to formal meditation. I meditate at least once a day when it seems natural to do so.

If something unexpected like a burst pipe occurs, unless I'm *really* centered, I do the usual swearing and ranting and getting into a whole story about how this is ruining my day and how are we going to pay for this? I let this pass and then I bring my mind back to the present with Truth and do what needs to be done to take care of it.

When I find someone attractive on TV or in person I enjoy the view. I am whole right here right now in Truth so the ego's forms of "salvation" no longer tempt me. I am so aware of Wholeness within and the passing nature of the personal experience that I do not cling to the ego's pleasures or suffer over its pains. I let it all come up and I let it all go, without judging any of it

When the Holy Spirit seemed like something "other" to me, I conversed with It as I would with any friend, albeit one Who was wise and all-knowing. At first It was Something that seemed far from me. Then for a long time It was my Constant Companion, always right here to talk to. Finally, the line between us blurred and I went from calling on It to simply experiencing Its Thoughts as my own. But it was never the words I used or their formality or informality that invited the Holy Spirit into my awareness. The words were for me to focus my thoughts for myself. The Holy Spirit didn't need them. The Holy Spirit came into my awareness because I was open and willing to experience the Holy Spirit.

112. Ask: Where is my rudder in this ocean of thoughts? (April 12, 2013)

"Over many years now I have experienced the light through the Course, *with intervals of seeming to fall back into darkness… To remember the warmth and Great Love from God that is in me when I write about it seems to vague out when my thoughts change back to human thoughts…It is also like living through the mirror into Alice in Wonderland's chessboard. In these multiple sets of realities I seem to be experiencing I find it very difficult if not impossible to live as a real self let alone Self. The moment I write this Help is there, and comfort pours into me, but I seem to be so impatient for the Great Love I have known again and again and want to be in constantly. But I keep on living in a body and the cycle returns again and again…Where is my rudder in this ocean of thoughts…"* -T

You are describing the typical vacillations of a serious student of *A Course in Miracles* or any other teaching that leads to an awareness of God (Truth). You are experiencing both parts of your mind. You have accepted God into your awareness, but not wholly yet. You are still afraid of It. You still identify with the ego (personal thought system) enough that its undoing feels like your undoing. So as painful as the ego is, it is at least familiar to you, so you swing back into it. This vacillation is the whole process of undoing the ego. It is very painful in the beginning because the contrast between the pain of the ego and the peace that comes from being aware of God is so stark. It makes the darkness of the ego seem even darker. It makes the pain seem more painful because you know there is Relief. But in time God will become more real to you and the ego will become less real to you. And you will not let your perception of a world of conflict stand in the way of your awareness of God and the peace this brings to you.

The *Course* reminds us that time closes over the experience of the Holy Instant unless we extend it into our day to day life. You do this by communing with God every day, by taking moments to practice the Holy Instant throughout the day, by making the Holy Spirit your Constant Companion, and by extending your awareness of Love to your experiences in the world. When something is ugly, tragic, or frightening, use its contrast with Love to remind you to turn inward and remember that only your experiences of the Great Love are real. These habits of bringing your mind into the present and turning it inward to God throughout the day will be your rudder. (For more on these habits see my book, *4 Habits for Inner Peace*, at www.lulu.com).

113. Ask: I judge my judgmental friend. What is going on here? (April 19, 2013)

"I have been a student of ACIM *for about 5 years, being brought to it by someone who has been studying it for 30 years and who considers himself to be a great expert in it. The trouble is he is*

a difficult personality who sometimes becomes very judgmental of people and situations. I think someone who is so into the Course *should not be like this and I point this out, in what I consider to be a calm and loving way. He, however, hates any criticism and gets very angry with me and accuses me of judging him, whereupon I point out (rather less calmly!) that he is judging me ... and so it goes on with us both getting very angry and shouting at one another. What's going on here?"* – Anonymous

What is going on is two egos (personal thought systems) battling for who is going to be "right" in the mistaken belief that being right will undo guilt. Your friend's judgments on others are his ideas of what is right. You judge him as wrong and you think that however you think he "should" be is right. Attack and defend. Attack and defend. You are both feeling guilty and terrified.

When your friend sees the ego in others it reminds him of the ego in his mind. He still feels very guilty about the ego in his mind. Otherwise, seeing ego in others would not bother him. Without guilt he would just observe the ego in himself and in others instead of projecting his guilt onto them.

He feels attacked and afraid when you judge him because he unconsciously agrees with you that he "should" be different. So he attacks you, the mirror of his own guilt, instead of recognizing that his feeling that he is being attacked comes from his own belief in his own guilt.

You, too, feel guilty for the ego in your mind. When you see him coming from ego it reminds you of the ego in your mind. In your guilt you attack him, the mirror in which you see your own guilty mind.

I'm going to take a whack at what else is going on with you. It scares you that someone who has been studying for 30 years still gives so much power to the ego in his mind. But remember that time studying the *Course* is pointless if it is not put into practice. Intellectual study alone will not bring peace. Willingness to work through your obstacles to peace will result in peace. You must be willing to use every situation as a classroom. When you cannot just observe another but you get an emotional charge from their attitudes, behavior, or words know that this indicates that you have something to learn about yourself. So you can be grateful to this relationship for bringing your belief in guilt to your conscious awareness. Now you can let your friend go his own way and bring your guilt to the Holy Spirit to work through.

114. Ask: Can you help me understand Separation and the solution to it? (April 26, 2013)

"Can you help me understand Separation, and the solution to it as the only problem humans have?..." – PM

God, or Reality, is formless, limitless Being. As a self in a body in a world you seem to experience a different reality. This experience of lack, limitation, and loss is obviously the opposite of God. So you seem to be "separate from God". Your belief in this other reality is your only problem because if you did not believe in it you would not experience lack, limitation, and loss in its many forms.

The "Atonement" is the solution to this problem. As ACIM uses the word, "Atonement" means correction of your perception that separation from God is real. This is accomplished through you becoming aware of God within you. When you are aware of God within you, you know that you have Everything. You no longer believe in the reality of lack, limitation, and loss that the personal self seems to experience.

115. Ask: Why do I identify so much with guilt? (May 3, 2013)

"I had an encounter with someone who I would classify as a narcissist. During a particular conversation, he lost control himself and became irrational and demanding. What followed is a long story but basically he blames the whole argument on me. We are no longer on speaking terms which, to be honest, is a good thing because he started to be nasty even before that conversation. Strangely enough, I felt guilty about it even though I tried my best throughout. I feel like this situation is teaching me that even though other people are having tantrums (and projecting their guilt on me), I don't need to sacrifice or blame myself. However, it is difficult. The question is: why do I identify so much with guilt in this situation? It's been a couple weeks and I'm still going over the gory details. Thank you." – Anonymous

You identify with guilt because you identify with the ego (personal thought system). You cannot undo guilt from the ego. You can only undo guilt by releasing the ego.

Since you feel that you did your best in the conversation your guilt is not about anything in the conversation specifically. His ego simply triggered your awareness of the ego in you. And to be aware of the ego is to be aware of guilt. Replaying this conversation is just the form that guilt is taking in your mind now.

To release yourself from the generalized guilt of the ego you must release yourself from the ego. Recognize that the ego is not you and guilt is not real. Then turn your mind inward to God (Truth) and remind yourself that only God within you is real. If you have a strong awareness that God is real this will detach you from the ego. If your awareness of God is not strong enough yet for you to detach from the ego, this practice will eventually lead you to detach from the ego. Until your awareness of God is strong enough for you to detach from the ego you will experience guilt.

116. Ask: Do we each share a projection or live in our own projection? (May 10, 2013)

"I get confused about if there is one projection that we all share or if we are each living in our own projection…" - Anonymous

It's both. Not-Truth is a universe of form projected from one split mind. This projection includes billions of versions of the split-mind which make their own projections of meaning onto the universe of form. These projections are what make the experience seem dense, multi-layered, complex, mesmerizing, and convincing to each seemingly-individual mind.

The shared projection, or macro-projection, is the larger story for space and time that is generally agreed upon by the split minds. This projection has no meaning in itself. Each seemingly-individual mind makes the macro-projection meaningful to itself through its own projections of meaning. These micro-projections are made from each self's individual story in time. So, for example, Letitia and Jose are looking up at a vast, cloudless, blue sky. They agree that the sky looks vast, cloudless, and blue. But when Letitia looks at the vast blue sky she sees an aspect of nature that she considers beautiful. And when Jose looks at the sky he sees a shade of blue that is the color of the favorite t-shirt of his abusive step-father. Letitia enjoys looking at the sky because to her it is just something pretty. Jose doesn't want to look at it at all because for him its color is infused with painful meaning.

For further examples of this just watch the talking heads discuss an issue on any TV news program. Each looks out at the same forms but through their own set of filters and values derived from their own personal story. So while they all seem to live in the same macro-world they actually respond to their own private micro-world. And each thinks that their "world", which is really their mind's unique filter through which they look at form, is "right". This is why everyone eventually conflicts with everyone else, even when they sometimes agree on much. So what they say actually reveals more about them than about the issues that they discuss.

So you seem to live in a blank macro-projection. It functions as a screen onto which you can project meaning or not. When you do project meaning onto the macro-projection both the macro-projection and your micro-projections seem like reality to you. But when you learn that you already have Everything (Truth, God) within you, you will feel free to withdraw meaning from a meaningless world. You will just observe it passing by as you rest in peace within.

117. Ask: So if I choose my illness do animals, plants, and children choose too? (May 17, 2013)

"So if I am choosing my illness, what about animals? What about plants? They get diseases, too. What about infants and small children who get sick? Are they all choosing, too?" - Anonymous

The entire universe of form, including all plants and animals, is a projection of not-Truth from the split mind. As not-Truth it is inherently limited, imperfect, and disordered. The split mind projects itself into not-Truth by projecting itself onto only one animal—humans. Your seemingly-individual split mind is a projection of THE split mind projected onto a specific human animal in the projection. So it seems as though humans have a choice where plants and other animals do not even though they are all equally not-True.

With regard to the body, choice occurs in your mind in two ways, generally and specifically. When you choose to identify with a body you choose all of the imperfection and disorder that comes with it. Then within this general choice you make specific conscious and unconscious choices that affect the body.

The body is under the physical laws of the universe of form. You are not a body so these laws have no effect on you, but when you identify with a body you think that what is happening to the body is happening to you. Under the laws of the universe of form body disorders are caused by the body's genes, its environment, its energy, and its behavior. You do not personally or individually choose the body's genes. They are part of the projection in which you seem to find yourself in your identification with a particular body. Sometimes you choose the body's environment; sometimes that choice is made for you (parents when you are young; pollution that you are unaware of, etc.). You do make choices that affect the body's energy and behavior.

For some, genetically or environmentally caused disorders show up earlier than it does for others. This accounts for disorders in infants and young children. Sometimes you may unconsciously choose specific forms of disorders or injuries. You may do this to get attention, to punish yourself, to play the martyr, to get rest, etc. You also make behavioral choices that affect the body's health (smoking, eating healthier foods, etc.). And you make choices that determine the energy in and around the body and this can result in diseases manifesting in the body.

As a version of the split mind you always have the choice to identify with a body (not-Truth) or with the other part of your split mind, Truth. But you are not likely to become aware of this choice until you reach an age where you think independently and you start asking questions about your true nature.

You cannot transcend the body and identify with it at the same time. You transcend the body by identifying with Truth instead. Until you are wholly identified with Truth you will experience the body and all of the limitations that come with it.

It is important to remember that disorders in the body are not wrong or bad or sinful. Like the body itself they simply are not True. A body in your awareness in any condition only means that you have not-Truth in your mind. And not-Truth is nothing. You can choose to focus on what is not True and be in conflict. Or you can choose to use experiences in the body to remind you to turn inward and grow your awareness of Truth. When you are aware of Truth the peace that you experience transcends all conflict, limitations, imperfections, and disorders.

118. Ask: How do I know which teachers to follow? (May 24, 2013)

"I'm new to A Course in Miracles. *There seem to be so many books about and teachers of* ACIM *and often what they teach seems to conflict. How do I know who to follow?"* – Anonymous

The only Perfect Teacher is the Holy Spirit within you. Teachers in the world are imperfect. We teach because we are still learning. Teachers are at various stages in their awareness of Truth. This can make it seem like we contradict each other when it is just that some are more aware of Truth than others. If we are truly open to the Holy Spirit then our teaching evolves as we grow more aware of God (Truth). And this can make it seem like what we teach now contradicts some of our own past teachings.

Teachers in the world are instruments of the Holy Spirit for you only when you follow the Holy Spirit within you. So be sure to first invite the Holy Spirit into your awareness when you choose to read or to listen to teachers in the world. Otherwise you will only reinforce the ego (personal thought system) in your mind. You will know that you are learning from the Holy Spirit when you experience clarity and liberation from guilt and fear.

You are automatically drawn to teachers who model what you want. If you want to intellectually understand ACIM you will be attracted to teachers who have a deep intellectual understanding of it. If you are looking for a spiritualized life in the world then you will be drawn to teachers who spiritualize the ego. If you want inner peace you will be drawn to teachers who have inner peace. As you grow aware of Truth your goal for yourself may change. You will find your attraction to teachers of your old goal falling away to make room for teachers of your new goal.

Only the Holy Spirit knows what you need right now to move you toward your goal. But you may not yet be confident in your ability to hear the Holy Spirit. Or you may feel blocked in your awareness of the Holy Spirit. So until you are more certain of the Holy Spirit in yourself bring your confusion and questions to a teacher who teaches from the Holy Spirit. Find someone who models what you want. And be sure that they help you to hear the Holy Spirit in yourself.

In time you will be able to bring your questions directly to the Holy Spirit. This practice will not only result in you having the answers that you need at the time but it will also strengthen your awareness of the Holy Spirit. And this is the real value in any spiritual study. In time, as the

Holy Spirit becomes a real Presence for you, studying will fall away. You will learn directly from the Holy Spirit within you.

119. Ask: What is meant by "spiritualizing the ego" and why is it undesirable? (May 31, 2013)

"What exactly is meant by 'spiritualizing the ego'? Does ACIM *discuss this? And why is it undesirable?"* - Anonymous

What is popularly called "spiritualizing the ego" is called "confusion of levels" in *A Course in Miracles*. It refers to confusing the seeming-levels of your mind: ego/perception/illusion with God/Knowledge/Truth.

"Ego" in the context of "spiritualizing the ego" means spiritualizing not just the personal thought system but all form. The personal thought system, the body/personality, and the rest of the universe of form are all not-God (not-True). But all forms have no meaning or purpose in themselves. The personal thought system, however, is a form without meaning but which *gives itself* the purpose of negating God (Truth) in your mind. It uses all other forms to do this. So what is called "spiritualizing the ego" really means "spiritualizing the ego and its tools", or more simply, spiritualizing not-God. And of course it is the ego in your mind that does this!

Simply, this occurs when you believe that both God and not-God (ego/ universe of form) are real and you see a relationship between them. The most obvious example of this is the ego's religions. They teach both that God controls the universe of form and that what happens in the universe of form affects God. They teach that both a spirit within you and a body and a world that seem to surround it are real.

The ego's spiritualizing of not-God shows up in many more subtle forms as well. Some of the more common ways are in any feelings of guilt with regard to God; "should" and "should not" beliefs with regard to God; the belief that your behavior in the world changes how God responds to you; believing that you have to earn, attain, or achieve God, enlightenment, awaken, etc.; the belief in an individual soul or spirit; the belief in pre-ordination and/or reincarnation and/or an individual soul or spirit "going on" after death; believing that unseen forms, like energy, are God; believing that "supernatural" or unexplained phenomena at the level of form are the same as God; viewing synchronicity as coming from God; wanting to change the personal self to be "good" or "spiritual"; wanting to change others or the world according to values that reflect spiritual beliefs; wanting to use spiritual awareness to manifest or attract a better personal life for the personal self; wanting to use spiritual awareness to heal the body.

Spiritualizing not-God is undesirable because it perpetuates guilt in your mind by giving meaning to not-God. This makes it real and valuable to you. This is why ACIM puts so much emphasis on sorting out God (Truth) from not-God (illusion). As long as you believe that the ego and its world have any reality you will believe (usually unconsciously) that you have attacked God. You will believe that God is a power outside of you and over you. And you will not be able to choose God over not-God because you won't be able to tell them apart. Undoing the confusion of God with not-God is really the entire process of attaining inner peace.

It is almost impossible to avoid spiritualizing the ego when you first become aware of God because the personal experience is so real to you. You expect that you are meant to change it to be more God-like rather than to let it go. And of course the ego wants to reinforce this for its own sake. The vast majority of those who embark on a spiritual path never get past this stage because, after its initial resistance to you turning inward the ego realizes that it can use spiritual ideas to validate itself. It does not care if you want to make it more "spiritual" as long as you continue to believe in it. So it is more comfortable to spiritualize the ego than to let it go. But the price for you in remaining at this stage is continued guilt and fear.

From the ego's point of view your awareness of God only has value if it can serve the self. Its constant question is, "What's in this for me?" But if you pursue an awareness of God to serve the self you will not find lasting peace. You will reinforce your belief in the self as your reality. And this will perpetuate guilt in your mind.

Another reason that spiritualizing the ego occurs is that you may see how your awareness of God as Reality has a positive effect on your personal experience. God is what your mind truly is. And the personal experience is a story unfolding in your mind. So both are in your mind, but they never intersect. The universe of form never touches God. And God never touches the universe of form. But *your awareness* of God corrects your mind back to its natural state, and this has a positive effect on the self's unfolding story in your mind. The personal self's attitudes, behavior, choices, and energy change for the better when you are aware of God as Reality. This changes the self's relationship to the world and the world's response to it. This can seem like there is a relationship between God and the world. But really it is just that your awareness of God affects your mind and this affects your mind's effect – the self.

If you want more peace and happiness than a spiritualized personal life can offer then you must recognize that your peace and happiness come only from the awareness of God within you, not from the effects of this awareness on the self's life. You must attend to the cause of peace and happiness (your awareness of God within), not to its incidental effects (the positive transformation of the personal experience). You may be grateful for these effects but you must recognize that they do not make the self real. The self is an idea in your mind. It is not you. God is your Reality. And only in an awareness of this can you find true, lasting peace and happiness.

120. Ask: How do I know if I am not pursuing worldly goals because of ego stuff? (June 7, 2013)

"...I am 23 years old. Since I graduated from high school I haven't joined any... form of education...What I feel in me is this... worldly desire for finding my goal/purpose in form. It feels like I cannot be fully happy while this remains unknown for me. Like just living ordinarily doing very little in form makes me unhappy...I noticed that the stories, articles about Finding Your Purpose make me sad in a way...But the truth is that the other part of me, the truer part, wants to let go of this so called Search for my Goal. I want to eventually come to the place within me where I can be happy with less or more activity, happy with not knowing clearly my worldly purpose, just being, living, as one beloved teacher said, Being happy with the void....nothing and eventually everything.

I guess what I seek to know, How do I truly know if I am not denying this desire for activity in me, because of fear of some ego hidden stuff, by saying that I really want to let go while it may be the opposite? What should I look at truly to know the truest answer? And what could be helpful in honestly detaching from it letting it go?..." – SM

Words and thoughts can lie. But feelings cannot lie. If you want to know what you *really* believe then look at your feelings. Your feelings of sadness when others talk about having a goal or purpose in the world are telling you that you still believe that fulfillment comes from having a goal and a purpose in the world.

You are experiencing what many students new to a spiritual path experience. You have a new goal of Truth. But you are not yet aware enough of Truth for this awareness to fulfill you. So you want to seek for fulfillment through the self's life in the world. This is natural at the beginning of the path.

The good news is your two goals are not mutually exclusive. You can grow your awareness of Truth as you pursue a goal and purpose in the world. In fact, you must use your experiences pursuing your interests in the world to grow your awareness of Truth. You simply have to bring your willingness to learn of Truth into every situation. You probably have already made the shift of seeing every situation as a classroom in which to learn of Truth. You will bring this point of view with you into whatever you pursue.

Your question about whether or not you are using your spirituality as an excuse to avoid taking risks and making efforts in the world is a good one. First, ask yourself if you are avoiding life in the world because you think that you "should not" have worldly desires because they are not "spiritual". Guilt may be your only obstacle. Remember that there is no god outside of you that you have to appease by making the "right" or "spiritual" choices. There is no reason for guilt. You make the choice to be aware of Truth because you want peace.

And, again, the Teacher of Truth (Holy Spirit) within you uses every situation to teach you of Truth, if you are willing to learn. As the Truth becomes true for you, your desires and goals will evolve naturally. You will eventually find your purpose in your awareness of Truth. But that takes time, and the Teacher of Truth knows this. It meets you where you are. And where you are is still very much in the world.

But if guilt for worldly desires is not the block, or if it is only one block and you still cannot move forward when you let it go, then you need to ask yourself what else you fear pursuing whatever goal you want in the world.

121. Ask: How did I create terrible things in my life that I did not want to happen? (June 14, 2013)

"I don't see how I've created my own life. Some terrible things have occurred and I didn't want them..." - Anonymous

(In *A Course in Miracles* "to create" means "to extend" or "to be one with". ACIM uses the word "make" for what is meant by "create" in this question).

Your choice for the limited, imperfect, disordered experience of not-Truth (universe of form) was not made by you personally or individually. It was made by the split mind of which your mind is one projected version. On the individual level you become aware of yourself as a mind in a specific form among a multitude of diverse forms. But you are not without choice or power. Form has no power over you and cannot cause you either conflict or peace. That is a choice you make with the mind. If you want the personal experience to be your reality you will experience conflict. If you want to be aware of the Truth (God) because It is the Truth you will experience peace.

The personal experience has no meaning in itself. Being not-Truth it is inevitably limited and painful. But suffering over it is your choice. Your projections of meaning, or judgments, from the personal thought system (ego) are what cause you to suffer. Instead, you can let these go. You can watch the self's pains and pleasures come and go while you rest in peace in your awareness of Truth.

On the individual level you do make choices and decisions that make up the self's life in the world. Your conscious and unconscious beliefs (thoughts) determine the personal self's attitudes, behaviors, choices, and energy. These determine its relationship to the world and the world's relationship to it. If you look back honestly over the self's life in the world you will see how you are responsible for certain choices, unconsciously or consciously made, that resulted in certain outcomes. You won't be willing to see this, however, if you confuse responsibility with blame, as the personal thought system does. When you can lay aside guilt and blame you will learn that taking responsibility empowers you.

For example, I was discussing with a client one day her early marriage to an abusive man. (She was long divorced from him by this time). She had married very young the first man to ask her because her self-esteem was low and she was afraid that she would not be asked again. He abused her as her boyfriend but she made the very young mistake of expecting marriage to change him. It did not. She wanted to know how she had "created" a situation where she was abused. I pointed out that she married a man that she knew was an abuser and she exclaimed defensively, "But I was young! I didn't know any better!" I said, "Yes! Exactly! And this is why you made a life with an abuser. You were young and inexperienced." I was not judging her, but pointing out a fact. Her guilt, however, made her hear facts as blame. She judged herself as wrong or bad or sinful for marrying an abuser when really she had just made a mistake. This judgment against herself (guilt) had prevented her from taking responsibility, which in turn made her feel powerless over the self's life. But once she realized how she had made this situation in her life (low self-esteem, inexperience, denial, wishful thinking) she felt empowered instead of guilty. She could change those things in herself that had led to this mistake. (And she mostly already had by then).

Painful things happen in this disordered experience that you do not individually choose. You are abused as a child. People die. Natural disasters occur. Disease happens. To avoid as much pain as possible you want to learn from these experiences. What part, if any, did you play in what happened to you? For example, if you live where there is often flooding in the spring you shouldn't be surprised if one May your car is washed away. You took that chance. This is not right or wrong. You had your reasons for living there and taking that chance. You do not need to judge yourself. You do want to re-evaluate your choices and take what measures you can to prevent a similar thing from happening in the future. Live and learn. And you do decide whether you want conflict or peace by deciding how you look at what happens in the world. You can use painful experiences to judge and punish yourself. Or you can see them as opportunities to turn inward and grow your awareness of Truth. Your awareness of Truth will then result in you learning at the level of form practical lessons as just described.

Your awareness of Truth also affects the personal self's attitudes, behavior, choices, and energy. At some point you made a choice for Truth and/or peace. And what you needed at that time came into your awareness: books, teachers, self-help programs, counselors, etc. And eventually *A Course in Miracles*. Whatever happened in the past, going forward your awareness of Truth will now show up as answers that you need, healthier decisions, and as an over-all more harmonious life for the personal self. If you put aside the personal thought system's judgments your painful experiences will not be "terrible". They will be opportunities to grow your awareness of Truth and practical lessons from which you learn.

122. Ask: I know I shouldn't want to fix the world... (June 21, 2013)

"I know as an ACIM student I'm not supposed to want to "fix the world" but I see so many problems and people in pain and I feel like I have to do something..." - Anonymous

Statements like "supposed to" or "should" with or without a "not" indicate that you feel guilt and fear. This means that you are reading *A Course in Miracles* with the ego (personal thought system). When the *Course* seems to inspire guilt and fear in you, know that these come from your mind, not from the *Course*. Ask the Holy Spirit (Teacher of Truth) in your mind for the loving way to read passages that scare you. The *Course* is a path to inner peace, not a path of righteous behavior to appease a punishing god.

It is true that you cannot want to fix something and let it go (forgive it) at the same time. If you want to fix something it is because you value it. And if you value it you must believe that it is real. So your feelings indicate that a guilty world in need of fixing is still very real to you. You haven't learned yet that the guilt that you see is projected from your own mind. And it is this guilt that seems to give the world of form substance and reality.

The ego (personal thought system) in your mind is a thought system of guilt. From it you project guilt onto meaningless form. So you will release guilt from yourself and the world when you release the ego. Since the premise for guilt is that you killed God, you will release the ego when God is real to you and you realize that there is no justification for guilt.

So before you can release the guilty meaning that makes the world so real to you, you must grow your awareness of God. And the Holy Spirit within you is the means to do this. The Holy Spirit is the thought system of God in your mind that can replace the ego. It meets you where you are. So you do not have to give up your interests and values, like fixing the world. Instead you want to bring the Holy Spirit with you as you pursue them. The Holy Spirit will use them as classrooms in which you learn from and of the Holy Spirit. Then, instead of being ends in themselves, they will be the means for growing your awareness of God.

You do not have to judge yourself for whatever honest values you have in the world. Your personal values are neither right nor wrong. They are all actually nothing. But with the Holy Spirit as your guide you can use them to grow your awareness of God. Eventually, God will be real for you and you will release your projections of guilt onto meaningless form. You will realize that there is no world. Only God is real.

123. Ask: How can I deal with deep feelings of sadness as I go deeper on the path? (June 28, 2013)

"How can I deal with deep feelings of sadness?....it happened when I started to go deep in meditation and spiritual path. It is as I have contacted a place of separation from God within me, which is almost impossible to ignore....I feel subtly very guilty of feeling sad. I also project a lot of people kind of trying to take me out of this dark place, and me feeling rejected for it... What I honestly get from the Course *is that I have to go beyond it, to see what's the truth beyond it, but in practical terms I feel confused on how this works. Should I give me permission to feel it? Should I also be soft with the part of me that wants to put some boundaries to don't feel rejected?...I would like to learn how to deal with it with the Holy Spirit..."* – NA

First, yes, always let yourself feel whatever you honestly feel. Repressing your feelings is the way to hold onto them, not to release them. And there is no reason to feel guilty for any of your feelings. Feelings are not facts. They have no effect on God (Truth) at all. They only show you what you truly believe. And you want to know this! How else can you undo false beliefs except by looking at them? And all negative emotions indicate false beliefs that are obstacles to peace.

Guilt is always at the bottom of what you feel in your identification with a self. "Sadness" is another word for "depression". Depression is anger turned inward. Anger is a defensive posture, so it means you are fearful. And fear is really always fear of punishment because you believe you are guilty. (Depression = anger = fear = guilt). You can peel away these layers with the Holy Spirit.

> I'm depressed. So why am I angry?
> I am angry. So why am I afraid?
> I am afraid. So why do I feel guilty?

It may help you to write out your responses. Invite the Holy Spirit into your awareness and then go deep with these questions. If you are not comfortable doing this alone with the Holy Spirit then you might want to work with a teacher or mentor.

You are actually already close to your answers because you stated that you have "*contacted a place of separation from God within*" yourself. You are already consciously in touch with the place of guilt (center of the ego) in your mind. Now you just need to find the exact shape that guilt takes for you in this circumstance.

You must feel rejected by people who try to take you out of your darkness because you feel that you are not understood. That may be a projection of you not understanding yourself. When you figure out what form guilt takes at the bottom of your sadness your darkness will lift and you won't need others to understand you. You will understand yourself, which is the only understanding that you really need. In the meantime, if you need to, then, yes, set boundaries with others to take care of yourself.

124. Ask: Will others be going with me as my life takes this new direction? (July 5, 2013)

"*...I have recently retired and have taken this opportunity to start going deep into my study of ACIM and my spiritual path in general. I have recently encountered a lot of confusion about what the direction of my life will be from here and if my wife and any of my friends and family will be going there with me. I have felt like I have to place all of these things in my life on the altar as it were and be willing to live with or without them. I am assuming that this is a somewhat normal occurrence but it is becoming very disruptive in my marriage as I express my confusion and the change in my energy and actions is being felt by both of us. I can tell that there is fear of the unknown present and I have given it to the Holy Spirit to show me the truth of the situation...*" - MG

It is common for students to become aware of internal shifts in their perspective and values as their goal changes to inner peace. And this is usually accompanied by fear that this will cause external shifts in their life. And it will, although not always as dramatically as the ego (personal thought system) makes you fear.

If your life is greatly dysfunctional then you are more likely to have some dramatic shifts in your external life that reflect your new goal of inner peace. These can seem to happen suddenly. For example, if your sense of self-worth has been very low the goal of inner peace itself indicates a healthy shift. You must value yourself at least a little to make inner peace a goal. This shift in goal changes your relationship to the world. The choices you made from a place of low self-worth will no longer fit you when you value yourself. This is why many students find themselves divorcing, filing for bankruptcy, foreclosing on their home, closing their business, losing their jobs, etc. For some this all happens at once! Often they feel they did not set these things in motion, but their shift in goal did.

Some external shifts will certainly happen over time. The ego's (personal thought system's) way of relating to others is dysfunctional. It is co-dependent. This means that when you come from the ego in your relationships with others you take responsibility for them or you ask them to take responsibility for you. So as you learn to look to God (Truth) for wholeness rather than to others this will change the way that you relate to others. You will no longer ask them to make you whole. You will no longer play a certain role with them to feel whole. You will be in a relationship with them simply because you love them and enjoy being with them. But if they expect you to ask them to play a part in your life that you no longer need, or you no longer play a part that they want you to play, then they will face the choice to grow with you, stay and be unhappy, or leave the relationship.

The ego is a thought system of conflict. And conflict means drama. When you choose inner peace it means you choose to let go of conflict and drama. You choose to detach from ego. To the ego in your mind as well as in others' minds this can feel like a death. So as your values change give others in your life the time and space to grow with you. Acknowledge their fears, reassure them of your love, and support them if they choose to grow with you. They may not follow your path. But they will need to grow in their own way to adjust to the changes in you.

125. Ask: How do I deal with obsessions and compulsions? (July 12, 2013)

"I am a recovering anorexic/bulimic, alcoholic, codependent. I have been studying ACIM for 2 years, and have felt the benefits of it. My one goal is "salvation", to know and be love. However, i have a lingering obsession, i feel that i must walk a certain amount each day. if i don't do it feel guilty because i feel like I broke an unspoken rule i established, and if i do it feel guilty because i feel like i'm giving into the obsession... i know ultimately guilt is the belief in separation. but knowing this and having this truly change me isn't coming on this point. my mind feels torn. so i guess the question is how to deal with obsessive thinking and compulsive behaviors... the problem is that my thoughts about the whole thing are totally conflicted. i think it is because of my history..." – KL

First, you may need to evaluate whether you need medication and therapy to deal with your illness. These will not remove your underlying belief in guilt but they may help you manage intrusive thoughts induced by a chemical imbalance that make it difficult for you to get down to your belief in guilt. Drugs and therapy are called for when you have thoughts that disrupt your life rather than just make you feel conflicted or uncomfortable.

Behaviors, like emotions, are caused by thoughts, so you only need to deal with your thoughts and your emotions and behaviors will change. You hit on what is going on with "I feel like I broke an unspoken rule I established". You set these rules for yourself to deal with guilt.

You feel that you need to be a good or right or perfect person to appease a punishing god. In the absence of rules given to you, you set your own in the hopes that this god will be pleased and not punish you so much for your intrinsic guilt.

The ego is the opposite of God so for it to believe in its own existence it must believe that it killed God. When you identify with it you believe that you killed God. You accept this because your limitless mind is not in its natural state when it identifies with a limited self. You are uncomfortable and you interpret your discomfort as guilt for killing God.

If you believe that guilt is real then you must believe that you will be punished. Any need you feel to be good or right or perfect or to control the world comes down to a belief in intrinsic guilt and a punishing god. (If God is dead how can It punish you? Don't expect the ego to make sense. That it knows deep down that God is not dead and that it does not really exist is why the ego is so insecure). The belief in guilt and a punishing god are the center of the ego thought system. It is not going to change, which is why you need to release the ego to be at peace. You do this by looking at your unconscious and conscious beliefs in guilt and fear so that you can release them.

In *A Course in Miracles* the word "God" refers to the Limitless Being that is Truth or Reality. God is your True Being, not a power over you. Whenever you feel guilt and fear, in whatever form, turn your mind inward and remember your experiences of God. Since you experience God, God cannot be dead. This undoes the ego's basis for guilt. And God is the Power within you, not a power over you. There is no power over you. You will need to remind yourself of this over and over as you root out all of the ways that you believe in intrinsic guilt and a punishing power over you. In time you will release your belief in guilt and your need to control the self and its environment will fall away.

(This article coincides nicely with the release of my new book, *Releasing Guilt for Inner Peace*. It addresses in-depth the ideas expressed in this answer).

126. Ask: Are not murderers, etc., guilty? (July 19, 2013)

"My problem with the Course *is it seems irresponsible to say that there is no such thing as guilt. What about murderers? What about rapists and child molesters? Are they not guilty? If we don't say that some behaviors are bad or wrong then the world would be even more chaotic than it is…"* - Anonymous

When *A Course in Miracles* says that there is no guilt it means that in God (Truth, Reality) there is no guilt. But in the mistaken construct of a reality (illusion) that we call a world there must be rules for living with each other in relative harmony. So there is in the world guilt under the law.

The guilt that the *Course* says does not exist would be an internal *feeling* of "I am wrong/bad" or "I have done something wrong/bad". This is the guilt that is not real. In the world, legal guilt does not refer to an internal experience of guilt. It refers to socially inappropriate behavior.

The ego (personal thought system) confuses them, however, to explain the internal guilt that you feel is real. Here is an excerpt from my recently released book, *Releasing Guilt for Inner Peace*, which might help clarify things:

When you are very young adults are supposed to teach you the boundaries and laws of your family, culture, and society. These rules of right and wrong form a social-morality. As you learn these you develop a social conscience. Your social conscience is an internal sense of what is right or wrong according to your family, culture, or society. It is what feels disturbed when you violate social-morality. Rules, boundaries, and laws vary among families, cultures, and societies. They also change over time as values change and more is learned about the world and human nature. Though arbitrary, social-morality is a starting point for living in relative harmony with others in the world.

When rational and realistic, rules, boundaries, and laws serve the well-being of a family, culture, or society. But the belief in an absolute-morality results in unrealistic and/or harsh social-moralities to control members of a family, culture, or society. Absolute-morality, if it existed, would be right and wrong behavior in the world as decreed by a power, or god, over it. Your unconscious belief in absolute-morality is your belief that guilt is an intrinsic aspect of reality. When you confuse absolute-morality and social-morality, social-morality becomes an attempt to control what is seen as intrinsic guilt.

A disturbed social conscience and feeling guilty are not the same experience. But the personal thought system hijacks your social conscience to "prove" your guilt. A social conscience refers to the self's behavior in the world in relation to others. If guilt does not become involved with it, your social conscience is assuaged through amends or a genuine change in values. Guilt, however, is the feeling that the imperfect and sometimes mistaken self is proof that you are intrinsically wrong or bad. Guilt cannot be swept away. Where your social conscience sees temporary mistakes easily corrected, your belief in intrinsic guilt sees eternal sins that can never be undone. It twists your social conscience into a useful source for guilt.

Murderers, rapists, and child molesters break social-moral boundaries and are guilty under the law. But they are not guilty in the eyes of God because they do not exist to God! There is no relationship between God and the world. Only the belief in intrinsic guilt makes it seem that there is.

127. Ask: Do you think all of the channeled material available now is authentic? (July 26, 2013)

"There seems to be so much 'channeled' material available now. Do you think that it is all authentic?" - Anonymous

I'm sure that the vast majority of channeled material out there is offered sincerely. I have not looked at any of it extensively. But I have looked into some of it and generally I've found the usual religion-like jumble of Truth and spiritualizing the personal thought system (ego) that indicates that the channeler is not very advanced in their awareness of Truth.

There are limitations to material channeled by people who have not yet spent the many years it takes to sort out the Voice of Truth in their mind from the personal thought system. They often do not realize that the personal thought system has gotten involved in their channeling. And even when the personal thought system is not involved their inward hearing is not perfect. They are the first student of the material that they channel. And the material often far outstrips their awareness of Truth. So they do not notice incongruities or ask for clarity. Sometimes this is because they feel that they are not worthy to question what they hear. And often they want what they channel to be "pure" so they are reluctant to involve themselves with it. But what they do not realize is that questioned and clarified material is purer because questions are how one gets past their own limitations in hearing.

A teacher who is advancing in their experience of Truth feels incongruities and inconsistencies, whether they channel material or they teach in collaboration with the Teacher of Truth (Holy Spirit) in their minds. They question what does not feel right. This leads to them receiving correction for what they misheard. Or it leads to them receiving clarification on the issue that seemed incongruent. Either way, it makes their teaching purer.

Critical thinking is an essential part of spiritual study because all spiritual material comes through imperfect teachers. So always invite the Teacher of Truth into your awareness when you study, whether the material is channeled or it is written from the teacher's own experience. When you feel confusion or you notice incongruities or inconsistencies discuss them with the Teacher of Truth. This will "purify" anything that you study. And it is a great way to grow your awareness of the Teacher of Truth within you, which is the only real value of study anyway.

128. Ask: How do I practically apply "salvation lies in your brother"? (August 2, 2013)

"'Salvation lies in your brother – the power and glory are in him.' The inference is that there is no salvation without your brother's. How do you respond to this in a practical way?" – TS

Helen Shucman and Bill Thetford were in a unique Holy Relationship where they were at an equal teaching/learning level. They were partners in salvation [correction of the perception of separation from God (Truth)] in a way that most students do not experience. They each, simultaneously, saw Christ (the part of every mind that is One with God) in their minds reflected in the other. As it says in the Manual for Teachers, these relationships are rare.

What this quote was saying to them was that the Christ that each saw reflected in the other was salvation for them because it showed them that they were not separate from God. They could see Christ in the other because the Christ Mind was in their own minds.

But you do not need to have a partner in salvation in the world as Bill and Helen did to learn from their lesson. You can see Christ in others even if others are not aware of It in themselves because Christ is in you. You "save" yourself by practicing seeing Christ in them to grow your awareness of the Christ Mind in you. Once you have even a dim awareness of Christ in your mind you can remind yourself when you are with others that that same Christ Mind is in them, too. You can remind yourself that Christ is all that is real and true in anyone. You can save yourself from the false perception that you are separate from God.

129. Ask: How can I declare myself an alcoholic when I am a holy child of God? (August 9, 2013)

"I've been in a 12-step program for many years. I'm no longer comfortable declaring myself an alcoholic because I know from A Course in Miracles that I am a holy child of God. But I have benefited from the program and part of me wants to continue in it. I'm in conflict and don't know what to do." - Anonymous

Your mind is an extension of God's Mind (Truth). God within your mind (child of God/Christ) is one with God. But your mind is split and God is not all that is in it. You also have a self and a thought system about the self in your mind. The self (body/personality) with which you identify and its thought system (ego) are not part of God. These are ideas completely apart from God. They do not come from God and they will never be one with God. And it is the self that has the disease of alcoholism.

When you stand up in a meeting and say, "I am So-and-so and I am an alcoholic" you are simply stating a fact about the imperfect self. You can state this while knowing that God within you is eternally perfect and unchanged by the imperfect self. God within you is the Power greater than the self the awareness of Which "restores you to sanity".

130. Ask: Why would I fear God? (August 16, 2013)

"A Course in Miracles says that I fear God. But I don't feel that I fear God. It also does not make sense to me. Why would I fear God?" - Anonymous

You think that you do not fear God but look at the evidence: Are you aware that God is your True Being and that only God is real? Do you recognize that the self and its world are nothing? If you knew these things you would experience only peace all of the time. Do you? If not, what is blocking your way? It can only be fear.

When you are identified with a self you fear God for many reasons. God is formless Being extending infinitely. It is an experience of wholeness unlike the limited experience of the self in every way. From the limited experience of the self God seems like the Great Unknown. And what is unknown is frightening.

You also know on some level that an awareness of God undoes the self. So when you are identified with a self you feel that God will "kill" *you*.

The personal experience is the opposite of God. It is the denial of God. Denial itself makes you fear what you deny. Why would you deny something unless it is undesirable? The denial that is the entire personal experience seems to imply to your mind that God is something to be feared.

Your denial also makes you unaware that the personal experience is a benign, meaningless idea of the impossible. You think that you have attacked God. You unconsciously feel guilty for it. And guilt makes you fear retaliation from God.

So you fear God when you are identified with a self because you do not know God and you think that God will kill you. Your fear is unconscious and so woven into the personal experience that you do not know that it is fear. The entire personal experience is guilt and fear.

Your fear of God is so huge that you are not yet even able to acknowledge it. But you can see the evidence of it in the guilt and fear that seem real to you. Recognizing fear is the essential first step in releasing it.

The catch-22 is that to overcome your fear of God you must be aware of God! This is why growing your awareness of God is so slow in the beginning. You must ask to help you overcome fear the very Thing that you fear. But just a little willingness and trust is all that is needed: "I'm afraid of You but maybe I've been wrong about You. I am willing to question my beliefs about You so that I can get to know You. I am open to Your help as I look at these beliefs."

131. Ask: Why are there ego-based conflicts at ACIM events? (August 23, 2013)

"I've tried to attend study groups in my area and I've been to ACIM-based conferences and I'm always disappointed to find the usual ego-based conflicts arising between the people there. I guess I just think that students of ACIM should know better…" - Anonymous

You are disappointed because you are looking for something at these events that they cannot deliver. If you are looking for God (wholeness; abiding love, peace, happiness) you will find It only within. If you are looking to understand *A Course in Miracles* better and to learn from others' experiences with it you may find these at these events.

Sometimes people confuse community with other people with communion with God. Humans are social animals and survive through cooperation. So joining with others is rewarded through the release of endorphins in your brain when you meet with others. This temporary feeling of well-being, or even of being "high", is often confused with the joy of communion with God. But euphoria and joy are not the same experience. Euphoria is a temporary chemical experience in the brain. Joy is the experience of Being (God). When you experience true joy you know that it is eternal even if your awareness of it wavers. If you want lasting peace and joy you will find their source only in an awareness of God within you.

You shouldn't be surprised that when people gather together they act like people! And ACIM students are just people. Many are there, like you, looking to fill needs that the event cannot deliver. This leads to conflict as they blame others for not fulfilling their needs. But you can attend these events with the quiet awareness of the Holy Spirit within you. Then you will ignore the inevitable manifestations of ego and use the events for deepening your understanding of ACIM.

132. Ask: How can I use my awareness of Truth to sing freely and effortlessly? (August 30, 2013)

"I am studying to be an operatic singer, and I am under the impression that when I become aware of Truth, my singing will spontaneously feel free and effortless, and my stage fright will disappear. Learning to sing involves a keen awareness of the body, and it is to this that my voice teacher directs me. Hence I have been completely preoccupied with doing things correctly. I can see how I have created a punishing god out of my body, and an 'absolute morality' out of singing freely. As a result, I fear and avoid singing and performing. What do I need to understand in order to release these fears? Is there some guarantee that my larynx will drop and open fully and permanently when I accept a certain Truth? I have enjoyed several thrilling glimpses of singing on an open throat, but how do I get it to be permanent?" – OT

What you need to understand is there is no relationship between Truth (God) and your singing or anything else in the world. Truth is unaware of anything in the world. But your *awareness* of Truth does have an effect on the self's attitudes, behavior, choices, and energy. When you are aware of Truth you find yourself led to the means to heal the self's false beliefs and the dysfunctions that are false belief's effects. However, this healing is only a manifestation of a healed mind. They are incidental effects and never the point if you want peace.

If you want to be aware of Truth because It is the Truth you will find peace no matter what occurs in the world. But if you want to be aware of Truth to serve a goal of the self (as in, singing freely and effortlessly) you will keep yourself in guilt and fear. You will be teaching yourself that the self is real and that it is you. You will believe that certain outcomes must occur for the self for you to be at peace.

Peace can be your goal while you still have goals in the world, but you will have to shift how you see your worldly goals. You will want to see them as means to your ultimate goal of peace rather than as ends in themselves. You cannot be attached to them, define yourself by them, or think of them as your salvation (the source of your wholeness, peace, love, etc.) or they will be obstacles to peace. You will want to recognize these goals are only temporary classrooms where you learn of peace from the Holy Spirit.

So you have to decide on your ultimate goal. And you will do that based on what you think will bring you peace. Only an awareness of Truth brings lasting peace. But if you think that singing with an open throat is what will bring you peace you are going to put a lot of pressure on yourself to find a way to do so. And this pressure will make it harder for you to do so. And, of course, you will not find lasting peace whether you sing with an open throat or not.

133. Ask: Exactly what is the ego and exactly how is it "vicious"? (September 6, 2013)

"Exactly WHAT is the ego and what exactly does the Course *mean by the ego turning 'Vicious'?" (Examples, please?)* – DC

The word "ego" means different things in different contexts. In psychology the ego is just one aspect of the human psyche (the other two being the id and the superego). Some use the term "ego" to simply mean "pride". *A Course in Miracles*, however, uses that word to refer to the thought system in your mind that opposes your Reality or True Being, Which it calls "God". The ego thought system focuses your mind on the self/body as your reality.

The ego does not really exist. It only seems to exist to you when you believe in it. So it is inherently defensive, always feeling it needs to prove its existence to you. This is why the *Course* says *"The ego is therefore capable of suspiciousness at best and viciousness at worst."* (T-9.VII.3)

The ego cannot harm you. It can only seem to harm you when you identify with it. In other words, it can only seem to harm what it makes of you when you agree with it. It has no power but it seems to have power when you believe in it.

Examples of the ego's viciousness are legion! It has both positive and negative thoughts, all of which are attacks because they are not true. But its negative thoughts are obvious examples of its viciousness. Every thought that you have of guilt, anxiety, fear of punishment, meaninglessness, unworthiness, and inadequacy is a vicious attack from the ego. Certainly it is at its most vicious if it tells you to kill the self. And its telling you that you are killing yourself by growing your awareness of God is a vicious attack.

Any time that you are not at peace you can be sure that you are listening to the ego. It does not matter if the thoughts are about you or about others. Often, the ego's attacks on you are subtle. They may even seem benign, but any thought that focuses you on the self and its body as your reality is an attack on you.

But the ego becomes overtly vicious when it is threatened. The threat can seem to come from another and seem to offend the ego. For example, when someone says something that "hurts" you in your identification with a self the ego viciously attacks them back.

Or the ego can be threatened when you disregard it. It is particularly threatened, and therefore most vicious, when your attention has gone to God instead of to it. It cannot understand God or join you There. It only knows that your attention has gone to Something Else and this is the ultimate threat to it. This is why you will find that an episode of peace or insight is often followed by dark, negative attack thoughts on you and/or others, often for weeks after you have experienced God in some form. Once you turn your attention back to the ego even a little it will do what it feels is necessary to hold your attention. And a vicious attack works as long as you believe in the ego.

134. Ask: What if I get comfort from ACIM but do not always believe it? (September 13, 2013)

"I get a lot of comfort from reading A Course in Miracles *but I have to admit I have not had some of the spiritual experiences that others say they have. I feel guilty to say this, but I'm not sure I really believe everything I read and frankly I'm not always sure I believe in a God..."* – Anonymous

First, I want to point out that the feeling of comfort that you have when you read *A Course in Miracles* is the Holy Spirit (Teacher of Truth) within you. So that is one spiritual experience that you do have. It's important to recognize that you do feel the Holy Spirit when you read ACIM so that you can recognize the experience in other contexts as well.

There is never any reason to feel guilty for being honest. In fact, you cannot move forward without first acknowledging to yourself what you are truly experiencing. There are two lies that people commonly perpetrate against themselves on a spiritual path that are huge obstacles to peace. One is thinking that "belief" is all that is required. But "belief" is only a decision to intellectually accept something as true whether or not you have experienced it as true. It's really a con that you play on yourself. You either experience God (Reality; True Being) as real or you do not. So "believing in" God means nothing. Experiencing God is the goal and leads to true peace.

The other lie that many perpetrate against themselves is blind "faith" in God. But you either trust God or you do not. Pretending to trust God when you do not really do so only increases your fear, stress, and guilt. Trust comes after many, many experiences of God because God is a wholly different experience from the one that you are used to in your identification with a limited body/self. You cannot force trust. You either feel it or you don't.

Acknowledge your doubts to the Holy Spirit, even if you are not certain It exists. You have nothing to lose being open and willing to experience God. If God turns out not to exist then everything stays the same. You won't gain anything, but you won't lose anything, either. And if God turns out to be true then you gain Everything. Even after many experiences of God I often fell into doubt and I'd say, "I don't know if You exist but I'm willing to experience You if You do." More important than the words was a feeling of true openness. And always something occurred within me to show me that my True Being is beyond the limited experience of the self.

In time, after many undeniable experiences of God, you will not give power to the doubts. The ego (personal thought system) will never accept that God is real, but it speaks only for itself, never for you. You will know that God is real and release the ego.

135. Ask: Do you pray that we don't go to war? (September 20, 2013)

"Liz, what do you do when you see something like we may go to war again? Do you pray that we don't go to war?" - Anonymous

As I released my projections of meaning onto the universe of form the world became very two-dimensional for me. So now the world is like a blank screen. It's a lot like walking around on a theatrical set in which no play is being put on. The set and props have no meaning without a story. So without me projecting a story, or meaning, onto events in the world they no longer stand out as special or significant to me. All of not-Truth (universe of form) is all the same. I see no difference between a hang-nail and a war and a butterfly and a rainbow. They are merely different expressions of not-Truth. I do not mean that things appear the same to me. The body's eyes see differentiation, size, degree, etc. But my *experience* of not-Truth has flattened out.

Of course personal opinions pop up in my mind about events in the world, but what are they but nothing thoughts about nothing? My thoughts about not-Truth are just another part of not-Truth. I observe them just as I observe the world. I let them come up and I let them go. I do not live there anymore.

As for prayer, to what would I pray? There is no power outside of me to petition. My experience is between me (split mind) and Me (True Mind), not between me and some outside power. Not-Truth and Truth are the two experiences *within* me. But they are diametrically opposed and they do not intersect. I do not ask Truth to change not-Truth because there is no relationship between them. And why would I want to change what isn't true unless I thought it was true? The problem, then, would be in me, not in what I thought was true.

And even if the world were true how would I know what had to happen in the grand scheme of things? It would only be the arrogance of the personal thought system (ego) to think I knew how the world should be. Perhaps what I judged wrong or bad was somehow necessary.

But of course, the world is not my reality, and only my judging it makes it seem real to me. My goal is to know Truth to be at peace so I am not interested in maintaining my belief in what is not real by seeking to transform it. I want to *transcend* my belief that what is not real is my reality. And I do this not by looking at it and praying that it will change to be what I personally want it to be. Nor do I look at it and then try to deny it. Instead, I accept that it is what it is and turn inward to Truth. Whatever I attend to with my mind is what is real to me and what will grow in my awareness.

136. Ask: How do you interact with the world when nothing has truth or meaning? (September 27, 2013)

"Liz, I think after so long and doing the Workbook lessons again I'm beginning to at least grasp where you are coming from- theoretically. But where the rubber meets the road I haven't a clue how to do all of this. I have a spouse, friends, family and work with schedules, plans and expectations to make and meet within all this nothingness that has no truth or meaning. How do you interact with any one close to you- much less to us, your students? If nothing you see, hear or touch has truth or meaning how do you live and find meaning in each day? Of course you go inside and commune with 'self' but this life goes on around you. Write a book or do a tape... You are in an existence here and now. Create a picture of what it looks like even to be 'present' with

you when you aren't present but closed off inside. Not knocking you or making fun of you. But I'm really missing something here." - LM

The self's life in the world is a projection of the mind and it is automatic. It is directed by the thought system in which I choose to center my mind: the personal thought system (ego) or the Teacher of Truth (Holy Spirit). On the outside, my life looks like a typical, ordinary life either way. But what is different is my internal experience.

When I am centered in the personal thought system I feel that I am in lack. The personal thought system teaches me that the way to fulfill the lack is to direct the self to get (whatever) to make me feel whole. "Getting" to fill the lack is my motivation for whatever I direct the self to do.

But when I am centered in Truth I feel whole and at peace. I do not feel a need to direct the self to get anything. So I don't live *through* the self; I merely observe its unfolding story, without judgment. I do not have a motivation for what the self does. I just find the self doing what it needs to do to take care of itself and its responsibilities in the world.

What you are missing is the experience of wholeness that comes from an awareness of the Truth within. Until you experience True Wholeness you will look to the self's life in the world as the source of your wholeness. You will have no choice because this will seem to be all that you have. You will feel that without you intensely directing it the self's life in the world will fall apart and you will have no hope of wholeness.

You ask how I find meaning in each day. I do not. I find deep, rich meaning within in Truth. I do not look to the day, to others, to what the body does, etc. for meaning. Those things just happen. It is the personal thought system that asks, "Why do I do this?" because it is looking for what it can get out of a situation, relationship, etc. But centered in Truth I have no reason to ask "why" about anything because I do not need to give it meaning. I am already in True Meaning.

I am not closed off inside. I am open inward to Truth, rather than outward to nothing. This leads me to be truly present, because if I am in nothingness, where am I? Certainly not truly here!

If I am not present to Truth when I am with another, then I am present only to my own projection of them. From the personal thought system I do not experience another as they experience themselves or as others experience them. From the personal thought system we all see through the filters of our own separate personal stories. But when I am with others and present to Truth I am present to What is true in their mind as well. Only the Truth in each of us is the same (one).

You are trying to understand with the personal thought system's intellect what you will only learn through experience. And when you learn it, it will be *you* that learns it, not the personal thought system. The experience I have now of the world as devoid of any meaning in itself did not happen through any effort on my part to experience it that way. It came as a surprise to me! Nothing on this path has unfolded the way that I expected. Nor has any of it come from me working directly on trying to make anything happen. My attempts to make things happen were always misguided and never worked. When shifts came they never came where or how I expected. Eventually I learned that all I have to do is to grow my awareness of Truth and to watch how my own mind projects meaning and makes the world that I seem to experience. So don't try to be where I am or even to understand it. Instead, invite Truth into your awareness right where you are in your life now. Let It lead the way and all of this will unfold naturally for you.

137. Ask: How do I deal with wanting to help without seeing it as real? (October 4, 2013)

"...You wrote somewhere that, at one point on your path, politics kept dragging you back into the dream. I'm totally like that, too. Thankfully I don't get stuck there like I used to. The emotional pull is nowhere near as strong. But it's still hard for me to see the corruption and say it isn't true. It's hard for me not to get involved somehow. Maybe it's because the town I live in is a political nightmare. I feel it's my responsibility to get involved! How do I deal with this sense of wanting to "help" without seeing it as real?
(By the way, I must admit I don't know if I am actually helping even if I think I'm trying!)" – SD

The first shift that happens for students of *A Course in Miracles*, often unconsciously, is that you see every situation as a classroom to learn of peace. This turns every situation from an end in itself to a means for peace. If you want inner peace this is the only shift that really needs to occur. So you do not have to give up your natural desires and interests. They will not get in the way of your attaining peace if you use them to attain peace. So pursue your natural inclination to help, remembering that every situation is a classroom where you can learn of peace from the Holy Spirit (Teacher of Truth). In time, Truth will grow real to you and you will recognize that the meaning that you see in a meaningless world comes from your own thoughts and beliefs. Nothing real disturbs your peace. Only your own thoughts can disturb your peace.

When you no longer see the world as real you will no longer feel a need or desire to "help". This is not to say that you will not help others. But you won't be coming from personal need or desire. You will simply be willing to help if that is the way things flow for you and you will not have strong feelings about helping or not.

138. Ask: What do you think about all the hype about germs? (October 11, 2013)

"What do you think about all the hype regarding germs, sanitizing, and hand washing? I'm asking because my partner and I have different habits around this, and I feel really disgusted by her behavior sometimes. I know that mentioning it to her will cause a fight, probably because I feel guilty for having these feelings. I'm afraid that by being close to her physically, I am risking becoming infected with something she has picked up in public. What's actually going on here?" – OT

At the level of form there are laws of cause and effect. Some things cause harm to the body. The experience of a self is inherently dysfunctional and will never be perfect. But it does make sense to know the laws of cause and effect relating to the self and its body to mitigate your discomfort in this experience where possible. As the story goes, germs cause illness in the body. You do reduce, but not eliminate, your risk of being infected or of causing infection in others through basic hygiene, like washing your hands after using the toilet or handling raw meat, washing more often when you have a virus, brushing your teeth, etc.

There are two questions for you to look at: First, are your hygiene habits rational and reasonable or driven by such irrational fear of infection that they are obsessive? Infections in the body are inevitable. But the body is not you. As you grow more aware of Truth you will be aware of Perfection within so you will release (forgive) the body. This shows up as you accepting the experience of the body as it is, without judgment, resistance, or a need to make it perfect.

Also, if you are irrational and obsessive about hygiene the body's brain may have a chemical imbalance that causes an obsessive-compulsive disorder that needs to be evaluated by a psychologist or psychiatrist. Medication and therapy may be helpful. In time, as you grow aware of Truth, you will recognize this disorder is also of the body, not about your Reality in Truth.

The second question is why do you feel guilty for feeling that your partner's habits are not up to par? Is it because you sense your hygiene standards are irrational? Or do you feel that you are judging her by observing her unhealthy habits? It may be an observable fact that her hygiene is not very healthy. Your judgment on her would be feeling that she is wrong or bad for not having good hygiene.

So you need to sort out what is fact (perhaps her hygiene really is not healthy) from projection of meaning, or judgment (she is wrong for having poor hygiene). You are never disturbed by fact, but rather by your own projections of meaning. They make guilt real to you.

Once you sort this out, if it is a fact that her hygiene is poor you will be able to discuss it with her matter-of-factly, without rancor.

139. Ask: What is your take on the Second Coming? (October 18, 2013)

"...what is your take on the second coming? I have often thought of it as fundamentalist bunk to police the converts. I must confess the ACIM's explanation, page 449 # 9, quite loses me . Is it something like a 'grand enlightenment for all people' or what?..." – ES

My "take on" the Second Coming as described in *A Course in Miracles'* Workbook, Part II.9, is in my translation of the Workbook, *Practicing A Course in Miracles,* Part 2.9:

"What is the Second Coming of Christ?

1. The Second Coming of Christ, which is as sure as God, is merely the correction of your mistakes, and the return of Sanity to your mind. It restores to you What you never lost, and re-establishes What is Forever True in your mind. It is your invitation to God's Word to take the place of your illusions, and your willingness to forgive all things, without exception or reservation.
2. The all-encompassing nature of Christ's Second Coming embraces all that you perceive, and holds you safe within it. There is no end to the release that Christ's Second Coming brings to you, because God's Extension is Limitless. Your forgiving lights the way for Christ, because it shines on everything as one. This is how you recognize the Oneness of your mind at last.
3. Christ's Second Coming ends the Holy Spirit's lessons for you, making way for the Last Judgment, in which your learning ends in one last summary that extends beyond itself, reaching up to God. It is the time when your entire mind is given to Christ, to be returned to Spirit in the name of God's Extension and Will.
4. Christ's Second Coming is the one event in time which time itself cannot affect. All that you ever made, or imagined for the future, is wholly released from your mind in it. Christ is restored as the One Identity of your entire mind, and God smiles upon you, God's Extension and Joy.

5. Pray that the Second Coming of Christ is soon, but do not rest there. It needs your eyes, ears, hands, feet, and voice. Most of all, it needs your willingness. Rejoice that you can do God's Will, and join together in Its Holy Light. God's Holy Extension is One in you, and you can reach God's Love through It.

<u>Mentor's Note</u>
From The Message of A Course in Miracles: A translation of the Text in Plain Language:

The 'Second Coming of Christ' simply means the end of your perception of separation from God, and the healing of your mind. (MACIM-4.4.10)

The Second Coming of Christ is not the return of Reality, but merely your awareness that It is always here. (MACIM-9.4.11)"

140. Ask: How can we have a healthier state of mind as we become parents? (October 25, 2013)

"My husband and I are trying to get pregnant and are seeing a fertility specialist. We are having procedures done to get pregnant and I've had a miscarriage in the past. How can I keep that heartbreak from hindering my future/our future? I know that our waking life is not real, but we want to raise and love a child we created together. What can we do to create a healthier mind state as we go through this journey to hopefully become parents?" – Anonymous

A truly healthy state of mind is one where you are aware that only God (your True Being) within you is real. When you know this you know that you are whole. You do not set up anything in the world to be your salvation. This means that you do not look to or expect anything, anyone, any situation, or any role in the world to make you whole or lastingly happy and at peace. So while you have desires, preferences, and inclinations you are not attached to satisfying them.

When a child is wanted a miscarriage or an inability to conceive are very painful experiences. But when you are aware that only God within you is real then you experience the pain and grief of any disappointment or loss without your deep sense of well-being being affected. The pain and grief are a process through which you pass, but you do not live there.

So as you work toward the goal of having a child, or any other goal, do not forget that you have accepted the new goal of inner peace for your life. And this goal is attained only through an awareness of God within you. Your goals in the world are now means to grow your awareness of God rather than ends in themselves (the source of your salvation). You want to invite the Holy Spirit (Teacher of Truth in your mind) into the process of attaining your goals. And you want to use any challenge or upset as a reminder to turn inward and remember that only God within you is real and eternal.

When you look to something or someone in the world to be your salvation it or they become an idol for you. An idol is a substitute for God. It is meant to be the source of your wholeness, happiness, and peace. One of the strongest idols that the ego (personal thought system) in your mind uses to replace the experience of God is the special relationship. In a special relationship you break down the boundaries between your personal identity and another's in an attempt to replace the Oneness (Wholeness) of God. I mention this because you wrote that "my husband and I are trying to get pregnant". While you and your husband are trying to have a child together and you may both be having procedures to increase the chances of this happening, only *you* are trying to get pregnant. Only you are risking the body's life and health and choosing to change it for the rest of its seeming existence. Only you are going to directly experience the consequences of this. It may be just a figure of speech to say "we" are trying to get pregnant, but I want you to look to see that there is no blurring of your identity with your husband's behind those words. It's ironic, but to release yourself from the personal identity and know your True Being in God you must have some measure of personal self-esteem and an awareness of the boundaries of the personal identity. You need self-esteem because you will not invite God into your awareness as long as you feel unworthy of God. And you cannot release an identity that is not clearly defined because you will not understand what it is that you have to release!

If you find that you have blurred your identity with your husband you may want to look into speaking with a counselor who can help you build your identity boundaries. Then, eventually, you will find yourself free to release it and to experience the healthiest state of mind.

141. Ask: As I judge others less I feel more alone. How can I be aware of the All? (November 1, 2013)

"I have an understanding that judgment, especially of other people, is a way that separation is maintained. Watching myself I can see how that happens…I recognize that is happening and turn away from it. My question is this: so far the only images of other people are ones of judgment…and all the mental production into presenting them as a separate person to my mind. When I don't do that as much, then I begin to feel more alone. I don't have the experience of 'other people' so much. I assume there is a deeper connection possible, to the All, to what is real, but so far that does not arise…" – RP

You have seen that there is no real connection between selves. The personal thought system's "connection" with others is an illusion maintained by judgment. You dropped the judgments and the sense of connection is gone. All along you were experiencing only your own thoughts.

When you detach from (truly forgive) the personal thought system's (ego's) judgments you don't want to simply turn away. You want to turn inward to Truth. Otherwise you just remain in another form of lack. You will experience wholeness (All) only in your awareness of your True Being (God) within.

As an individual, as you grow aware of the Truth within you and truly learn that the world is an illusion, a feeling of being apart from others and the world will develop. This is what it means to be detached! If you are uncomfortable when you feel this, however, it indicates that you are still attached to the self. You have not wholly detached. It is a signal to turn inward to experience your wholeness in Truth. In time your detachment will be complete and you will no longer be made uncomfortable by it. You will experience only Wholeness.

142. Ask: If we are all one how can we have such disparity? (November 8, 2013)

"…When sitting with family yesterday, it occurred to me that each of us has such a wide and varying approach and take on what is real. If we are all one, and not various and individual souls/persons, how can we have such disparity in our beliefs? Why isn't your awakening or

Jesus' awakening more of an influence on all of us if we are one consciousness? Why does guilt seem so individualized when we are not individuals?" - JG

You will notice that *A Course in Miracles* says that your perception of yourself as an individual mind (ego) among other individual minds (egos) is an illusion. You are not experiencing the one and only Mind (God) when you perceive the disparity of many minds. You are looking at an illusion. It is this mistaken belief in what is real that ACIM seeks to help you transcend.

It isn't really accurate to say that "we are all one". It is more accurate to say "there is only one Mind". Any time you apply a plural to "mind" you are looking at the illusion. But you can turn away from the perception of many minds and turn inward, away from the ego, to the one-Mind-that-is.

Jesus and other seemingly-individual teachers who are aware of the one-Mind-that-is can point your seemingly-individual mind inward to It. But your awareness of the one-Mind-that-is will influence you only to the degree to which you are open to It. In your seemingly-individual mind you alone have the choice of what influences your mind and how much it influences it.

Guilt only seems individualized when you think that individuals are real. In fact, it is the belief that individuals are real that is the source of guilt. It is the belief that formless Reality (God/the one-Mind-that-is) has been attacked and a new reality of many-minds-in-form has been made real. So when you look away from individual minds and turn inward to the one-Mind-that-is you see that there is no guilt. Nothing has been attacked. Only one Mind is real.

143. Ask: How can I accept that there is no ultimate responsibility for my actions? (November 15, 2013)

*"ACIM asserts that the physical universe and all it contains...are total **illusions**...ACIM tells us we are 'sin' free...and thus all acts we commit, regardless of their impact on others, are consistent with the illusion. ACIM tells us we must only 'Forgive' our Brother in the Son of God, recognizing that our Brothers' acts against us are equally unreal. Every other spiritual path or religion I'm aware of maintains that **we** are responsible for our actions in our present lives (implicitly asserting they are REAL) and will eventually be held accountable for them in some way, either in the present, directly in the afterlife or during some form of reincarnated future lives...This too, is disavowed by ACIM. The implication is that e.g., serial killer Jeffrey Dahmer and Mother Teresa are not only loved equally by God but are equally open to receiving all of God's Love without any consideration of past acts. It is profoundly difficult to accept the rejection of any ultimate responsibility/accountability for our actions...this connection is counter intuitive and I cannot find credible evidence (or argument) in ACIM persuading me to accept it..." - RM*

You never will find an acceptable argument to understand this. True forgiveness is understood only through the experience of God (True Being) as Reality. This does not come through the intellect. It comes through the experience of God within you. And you experience God when you are willing to experience God.

Ultimate guilt is supposed to be the "proof" that the ego is reality. Its story for you when you identify with it is that you attacked a god and made a new reality (the universe of form, including egos). This is the primary "sin" or guilt. Anything that then happens in this new reality is therefore an extension of that original guilt. To undo this you are supposed to live by certain (arbitrary, varying-by-culture) rules. If you do not you are compounding your guilt. So if you say that this has not happened, that Reality (God) is not touched by any of this, and there is no guilt you are effectively saying that the ego does not really exist. It is a mistaken experience. This is, of course, what *A Course in Miracles* says. But you cannot expect the ego to accept this. *You*, however, can become aware of this fact apart from the ego because your Reality in God is not changed by this mistaken experience.

In the world we need rules to live in harmony with each other. So there is a need for legal definitions of "guilt" in the context of the world. And there is cause and effect at the level of form so you do experience the effects of your actions in form. But there is no ultimate morality decreed by a power outside of you. "God", as ACIM uses the term, refers to True Being, not to a power-over. There is no power outside of you with power over you. There is only True Being and when you seem to forget It you think that you are a separate being among many other beings. This misperception is all that you need to correct if you want to be at peace.

Certainly all religions and most spiritual paths seek to spiritualize the ego. They are not interested in transcending the ego but in validating it as reality. So they teach that the egoic experience is real and has an effect on God. This is one reason why *A Course in Miracles* is different from most other paths. It leads you out of your misperception rather than further into it.

ACIM does not imply that Jeffery Dahmer and Mother Teresa are equally loved by God. What ACIM says is that the entire limited experience of form, including selves (bodies/personalities), is not real. What seems to happen in the universe of form has no effect on God (Reality) whatsoever. So Dahmer and Mother Teresa are not equally loved by God. Both are equally unreal. Neither exists for God. Realizing this is true forgiveness.

The belief in ultimate guilt and fear of punishment from a power that you have defied are the ego's defenses against God because they keep you from looking inward and seeing God. As long as you want the ego to be your reality you will be resistant to releasing the belief in an ultimate morality.

144. Ask: Are you saying that no form exists for God? (November 22, 2013)

"On reading your (last) blog...I was struck by a statement...:

... 'What seems to happen in the universe of form has no effect on God (Reality) whatsoever. So Dahmer and Mother Teresa are not equally loved by God. Both are equally unreal. **Neither exists for God.** *Realizing this is true forgiveness.'*

... Perhaps it is my ego that feels alarm, or perhaps I don't quite understand the statement. Are you saying that no form exists for God and that we are connected to the True Being only through our true self (which is neither our body nor ego). Perhaps I am clinging to my childhood Christian belief that nothing goes unnoticed by God and something to the effect that God knows how many hairs are on everyone's heads. If none of this form life exists for God, what is the point of it all?..." - MI

You read it correctly. God (as *A Course in Miracles* uses the word) is Formless Being. Only God is real. In God there is only God (the meaning of "Oneness"). So God knows only God. This means that God only knows God in you. Form is not of God and is unknown to God.

God, being All, must contain the idea of Its Own opposite. But being All, God cannot have an opposite. So the idea of the opposite-of-God is undone as soon as it is thought. It has no purpose. It simply is. But what it is, is a meaningless, impossible idea. This is why ACIM calls it an "illusion". And overcoming your belief in this illusion is what ACIM is for.

The part of God's Mind where this idea seems to occur is what ACIM calls the "Son of God". The Son of God's mind is never actually apart from God. So it is split between God and not-God. Since God is timeless, limitless, and formless, not-God is time-bound, limited form. Into this universe of form the Son of God projects billions of versions of itself. Each seemingly-individual mind is split between God (Christ Mind/Holy Spirit) and not-God (ego thought system). As a seemingly-individual mind you project from ego meaning onto meaningless form. This makes it seem real to you. This makes it seem to have the (unconscious) purpose of keeping you apart from God. Your belief in form as reality is the source of guilt in your mind. But because the universe of form has no intrinsic meaning you can choose instead to give the experience of form another purpose for you. You can choose to use it to lead your mind back to its Reality in God instead of away from It. If you make this choice (you do not have to) then the Holy Spirit (the teaching aspect of your Christ Mind) will guide you in this process.

As a student of *A Course in Miracles* you must question every spiritual, religious, and secular belief you have ever had about truth and reality (what ACIM calls "God"). Some of these may be treasured beliefs and at first you may grieve to lose them. But when you look at them closely you will see that guilt is hidden in them. Then you will be relieved to release (forgive) them.

The ego is just a thought system in your mind. It does not have feelings. The alarm that you experience reading the above statement is your own. You are experiencing the shock and fear that is common to new students of *A Course in Miracles* when they begin to get what ACIM says. So your alarm is actually a good sign! It indicates that on some level you are getting it. This is the beginning of your undoing of your belief in the ego as your identity. It is uncomfortable but it will pass as you realize how the awareness that only God is real sets you free from guilt and fear.

145. Ask: What is my personal responsibility in the awakening? (November 29, 2013)

"...In the chapter about 'What is the last Judgment?' (Workbook part II, #10) Jesus says:

*'You are still My holy Son, forever innocent, forever loving and forever loved, as limitless as your Creator and completely changeless and forever pure. Therefore **awaken** and return to Me. I am your Father and you are My Son.'*

My question is: Can you talk about the verb <u>awaken</u> in this context and my 'personal' responsibility in the awakening?"– ER

This phrase was not meant as an instruction, but simply as a reassurance. It's saying that you have nothing to fear from God (your True Being) because God continues on within you untouched by the personal experience. So therefore it is safe for you to become aware of (awaken to) God within you again.

You do not have to make the choice to be aware of God. This is a choice that you make for yourself because you want to be at peace. If you do make this choice then your "responsibility" is to be *willing* to be aware of God. This is not a passive process. Your willingness means that you are open to looking at and undoing with the Holy Spirit (the part of your mind that is aware of God) the unconscious and conscious beliefs that block your awareness of God. These blocks come up naturally as you go about life in the world. They are anything that disturbs your peace or distracts you from your awareness of God as your True Being.

146. Ask: Why do babies continue to be born to learn and grow? (December 6, 2013)

"...I have been studying ACIM for 6 years now and I understand and have accepted that some things just have to be taken on faith. I want to get your views on this: Given that this world of form is illusion—given that the ego is typically in charge here and that we have maintained this mode of thought because we rebelled against a god and created this mistaken experience; What is the best way to wrap my mind around the idea that babies continue to be born (Souls) coming to Earth School—to learn lessons and grow in knowledge and divinity. That is one avenue of thought that I have always heard. Does this make sense because the Holy Spirit uses our errors and mistakes to further God's Divine purpose for us? That Souls continue to be reincarnated and come to Earth to gather experience, or so that God can experience through us? Sometimes it feels like this doesn't make sense to me— simplistic, then again— I have not found an answer on my own." – AG

You do not have to take anything in *A Course in Miracles* on faith. It is a course in the practical application of the ideas in it that will lead to an awareness of Truth. It does not ask you to accept concepts but to open yourself to experiencing God (True Being) as Reality. God is not a concept but an experience.

There has been no rebellion against a god. The word "illusion" means you are experiencing something that is not real. Only the ego (personal thought system) in your mind tells you that you are guilty for leaving or attacking or killing a god. The central teaching of ACIM is that this has not occurred. You are in God (True Being, not a power-over) now, only you are unaware of this when you think that the universe of form is reality. If you want to be at peace this lack of awareness of Truth is all that you need to correct.

The universe of form is the idea of the opposite of God. It does not come from God, it has nothing to do with God, and God has nothing to do with it. Nothing in it has a God-given purpose. It is simply the idea of the opposite of Reality, which is why it is an illusion. So there is no ultimate reason "why" anything happens in the world, including babies being born. What happens in form is just the way the story goes.

The idea of time is the illusion on which all other illusions rest. The idea of time makes it seems as though you left God long ago and that you will be with God in some indefinite future. But really you are in God now. So the story for the world is just an idea unfolding in your mind now. This is why ACIM emphasizes the Holy Instant. In this Holy Instant you turn away from the story and rest in God now. Then when your mind returns to the story of time it brings the awareness of God with it. And the story of time is less and less enthralling as you realize that only God is real.

The importance of practicing the Holy Instant cannot be over-emphasized. It is the central, transforming practice of ACIM.

There is no such thing as "souls" or individual spirits. There is one Spirit, Which is called "God" in ACIM. Since God is the only Being individuality is part of the idea of the opposite of God. Only God within any mind is real. Everything else is an illusion. Reincarnation is an ego-concept meant to give reality and meaning and purpose to the ego, none of which it has in Reality.

God is whole and complete and does not need to learn anything or to perfect Itself. So it does not need to experience anything through you. The world has no purpose to God. Only when one believes in ego do the ideas of "error" and "correction" or of "learning" or "perfecting" have meaning. They are not real. One finds they experience themselves as form, the experience becomes painful or they sense that there is Something more, and they may unconsciously or consciously call on Truth to help them. If they accept the help offered the Holy Spirit (the awareness of Truth in their mind) will use their experiences in form to grow their awareness of Truth. And ultimately what one learns is that God within them is already whole and complete. They "need do nothing" for "salvation". What seeks to learn or grow or correct or perfect or attain divinity will never attain these. Your belief in it is your obstacle to God. You only need to release (forgive) it for your mind to be in its natural state of wholeness (God) and to be at peace.

147. Ask: Does it make sense for me to spend time caring for the natural world? (December 13, 2013)

"...The Course *challenges me in two ways that I haven't yet figured out. First, as an example, I recently finished my cherished monthly National Geographic that describes Lions and their often brutal behavior toward their population and also their cubs. That makes me wonder (not facetiously), did they also have a 'tiny mad idea' of separation or are they or their behavior illusions of ours? That leads into my second question as an environmentalist who grew naturally into being appalled by man's arrogance in manipulating and destroying what we see as our natural world. My concern is that thinking this is our illusion, our creation, our dream, doesn't that reinforce that role of human as ruler of all we see, to be used for whatever selfish ego based experience we desire? So I wonder, does what I spend my time on in advocacy, conservation and care for the natural world still make sense?..."* – DM

To answer your first question, here is a response to a question about animals from the May 17, 2013 article: "The entire universe of form, including all plants and animals, is a projection of not-Truth from the split mind. As not-Truth it is inherently limited, imperfect, and disordered. The split mind projects itself into not-Truth by projecting itself onto only one animal – humans. Your seemingly-individual split mind is a projection of THE split mind projected onto a specific human animal in the projection. So it seems as though humans have a choice where plants and other animals do not even though they are all equally not-True."

So, just like the self (body/personality) with which you identify, animals are just part of the projection, or "dream". Like all form, they and their behavior are meaningless. Any meaning (right/wrong, good/bad) that you see in form is projected from your seemingly-individual mind. You are responsible not for what you see but for how you see it. And how you see the universe of form determines whether you are in conflict or at peace.

If you believe that the world is real then you believe (unconsciously) that you attacked or killed Reality to make this other reality. Reality then seems like Something apart from you. It seems like a god with power over you. You believe that this god decrees an absolute morality. Your belief in an absolute morality and guilt lead you to experience strong judgments, and the feelings (anger, despair, etc.) that they cause, about the world. This is the whole package that comes with your belief in the self as your reality. You cannot identify with a self and escape the belief in guilt.

But if you are aware that the world and the ego's projections onto the world are only the idea of the opposite-of-Reality and that Reality is unchanged by this mere (tiny, mad) idea, then you will not have strong feelings about them. You will accept that the world, being the idea of the opposite-of-Perfection, is inherently imperfect. You will seek to transcend your belief in the world rather than to perfect what will never be perfect.

Whether or not your environmental advocacy makes sense to you is only something you can answer for yourself. It is never enough to read or to hear from others that the world is not real. You will have to experience this for yourself for a real shift to occur in your relationship to the universe of form. While the world is still real to you it will not serve you to pretend otherwise. If you want to grow your awareness of Truth (Reality) you have to invite Truth into your awareness right where you are now. Guilt is an obstacle to peace. And whatever disturbs your peace presents you with an opportunity to look at your deep-seated, often unconscious belief in guilt. So whatever disturbs your peace presents you with an opportunity to undo your belief in guilt and to grow your awareness of Truth.

Certainly, as Truth becomes true for you your relationship to the world will change. You may continue in your advocacy from another approach reflecting your awareness of Truth. Or you may find that it falls away naturally as you become aware that the world is not real. Only time will tell. In any case, you do not have to judge one way or another what the self chooses to do in the world. It may have temporary meaning for you but it is all equally meaningless in Truth.

148. Ask: Does ACIM teach that consciousness expresses itself in form? (December 20, 2013)

"I am trying to reconcile the teaching of the Course *which teaches everything is an illusion that is not God with the teachings of other spiritual teachers of consciousness which state that everything we see is ultimately consciousness. For example, Eckhart Tolle teaches that when you are with nature, you can sense the presence beneath....consciousness expressing itself as that form. In the* Course *it seems to teach that everything is illusion. Does the course not believe that consciousness expresses itself in form?"* – MB

Because you seem to experience a reality that is apart from Reality (Truth, God), *A Course in Miracles* discusses your mind as though it has two levels – Truth and illusion. The level of Truth it calls God, Reality, or Knowledge. The level of illusion it calls perception, consciousness, or awareness. Truth is formless so form is an illusion. Consciousness, then, is not Truth. It is form and expresses itself through form.

At its highest, consciousness is an *awareness* or *perception* of Truth, but not Truth Itself. And this level of awareness is what prepares you for the "last step": to *be* Truth. So it is still an illusion, but one which prepares you for Truth. Without this preparation the contrast between Truth and illusion would be too stark for you to accept Truth.

Semantics can get in the way when you are studying spiritual teachings. It's hard to know what others mean by "consciousness" or "awareness". They often do not use those words the same way that they are used in ACIM. So some may use them to mean what ACIM means by "God" (True Being) for example. And others may use those words in the same context as ACIM.

So as far as those words are used by ACIM it is correct to say that consciousness expresses itself as form. "Consciousness" as you used it in your question means the "Son of God" or the "split mind" – the part of God's Mind that seems to be split off from God and projects the universe of form. As a projection of this split mind your seemingly-individual mind is split between God (Christ/Holy Spirit) and illusion (ego). And on a seemingly-individual level your awareness of (consciousness of, perception of) God affects your attitudes, behavior, choices, and energy. So your awareness of God affects your relationship to form at the level of form. But God never takes form or expresses Itself as form. The experience of God (Formlessness) is completely apart from consciousness (form).

149. Ask: Does thinking ever stop? (December 27, 2013)

"...A question occurred to me thinking about consciousness/knowledge/awareness. I can experience awareness of Christ around and within me; I can 'sense' this awareness as being enveloped in the arms of Christ/God/Holy Spirit; and I wonder: what about abstract thoughts, i.e. connected to ideas of logic, are they—where? Form? I remember reading/hearing a long time ago that real thinking never stops. Do you agree?..." - T

Once, many years ago, while meditating I slipped into a Place Where there was no thought or ideas. I had expected there were no words in Truth but not no thoughts or ideas at all. I experienced pure *being*. No forms (thoughts, ideas); no doing (thinking). It was so alien to my usual experience that I would not have been able to conceive of it if I had not experienced it. It what total bliss! What release and freedom! No boundaries of any kind. I had no idea what a burden thoughts and thinking are, no matter their form. So I will say that, thankfully, thinking does stop.

All thought is form. Some thoughts are helpful (from the Holy Spirit/Teacher of Truth) and some are not (from the ego/personal thought system). So if you have thoughts you know your mind is at the level of perception/consciousness/awareness (not-Truth) rather than Knowledge (Truth/God).

150. Ask: I was wondering about other things that could be considered magic... (January 3, 2014)

"...I was wondering about some other things people do that could be considered 'Magic'. I would say that the use of vitamin supplements, or at least ones designed to do certain things(fat-burning, heart health)...birth control (to 'correct' the problem of fertility)...using sunlight for anything...using creams, bicycles or other equipment to lose weight or firm the body... mood music to help relax... Just trying to have a better idea of this that's all. I know not to judge myself or others for using these things... I guess, the thing would be to forgive our use of them... If we wind up dropping using some of these things, fine...if not, fine too..." - CS

Very simply, "magical thinking", as *A Course in Miracles* uses the term, means the belief that healing the body heals you. You are mind so real healing means healing your mind. And since your one problem is your identification with a body, healing your mind means releasing your identification with a body. So while certain medications, supplements, treatments, etc. may seem to work on the body they cannot heal *you*.

"Magical thinking" is similar to the "special relationship" in that both come from and reinforce the idea that the body is you and that "salvation" (wholeness; lasting happiness and peace) comes from something outside of you. Where magical thinking is the belief that outside sources of healing for the body will make you whole, the special relationship is the belief that finding another body to love the body as you decide it should be loved will make you whole.

You are correct that there is no reason to judge efforts to heal the body. They are not right or wrong. They are meaningless, just as the body, whatever its condition, is meaningless.

151. Ask: Would you comment on the passing of Ken Wapnick? (January 10, 2014)

"Please would you consider sometime commenting in your blog to the passing last week (December 27) of Kenneth Wapnick. You never commented on those individuals who helped transmit the Course *and I know that you exclusively used the UR text that was in the public domain. But I would love to know how you would estimate the contributions of someone like Dr. Wapnick to bringing ACIM into the culture. He and Helen worked side by side to refine the text and then the workbook before it was ready to be made public. He devoted 40 years of his life to ACIM..." - SS*

Someone told me that at the Foundation for Inner Peace website in reference to Dr. Kenneth Wapnick's passing they quoted from *A Course in Miracles*: "There is no death. The Son of God is free." What more is there to say? I am certain that Dr. Wapnick would not want anyone dwelling on "Ken" and would rather that you turned inward and remembered your Reality in Truth.

I did not know or study the teachings of Kenneth Wapnick so I do not have any personal feelings about his passing. I had heard that he was ill, and he was in his 70s, so I was not surprised.

As for estimating his contributions to the culture: If I want to get into my personal story I would certainly be grateful to Helen and Bill and Ken for bringing ACIM into the world. But I really don't live in a story for the world anymore. Individual people and events no longer stand out to me. So the relative worth of an individual or event over others has no meaning to me. It is all the same and has become rather flattened out. It is all equally unreal. So anything I would say would feel inauthentic and made up to me.

I'm sorry if what you want is a eulogy of Ken Wapnick from me. But the reason I did not write one last week (the week after his passing) is that I honestly have nothing to say.

But it seems like you may have some strong feelings about Dr. Wapnick's work and passing. Perhaps there is some ACIM venue online (blog, community, etc.) where you can express them.

(By the way, I used the first and second published editions when I studied ACIM. And for my translation of it into plain language I used the first published edition, which is in the public domain).

152. Ask: Can you send an article about release from physical pain? (January 17, 2014)

"...Can you send one (article) that deals with releasing physical pain, please?" – TN

Physical pain is an inevitable part of the experience of identifying with a body. But suffering is optional. Suffering is the psychological effect caused by the unconscious or conscious beliefs that you have about the pain. These are usually that you are being punished by a god or that you are a victim of another or of a god. These beliefs make you suffer over the pain and may even prevent you from seeking relief from the pain. If you feel guilty you may feel that you deserve to suffer. And if you want to remain in the role of victim or to make another guilty for your pain you may not be willing to be relieved of pain.

You will be completely released from physical pain when you no longer identify with a body. In the meantime, you can ask for guidance in overcoming physical pain. The answer may be a medication or a treatment in the world. These may be conventional or alternative medicines or treatments. You may find that some pain is caused solely by the desire to suffer, as mentioned above. In this case changing your thinking may be all that is needed to free you from pain. In any case, as soon as you decide you do not need to suffer you will be open to relief from pain, however this shows up.

If you are in pain, with an open mind ask the Holy Spirit (Teacher of Truth) in your mind for the way to deal with and/or to overcome the pain. Be willing to look with the Holy Spirit at your deep-seated beliefs about guilt. And do not judge the answers that are suggested or that show up for you at the level of form or you will not find the relief that you seek.

You will find that as you release yourself from identifying with the self all pain will fall into the background of your awareness. You will see that, like all form, pain is not "bad" or "wrong"; it is neutral. It has no meaning in itself. It is simply an unpleasant sensation. If you do not give it meaning it does not intrude on your peace, it passes faster, and you accept relief from pain sooner.

153. Ask: How do chakras relate to ACIM? (January 24, 2014)

"...Generally, how do Chakras relate to ACIM? They seem to be part of Not Truth, but are they still helpful in pointing us towards Truth itself and where we are trying to compromise its inclusion in our lives? How do they fit into the big picture?..." - A.N-G

The concept of "chakras" comes from the Hindu religion. They are the label given to the idea of a nexus of non-material energy with the material body. So you are correct that they are part of not-Truth.

It is hard to see how they could point you toward Truth. Some make the mistake of thinking that anything that is unseen—like energy—is the same as "Spirit". But energy is form and Spirit is Formlessness. You may find some practice involving chakras helpful to your life in the world, but this would not be a spiritual practice in the truest sense. It also would not be "right" or "wrong" or "good" or "bad". Like all form, from the perspective of Truth, it is meaningless. The question you have to ask yourself is if any practice involving chakras blocks your awareness of Truth. If it does, then it will be an obstacle to peace and you may want to consider dropping it. If it does not and you benefit from it in some way then you probably want to continue with it.

154. Ask: Since Reality is eternal doesn't it follow that Its opposite is eternal, too? (January 31, 2014)

"It occurred to me today, that the dream(s)/'life' we imagine ourselves to be in, must also be eternal. As true reality is eternal, then does it not follow that the illusory opposite of oneness, although not real, must also be eternal? If so, is the only escape from the bombardment of conflict, etc. is to continually be aware of the Truth throughout all the dreams of separation for all eternity?..." – JR

Truth is Eternal, which means It is timeless, not time without end. So time is the idea of the opposite of Truth (Eternity). Since Truth is One, or the same throughout Itself, time can only ever be an idea. It is an illusion. It has no reality.

There is a trap of believing in two realities that students of *A Course in Miracles* fall into. One reality they call "God" or "Truth". This is formless Being. The other "reality", the experience of form, they label "illusion" without thinking what "illusion" really means. An illusion is something that appears to exist but does not really exist. And that means that it does not exist *right now*. It does not mean it will cease to exist at some future time.

So when you seem to be in time you are really only thinking in terms of time (past/future) *right now*. And, yes, this creates your sense of conflict because it is not true. And, if you want peace, the appropriate response to your conflict is to bring the eternal (timeless) Truth to your awareness *right now*. This is what ACIM calls the "holy instant", the most essential practice there is if you want peace.

155. Ask: Are we to accept intrinsic guilt as an article of faith? (February 7, 2014)

"You describe guilt, the source of our troubles, as being intrinsic which also means inherent ie. we are born with it. This sounds similar to the way Christians accept the concept of Original Sin as an article of faith. Are we too to accept intrinsic guilt within the context of the Course *as an article of faith or is there some explanation which thus far eludes me?"* - ES

It's important to understand the distinction between what Christians teach and what *A Course in Miracles* teaches with regard to guilt. Christian's teach that you, or a distant ancestor or yours, have defied a god outside of you with power over you. This is a sin and your guilt for it is real and you will be punished for it. *A Course in Miracles* teaches that you simply have forgotten True Being (which it labels "God"). This is not a sin, but a mistake which causes your pain. There is no one and nothing outside of you to punish you for this. The concept of guilt is a false belief of the ego (personal thought system) meant to keep the ego in your awareness. Guilt is the ego's defense against you turning inward, finding Truth, and undoing your belief in the ego as your reality. So while guilt is intrinsic to the ego, it is not intrinsic to you. You can free yourself from guilt by releasing yourself from the ego.

I go deeply into all of this in my book, *Releasing Guilt for Inner Peace* (learn about it at my website, www.acimmentor.com) and here's an excerpt to help you recognize the many unconscious and conscious ways that guilt shows up:

"Some ways that a belief in guilt shows up are fear of a god, expectation of punishment, generalized unworthiness, generalized inadequacy, self-loathing, judging yourself, judging

others, thinking that others are judging you, taking others' attitudes and behaviors personally, confusing responsibility with blame, defensiveness, secretiveness, dishonesty, generalized anxiety, generalized fear, generalized anger, martyrdom, perfectionism, being hard on yourself, self-medicating with a substance or behavior, an inability to be alone, an inability to tolerate quiet, an inability to meditate, an inability to be present, busy-ness, nightmares, worry and anxiety about the future, worry and anxiety about loved ones, thoughts and images of you or loved ones or strangers being tortured, the need to be right, the need to win, over-achieving, the need to fix others, the need to fix the world, sacrificing, co-dependency, fear of success, fear of good outcomes for you, masochism, self-destructive behavior, self-sabotage, interpreting neutral events (natural disaster, disease, etc.) as punishment or proof of guilt, interpreting others' behavior as punishment or proof of your guilt, and spiritualizing the self. Examples of many of these responses are given throughout this book…

…You may think that you do not believe in guilt. You may think that you do not feel guilt. The personal thought system is very good at keeping guilt out of your conscious awareness. But you can see by the list…above how when you identify as a self guilt pervades your responses to and interactions with the world. If you have any of these responses at any time, you unconsciously or consciously believe in guilt and experience guilt."

You do not have to take it on faith that guilt is an intrinsic part of the ego. You can see examples of its pervasive centrality to the ego thought system in your own experiences as well as by observing everyone else in the world.

156. Ask: What does it mean that ACIM is a required course? (February 14, 2014)

"What is exactly meant in the ACIM introduction that this is a 'required' course? Please expand on 'required'." – H

Your mind is not in its natural state when you identify with a self in a body in a world. So you feel limited, incomplete, and in conflict. If you want peace you "require" correction of your perception that you are not True Being (God).

In your unnatural state you look ceaselessly to fill your sense of lack and to resolve your conflict. But you look to correct these through the ego (personal thought system) and its world, which will never work because their purpose is to replace True Being. *A Course in Miracles* is one form of the "required" lesson plan that you need if you want true, lasting peace because it brings Truth back into your awareness. Only a lesson plan that brings Truth into your awareness will bring you the peace that you seek.

It goes on to say that if you want peace your choice is not *what* you have to learn but *when* you learn it. Some choose to learn sooner than others. And of course the vast majority never chooses to learn it at all.

157. Ask: Are tyrannical leaders unconsciously seeking inner peace? (February 21, 2014)

"I am re-reading again your Four Habits for Inner Peace and something struck me. On page 70, you write, 'You do not feel a need to change others or the world so that you can be at peace.' Could it be stated that perhaps Hitler, and others like him in history, subconsciously were really

seeking inner peace and thought that the only way for him to attain it was to mistreat, control, and kill millions of other people?" – CS

Yes, exactly.
I began *4HIP* with the Introduction:

"... If you pay attention you will notice that you seek for peace all of the time in everything that you direct the personal self to do. Your desire for peace is behind every goal that you set. You believe, sometimes consciously, sometimes unconsciously. that in the next thing that you get, in the next place that you go, in the next goal that you attain, or in the next person that you meet you will find the peace that will not leave you...

...So it is never a question of whether or not you will seek for peace. The only real question is: Are you going to seek for peace where it is or continue to seek for it where you will never find it?..."

As *A Course in Miracles* points out, when you identify with a self you have only one problem and it has only one solution. The one problem is that you are not aware of your True Being (God). So you feel emptiness, limitation, pain, loneliness, and lack. The only solution to your problem is to be aware that you are already whole and complete and limitless in Truth. Until you have this awareness you will engage in "faulty problem solving" by seeking to change the self with which you identify, others, and the world to make you feel whole.

The basis for compassion is the recognition that everyone in the world is struggling to fill their sense of lack in futile, inappropriate, and dysfunctional ways unless they open themselves to Truth. For most people, their dysfunction only touches themselves and those near them. But for a few charismatic leaders their dysfunction plays out on the world stage and affects countless others.

So when you are tempted to be angry with someone (including yourself), whether they are close to you or are in public life, for their destructive, dysfunctional behavior just remember what motivates them. Then you will find compassion replacing anger.

(Please be aware that compassion does not mean that you condone or have to put up with destructive, dysfunctional behavior. It simply means you understand the pain that motivates it. Boundaries are appropriate and healthy for everyone involved).

158. Ask: Don't I have to uncover my barriers to peace? What are they? (February 28, 2014)

"When Jesus says in the Text:

'Your task is not to seek for love, but merely to seek and find all of the barriers within yourself that you have built against it. It is not necessary to seek for what is true, but it is necessary to seek for what is false.' (T.16.IV.6:1,2).

What does this mean? Is Jesus saying that love is our true reality and that we cannot ever lose that true nature? Yet, our training is incomplete—isn't it—if we let our fears, misgivings and regrets over our three-dimensional linear existence get in the way of seeing our true inheritance of being eternally one with love? So would the practical application of this Text section be to study what negative thoughts or habits I have? Any non-loving thoughts or actions are the barriers to knowing oneness with the eternal, right? I know that you have written in your 4 Habits book that peace can be uncovered or developed by focusing on Truth exclusively, which seems different from what Jesus says in the Text. Throughout the Workbook Jesus says that we should be rigorous in examining our thoughts ("Effects leave not their Source")—or else there wouldn't have been a Workbook, I guess. Please could you comment on exactly what are all the barriers within myself and all that's false?" –SS

Yes, you are correct that Love is your reality and you cannot ever lose It. It's always here and all you lack is an awareness of It. So all you need to do is remove your obstacles to being aware of It.

In fact, in the book that you mention, *4 Habits for Inner Peace*, I did not say that peace can be developed by focusing exclusively on Truth. I made the same point that is in the quote and that you make in your question. You cannot grow your awareness of Truth without looking at and undoing your obstacles to being aware of Truth:

(From the introduction to 4HIP): *"In theory you could wholly accept Truth this instant and be wholly at peace right now. But in practice attaining inner peace is a process that usually takes many years. Practicing the four habits for inner peace in this book will bring up your obstacles to peace much faster than if you were not consciously seeking for peace. This brings you the opportunities that you need to work through them and reach peace at an accelerated pace."*

(From the introduction to Part II of 4HIP):*" ... Each of these obstacles takes the form of thoughts in your mind. You will naturally bump into these thoughts as you attempt to bring and hold Truth in your awareness. Bringing them up from your subconscious and undoing them is the process necessary for you to be wholly at peace."*

The book I wrote as a companion to *4HIP*, *Releasing Guilt for Inner Peace*, takes you through the process of recognizing and undoing guilt, the chief obstacle to peace. In short, as you go about your day guilt will naturally rise to your awareness through feelings that disturb your peace. Feelings are caused by unconscious and conscious beliefs. So feelings that disturb your peace tell you that you believe in guilt, no matter what you *think* you believe or what you *want* to believe. Feelings that disturb your peace are opportunities for you to see and undo your unconscious belief in guilt.

This is a long process. As *A Course in Miracles* points out, it takes some preparation to look at the guilt that is central to the ego (personal) thought system. Your belief in guilt makes it seem too horrible for you to look directly at it. It's slow going because in the beginning you are in a Catch-22: To undo guilt you have to learn to trust the Thing (Holy Spirit, the Teacher of Truth in your mind) that you fear because of guilt. So you take 3 steps forward and 2 steps back for a long, long time. But as Truth becomes true for you, you will trust It and become more and more willing to question the reality of guilt.

159. Ask: If individuality falls away how was Jesus able to dictate ACIM? (March 7, 2014)

"...If we are not really individuals once we leave this illusional world how was Jesus able to communicate as a former individual self to dictate the course? Is there a memory of who we once were (which would explain near death experiences where people meet loved ones) that remains with us when we return to our oneness? Is all of who we thought we were here in this

illusion forgotten? If that is the case, it makes Jesus claim of being a former body confusing to me…" - Anonymous

The story of Jesus is one of a man who became so aware of God (True Being) that he stopped identifying as a man and identified with God instead. In *A Course in Miracles* this awareness is called "Christ". The potential for this awareness is in every mind because God is in every mind. But for some "Christ" is too abstract an idea so they need a concrete symbol. "Jesus" can be a symbol of the Christ in every mind and some find this useful. Others need a role model that they feel they can follow and their story of Jesus serves as that for them. And for still others, it is too frightening for them at first to think of Christ within their own mind. In their guilt they do not feel worthy and fear that they will be punished for thinking that Christ is within them. So they temporarily need Jesus as a way to keep some distance between themselves and Christ.

Helen Shucman heard Christ in her own mind and she identified It as "Jesus". Just as your personal story is just a story anything that you think about Jesus is just a story, too. There are as many stories for Jesus as there are people who think about Him! As ACIM points out, we make an ego not just for ourselves but for everyone we meet. It is the same with those we never meet but just think about. But if you are open to Truth then the idea of Jesus can serve as a useful symbol of Truth until you no longer need symbols.

In my experiences of direct Revelation of God there is only one Being extending infinitely and eternally. There is no memory or thought of this personal experience. In God there is only God. To understand this is to understand the true forgiveness that the story of Jesus can represent.

160. Ask: Which Workbook lessons helped you bring your awareness back to Truth? (March 14, 2014)

"…What are your favourite Workbook lessons? Which ones have you personally found to be the most useful for bringing your awareness back to Truth? Are there any which you found yourself repeating more frequently than others, as you trained your mind?" – OT

This June it will be 30 years since I started *A Course in Miracles*. I did the Workbook right away, at the same time that I also dove into the Text and Manual for Teachers (I was hungry for it all!). So it has been a very long time since I've done the Workbook. I do not remember which lessons resonated with me back then. I do know that I thought I did a lousy job of it. But a lot more of it sunk in than I was aware of at the time.

I can say that the idea in one of them which says something like, "We say *God is* and then we cease to speak" was one I was brought back to again and again in many different forms by the Holy Spirit (Teacher of Truth in my mind). The most transformative practice for me has been to simply open my mind to God (Truth, Reality) without any goal but to be aware of God. This practice has brought the greatest insights and shifts toward peace.

Much later I was given another thought by the Holy Spirit which helped to keep my mind centered in Truth: "Only God is Real." Whenever I was tempted to get caught up in the world I'd use this thought to remind me that only my experiences of God are real and that I can let go of the rest.

(The following 4 articles are a dialogue with the same questioner).

161. Ask: (#1) Why do you and other teachers charge money? (March 21, 2014)

"I would really like to know why all spiritual teachers I've come across including yourself ask for money in return for teaching people about God. No one has ever answered me this question, so please answer me. Why are you making the Truth corporate? Jesus didn't ask for money or anything in return to teach people about God." – KR

       I cannot speak for others, but I offer a service that no one needs but that some may want. Obviously God (True Being) is in every mind so no one needs me to bring God to them. But some want to grow their awareness of God and I offer assistance with that. And just as everyone brings to their work, I offer my time, energy, attention, education, and experience. I ask for money in exchange for all of this because money is required to exchange for things that facilitate living in the world. So my business is just a business like any other. It is not somehow "special" just because the services I offer are of a spiritual nature. My services are intended to point people inward toward Truth if they are open to It. But like all form it is not Truth itself.

       I do not claim to be Jesus or even like Jesus. I cannot speak to His motivations because of course there are as many Jesus's as there are people who think about Him! What someone tells you they see in Jesus tells you about them and nothing about Jesus.

       Please look to see if you are giving absolute-moral meaning to money or the earning of money. Like all form, money and the earning of money has no meaning in itself. Any meaning that you see you give to it. And giving absolute-moral meaning to things in the world comes from the belief that guilt is real and that you will be punished. Behind this is a belief that there is a god outside of you who decrees an absolute morality that you must follow in the world or be punished. Of course, this god does not exist. It is a construct of the ego meant to hold guilt and the ego in your mind. But believing in this god is the source of guilt and fear. This belief is what you must undo with the Holy Spirit to be at peace.

162. Ask: (#2) By making people your clients aren't you reinforcing separation? (March 28, 2014)

"Thank you very much for answering. I'm so happy that at least one spiritual teacher answered instead of ignoring...I'm also a student of A Course in Miracles, *I've recently started studying of my own accord. Jesus says there's really only one of Us in reality and that this world is a dream, a hallucination of the One Mind. The belief that we are separate from Him and God is the only belief that needs healing. We are all the Sonship. Therefore answer me this, would you ask for money from your family? By making people as your 'clients' instead of brothers and sisters of the One Family, aren't you reinforcing the idea of separation? Therefore contradicting your 'teachings'? People may assume that you're a con artist instead of a 'spiritual teacher' in that case, making millions off 'spirituality' when in reality Truth is abundant and available to anyone at anytime. I am slightly aware of the Holy Spirit within me since I started studying the* Course. *It is not my place to judge or condemn you in any manner, but these questions are genuine and have been in my mind for a long time...Also, please do me a favor and ask your readers to question everything and not take things for granted. Ask them to read the* Course *to learn directly from the Holy Spirit and not from their projections. Thank you."* – KR

We are one in Truth (God), meaning the Truth in each mind is the same Truth. But we are not one as people. One formless Being (God) is reality. The illusion is the idea that there are separate minds in separate bodies in a world. So the goal is not to make the illusion like Truth, but to let it go to be aware of the one and only Being-that-is. The goal is to become aware that the universe of form is not Reality, but that the one Being that is the Truth in your mind is Reality.

And yes, I would take money from my siblings for my professional services. I used to clean houses for a living and my parents, one of my sisters, and my nephew were all clients of mine at some point. They all paid me full price for my professional services. The fact that the work that I do in the world now is spiritual in nature does not make it somehow different from any other work I would do in the world. It is no different to me than housecleaning was. It is just a job that I enjoy and that comes naturally to me.

The reason I do not feel guilty for taking money for my services is that I do not judge money, or needing to earn money to live in the world, as "wrong" or "bad". This is simply the way that the world works. I accept this without judgment because the world is not my reality. Judging the world is what made it real to me. But I have learned that Truth is my Reality. This is not just theory for me. It has become my experience.

I am not conning anyone. I'm very open about what I do. Also, I do not make millions! That would be nice, but it is not necessary to me. My income from mentoring, the donations people send me for my newsletter, and the royalties off my books came to a grand total of $30,000 (gross) last year. (And it was only that high because one of my royalty checks from O-Books for 2012 came in 2013). This is the most I have earned in a year since I started mentoring in 2006.

I think you may be locked in the old, religious habit of spiritualizing the ego. That's when you think that there is a connection between the Truth and what you do or do not do as a person. There is none. The Truth is untouched by anything that happens in the universe of form. Being aware of this is what *A Course in Miracles* teaches is true forgiveness. The Truth in you is already whole and perfect and untouched by the personal experience. You do not have to make the self be "good" or "right". You do not have to perfect it and make it Truth-like. If you want peace you only have to be willing to release the personal as your reality so that you can become aware of your Reality in Truth.

There is no god outside of you holding the self accountable so there is no reason to judge what the self does in the world. It has no meaning in Reality, and judging it is what makes it real to you and causes any sense of separation.

163. Ask: (#3) How can there not be a connection between Truth and you as a person? (April 4, 2014)

162) "…*You have said, 'I think you may be locked in the old, religious habit of spiritualizing the ego. That's when you think that there is a connection between the Truth and what you do or do not do as a person'. By judging me as thinking from 'old religious habit of spiritualizing the ego' haven't you contradicted yourself and judged me from the ego?*

Also, how can there not be a connection between the Truth and what you do or do not do as a person? That's clearly separation thinking because WE ARE TRUTH. How then am I so calm and less stressed out since I started studying the Course? *As I study the* Course *and Jesus points me gently towards the Truth I feel peaceful even for a little bit, why is that? If there is no connection between Truth and what I do as a person?*

You have said you spend your experience, energy and time with your clients in exchange for money- so aren't you valuing your worldly abilities in this dream world therefore reinforcing the ego?..." – KR

There is a difference between judging and merely observing. Judgment applies a meaning (right/wrong, good/bad) and results in an emotional charge. When you merely observe you do not give any meaning (right/wrong, good/bad) and you feel no emotional charge. I was simply asking you to look at your thinking. I was not implying that your thinking was right or wrong or good or bad, but that you may find it is an obstacle to peace.

The self is not Truth. The self is the illusion that *A Course in Miracles* talks about. The Truth (God) within your mind is reality. The body/personality/ego is not reality. You are calm since you started reading the *Course* because it points you to the Truth within yourself. But if you want to experience *only* peace you will have to release yourself from your identification with a self.

When I say that there is no connection between what you do as a person and Truth I mean that what you do as a person has no effect on Truth. Truth goes on untouched by the self in any way. The self is only a projection of your mind so your *awareness* of the Truth affects your projection of the self. But what the self does or does not do does not affect Truth in any way. So there is no reason to give meaning (right/wrong, good/bad) to what the self does.

It is this teaching – that nothing real is occurring in your experience of a self in a world because God (Truth) goes on untouched by any of it – that sets *A Course in Miracles* apart from other teachings. It is a teaching in absolute forgiveness that releases you from guilt and fear of punishment. Of course other teachings – Hinduism, Buddhism, for example - teach that the self and its world are all an illusion. But as far as I know only ACIM actually helps you do the psychological work necessary to release yourself from the unconscious and conscious belief in guilt that is the primary obstacle to peace.

Yes, this self in my mind exchanges its experience, energy, etc. for money because I have evaluated these as worth something. I leave it up to others, however, as to whether or not what I offer has value for them. That is the way that the world works. But I no longer evaluate myself by what the self has to offer. If I did, then, yes, it would reinforce the ego in me and be an obstacle to peace. But the Truth is true for me now and I let go of the self – which means I let it be, and let it do what it does, without judgment.

What changes as you go along in this process is not what you do in the world, but from which thought system you approach the world. So your life in the world looks like any ordinary life, but you experience peace within because you come from an awareness that Truth, not the self, is Reality.

164. Ask: (#4) How do I know if I've misunderstood something I've read? (April 11, 2014)

"So what you're saying is I shouldn't derive my sense of self from this world because it's not real? Why does it feel real to me? I've realized I misunderstood my readings of the Course, *so now I'm doubting whether to continue studying the* Course *or not. How do I know if I've misunderstood something or not?" – KR*

It feels real to you because you were born into this consciousness and you don't question its reality until something happens to make you question it. Workbook Lesson #132 discusses this a bit:

"There is no world! This is the central thought the course attempts to teach. Not everyone is ready to accept it, and each one must go as far as he can let himself be led along the road to truth...But healing is the gift of those who are prepared to learn there is no world, and can accept the lesson now. Their readiness will bring the lesson to them in some form which they can understand and recognize. Some see it suddenly on point of death, and rise to teach it. Others find it in experience that is not of this world...And some will find it in this course..." (W-132.6-8)

For most who have an experience that shows them that the world is not reality there is an *unconscious* readiness to learn Truth that opens them to the experience.

As you study the *Course* you will find things that do not line up with what you have believed before. And you will find things that do not line up with what you thought you already understood in the *Course*. This is how you will know that you have not understood. And this is why it takes many, many years of deep study with the Holy Spirit. It is a process of undoing a belief system that you thought was real. It is a life-long process that starts with a lot of confusion and even disorientation but leads to true, lasting peace, joy, and clarity. I have found these past 30 years worth it because peace has come to stay for me, but I can tell you the beginning was very hard and I often regretted starting it! Whether or not you are ready to learn it is not something I can judge. And you may not be able to judge for yourself. This is something for you to bring to the Holy Spirit.

165. Ask: Since my body is an illusion what's the point in taking care of it? (April 18, 2014)

"...I understand that everything is an illusion, just as Einstein discovered with his telescope, no matter just energy. But what I'm having a problem understanding is, since my body is an illusion, what's the point in trying to eat properly and taking supplements and curing disease naturally that enters my body, all of which are illusions?..." – AM

Before I get to your question, let me clarify that Truth is formless so the universe of form is the illusion. There is no relationship between Truth (Formlessness) and illusion (form); they are diametrically opposed. What Einstein discerned and then proved with math (not a telescope) about matter being made up of energy (form, too, though invisible) is an explanation for how the universe of form works. He did not reveal what *A Course in Miracles* means by "illusion". This will never be revealed through science because science always validates form, visible or invisible. Science "proves" that form (illusion) is real. Truth cannot be "proven" through objective "evidence". Truth is a wholly subjective experience.

Your question is a common one and one that comes from what I call the "pouting ego (personal thought system)". You have read in a book that the body is an illusion. This makes the ego uncomfortable so it goes on the attack and gets petulant: "If it's not real then why should I take care of it?" Of course, the ego will never see or understand that the body is not real. And if you really understood that the body is not real you would not have this question. You could just as easily ask, "Since the body is not real, why should I *not* take care of it?" From the perspective of Truth it does not matter one way or the other what you do with the body. The decision is always one within the illusion.

Motivation ("why") and judgment are ego postures. When you are aware that the Truth is true you do no seek for motivation for or judge what the body does or does not do. You forgive it, which means you let it be without judgment. You find yourself taking care of the body according to what it needs in the context in which you find it. Your care for the body comes naturally without a "why?"

If you are not yet at a stage where your care for the body comes without thought then use your concern for the body to grow your awareness of Truth. Ask the Holy Spirit within you, "Do I need to do anything to take care of this body? If so, what? I'm open to Your guidance."

166. Ask: Where and when do folks buy into guilt? (April 25, 2014)

"I am continually confused by most everything about the meanings in ACIM *of the concept of guilt. I was brought up in a home that taught that God loves us unconditionally and is present everywhere; that we reflect Him and all his qualities; that we are already "perfect" in reality. Being "perfect" as a young person took time to take in however, being a good person did not. Where and when do folks buy into guilt? Human guilt is another thing. Most of us feel human guilt easily which impedes our human and spiritual growth but can be a teaching tool, I think. Is there a time when we 'should' feel guilt?"* – LK

Very simply, when you identify with limited form (the self) you are aware on a deep, unconscious level that your mind is not in its natural state of limitless, formless Being (what *A Course in Miracles* calls "God"). So you are uncomfortable. To preserve itself in your mind the ego (personal) thought system in your mind tells you that your discomfort is guilt, or a deep sense of being intrinsically wrong or bad. In your identification with the ego your natural state of Being seems "other" to you. It seems like a power outside of and over you. You believe, when you identify with an ego, that the source of your guilt is that you have undone, killed, attacked – take your pick – this "god" outside of you. The ego tells you that this god is going to punish you and ultimately kill you. This is what you believe, unconsciously and/or consciously, when the universe of form is real to you.

You can see why guilt is central to the ego thought system. There is no guilt in your mind without the ego. And there is no ego in your mind without guilt. This is why to undo guilt in your mind you must release the ego thought system.

The source of guilt in your mind is the ego thought system, not any teaching in the world. The world reinforces guilt for the most part, because everyone in it believes, unconsciously and/or consciously, that the ego in their mind is them and that guilt is real. Sometimes there are situations where guilt is somewhat mitigated, as you described in your upbringing. However, guilt is in your mind as long as the ego is in your mind. Of course you can learn that guilt is not real and detach from the ego. This is what teachings like ACIM are for. This is a long process of first learning to recognize all of the ways that guilt shows up and then undoing all of the ways that you believe that guilt is real. (For a partial list of the common ways in which guilt shows up see article #155).

Guilt is never justified. In my book, *Releasing Guilt for Inner Peace*, I make a distinction between *guilt* and a *social conscience*. They are not the same, though the ego will twist your social conscience into a source for guilt:

"When you are very young adults are supposed to teach you the boundaries and laws of your family, culture, and society. These rules of right and wrong form a social-morality. As you learn these you develop a social conscience. Your social conscience is an internal sense of what is right or wrong according to your family, culture, or society. It is what feels disturbed when you violate social-morality. Rules, boundaries, and laws vary among families, cultures, and societies. They also change over time as values change and more is learned about the world and human nature. Though arbitrary, social-morality is a starting point for living in relative harmony with others in the world.

When rational and realistic, rules, boundaries, and laws serve the well-being of a family, culture, or society. But the belief in an absolute-morality results in unrealistic and/or harsh social-moralities to control members of a family, culture, or society. Absolute-morality, if it existed, would be right and wrong behavior in the world as decreed by a power, or god, over it. Your unconscious belief in absolute-morality is your belief that guilt is an intrinsic aspect of reality. When you confuse absolute-morality and social-morality, social-morality becomes an attempt to control what is seen as intrinsic guilt.

A disturbed social conscience and feeling guilty are not the same experience. But the personal thought system hijacks your social conscience to "prove" your guilt. A social conscience refers to the self's behavior in the world in relation to others. If guilt does not become involved with it, your social conscience is assuaged through amends or a genuine change in values. Guilt, however, is the feeling that the imperfect and sometimes mistaken self is proof that you are intrinsically wrong or bad. Guilt cannot be swept away. Where your social conscience sees temporary mistakes easily corrected, your belief in intrinsic guilt sees eternal sins that can never be undone. It twists your social conscience into a useful source for guilt."

The book goes on to give examples to explain this further. And, as you can tell by the title, it eventually goes into how to release guilt by undoing your unconscious and/or conscious belief in a god outside of you.

167. Ask: Can I love and respect nature and still be serious about ACIM? (May 2, 2014)

"...I have always felt a tremendous affinity to the Native American ways and their utter respect for a great Spirit and as keepers of the earth planet. So, here is the "angst" for me...I am clear that ACIM is my primary path, but the connection to the earth, animal totems, etc really speak to me. Yet, I know from the ACIM perspective, there is no world and the emphasis isn't on saving something that isn't 'there'. Natives saw 'spirit' in everything...trees, mountains, streams, corn, buffalo. Is it compatible to have and tend the 'love and respect of natural beauty' and be a serious student of ACIM? I remember Ken W saying that frustration with inanimate things was as significant as anything else. Clearly, I'm confusing some things here..." – KL

Your desire to love and to respect the natural world would only be incompatible with your study of *A Course in Miracles* if it prevented you from being aware that the Truth is in your mind, not in the world of form. As you grow in your awareness of Truth the self will still have its personality. It will still have its preferences, its interests, its likes and dislikes, etc. These are neutral, or without meaning in themselves. What changes is you stop looking to these to be your "salvation" (source of wholeness, happiness, peace).

When one is in nature they often allow their mind to process out its thoughts and they become aware of the quiet Truth (Spirit) beyond all the thoughts. They experience peace. Sometimes they project the source of this peace onto nature. They feel that nature brought them the feeling, rather than that they felt something within that they then projected onto nature.

Also, when you quiet your mind you slow down its processes and you can become aware of the unity, or one mind (what ACIM calls the "Son of God"), behind all forms. Ancient cultures did not have the distractions that we have today. They lived and worked in abundant quiet. So they tended to be very aware of this unity, as well as of cause and effect at the level of form. At first this unity was conceived of as many gods. Later it was conceived of as one god. But the True Being that ACIM calls "God" transcends the one mind that projects the universe of form. God is not responsible for the universe of form and has nothing to do with it. So what you have to sort out is your experience of God (True Being) within from your awareness of the unity of the universe of form.

This sorting out of Truth from illusion is really the whole process ACIM leads you into. There are many illusory experiences that have been labeled "spiritual" by the world that really have nothing to do with Truth. Confusing them keeps you in guilt so sorting out Truth and illusion is essential if you want to be at peace.

168. Ask: How did you deal with ego rebounding? (May 9, 2014)

"I read somewhere in your story, or a blog post, that at some point in your journey with the Course, *you experienced heavy ego 'rebounding.' I am 1/3 through the workbook. I find there's strong correlations for me between a day or few days of inner peace, much less ego chatter, etc, followed by very persistent, loud, insistent(!) ego noise and demands. Some mornings after a previous day of consistent meditation are particularly noisy. How did you deal with ego rebounding, and what do you recommend for those periods when my ego's voice, and its resistance to any of my meditative work, is strong?"* – M

Yes, you have described the ego's rebounding very well. This is the process. You experience peace or an insight and as soon as you even so much as glance (usually unconsciously) in the ego's direction it does whatever it needs to do to hold your attention. And it's usually not something nice! This will go on as long as the ego still seems to have something you want and/or you are afraid of God (True Being).

After long, futile struggle I eventually learned to just accept the rebound. I accepted that it was happening because I still believed on some level that the ego had value and/or was "safer" than Truth. I accepted that I was in a long process of undoing that belief. Accepting the process and where I was in the process did not undo all of my discomfort but it did lessen it considerably.

On those days when the ego was particularly raucous and I couldn't meditate I just accepted that, too. I made the attempt and tried to just be with the resistance, observing it and letting it go. But if it was too uncomfortable I would just go do something else. Throughout the day I would turn my mind inward to Truth whenever I remembered. And if I couldn't feel It I would remind myself that it was still there. The sun still shines even if, from my point of view on earth, the clouds seem to obscure it for a time.

And I've learned that ego episodes always pass. This was something that I would remember in the midst of them, too.

169. Ask: What did you mean by the world had "flattened out" for you? (May 16, 2014)

"In an earlier article you said something about things not standing out to you anymore and that the world has "flattened out" for you. Can you explain what you meant?" - Anonymous (May 16, 2014)

One of the first things that even new students report to me is that when a "crisis" occurs they find that they are not as upset as they once would have been. They are disturbed by this even though peace is what they want! This is the beginning of the "flattening out". Things in the world that once stood out as significant and to which you once had a strong positive or negative reaction now evoke much less of an emotional response. Very dimly you have accepted that peace is real and that the world is not so the ego's responses to the world no longer have the meaning for you that they once did.

It takes a long time, but this awareness does grow to a point where you live in peace and are not much affected by the world. This has happened for me. When something happens in the world that I judge as "good", whether in my story, someone else's story, or in the news, what I feel is "That's nice." And then I forget about it. And when something happens that I judge as "bad" I experience, "Rats. I was hoping that would go another way. Oh, well." And then I forget about it. Truth and peace are more real to me than the world now. I still perceive the world and all of its happenings. I still appear to be involved in it. But my internal experience of it has radically changed. I am not attached and I do not define myself by what does or does not happen in the world. It is all just passing before me as I rest in peace.

This will happen for you, too, as Truth and peace become real for you. Experiences that once evoked highs and lows will instead evoke temporary, passing emotional blips. Drama is the ego's substitute for peace. It validates the ego and in your identification with it you think the highs and lows are "life". But you will eventually recognize that peace is Life.

170. Ask: Why do you say to bring problems to the Holy Spirit? (May 23, 2014)

"Some teachers say to not bring worldly problems to the Holy Spirit. The Holy Spirit does not come into the world and fix them. But you seem to suggest that we do so. I'm confused..." - Anonymous

I do not suggest that you use the Holy Spirit (Teacher of Truth in your mind) as a problem solver. I suggest that you use your perceived problems as opportunities to grow your awareness of the Holy Spirit.

Whatever you perceive as a problem is never the real problem. The real problem is that you feel that you are not your True Being ("separate from God") but that you are a self in a body in a world. All of your perceived problems are an expression of this one problem. You overcome your real problem by becoming aware of your True Being (God) through the Holy Spirit. The Holy Spirit is the thought system in your mind that replaces the personal thought system (ego) when you decide that you want to know Truth. It meets you where you are in your perception that you are a self in a world. It gently awakens you to your reality by using your experiences in the world to remind you of your Truth.

For example, often new students of *A Course in Miracles* feel guilty for wanting things in the world. ACIM does say that your desires are obstacles to peace when you see them as ends in themselves ("if I get this I will be at peace, whole, loved, etc."). But this does not make them wrong or bad; only obstacles to peace. So it teaches you to use them as means to peace instead. It tells you to share them with the Holy Spirit. This does not mean to passively ask the Holy Spirit to take your desires and to sit and wait for something to happen. Your obstacles to peace are in your mind and you have to look at them to remove them. So you acknowledge the Holy Spirit in your mind and with It you look at all of your thoughts about what you desire: *This is what I desire, this is why I want it, this is why I feel guilty, this is what I fear, etc.* This is how you connect with and learn to hear the Holy Spirit in your mind. And it gives the Holy Spirit an opportunity to undo your guilt and fears with you. The side effect of this is clarity around and removing obstacles to your attaining your personal desires. So, as you say, the Holy Spirit does not come into the world to make things happen. What happens in the self's life is an effect of your mind.

Another example is when you have to make what you consider to be an important decision in the world. You acknowledge the Holy Spirit in your mind and with It you look at the decision from all angles: *These are the pros, these are the cons, this is what I want, this is what I fear, etc.* This process makes you more aware of the Holy Spirit so decisions in the world become means to be more aware of the Holy Spirit. And it brings clarity to your mind that will result in you being clear on the decision.

So the point of bringing your worldly questions to the Holy Spirit is to bring the Holy Spirit into your awareness. Solutions and answers and greater harmony in your life in the world are the side-effects, not the purpose, of this practice. But for a long time you will have two motivations for bringing your problems to the Holy Spirit. While problems in the world are still very real to you of course you want solutions to them, even while you are willing to use them to grow your awareness of Truth.. But in time you will discover that in the Holy Spirit you have the wholeness that you seek. The side-effect of a more harmonious life in the world is nice but it is also irrelevant to your peace of mind. In fact, it is an *effect* of your peace of mind, not its cause.

171. Ask: How do I overcome my fear of death? (May 30, 2014)

"I have been a student of A Course in Miracles for many years but I have to admit I still fear death. How do I overcome this?" - Anonymous

What you experience as fear of death is really not *your* fear but the personal thought system's (ego's) fear of ceasing to exist. So you will overcome the fear of death when you release yourself from the limitation of identifying with a self and you identify with Truth instead.

There is no death. The Truth within you is eternal. It has no beginning and no ending. It just is. Growing your awareness of the Truth within you brings you peace of mind precisely because It *is* eternal and never changing.

There is no death for the self, either, because it doesn't really exist. It was never really "born" so it never "dies". It is just a mistaken way of thinking about yourself *now*. It is an idea that you can just put aside *now*. And that is not death, but reawakening to your Reality.

Meditate on these facts. You may find that over time you have to revisit them again and again. But as your awareness of the eternal Truth in you grows you will find that you are released from the fear of death.

172. Ask: Do words have power? (June 6, 2014)

"Do words have power? Some teachers say we shouldn't swear, be careful what we say about what we want or wish, etc. because words are powerful..." - Anonymous

No, words do not have power. They are empty symbols that have no meaning in themselves. They only have the meaning for you that you give to them. Your unconscious and conscious *beliefs* are powerful. Only they affect you and your words can symbolize them or they can contradict them. Words can lie. Feelings do not lie. Your feelings reveal to you what you truly believe, no matter what you *say* to yourself and/or to others.

(For example, it's very common for students of *A Course in Miracles* to say, "I know the world isn't real, but..." because they've read in ACIM that the world is not real. But they clearly still believe that the world is real or there would be no "but" after they said it wasn't real to them! Their words contradict what they truly believe and if they looked at their *feelings* they would have to acknowledge this).

If you believe that a word or phrase is "wrong" or "bad" you may feel guilty for using it. But the source of your guilt would not be the words. The source of your guilt would be your belief that there is an ultimate morality decreed by a god outside of you that you violated by using that word or phrase. You may also feel guilty for the feelings that the words express when the words *are* in line with your feelings. But, again, the source of your guilt would not be the words but your belief that your feelings, and the beliefs that they represent, violate an ultimate morality.

173. Ask: My rationale for my form of study is that ACIM is a hologram. What do you think? (June 13, 2014)

"...I recently read that the Course *is like a hologram (whatever that might be) in the sense that any part of it contains the whole. I've had an unconscious intuition about that and used it as a rationale for studying the* Course *the way I do - reading books that clarify its essence, not doing the daily lessons, not buying the Jesus connection etc. What do you think?"* – ES

The kind of hologram to which you refer is one where a picture is made up of many pictures of the picture itself. For example, if you looked at each individual pixel in the picture you'd see that it is a miniature picture of the picture itself, shaded for its particular part in the macro picture.

It is true that as you become familiar with the themes of *A Course in Miracles* you will come across phrases, paragraphs, and sections that will make you declare, "Why, that sums up the whole Course!" Perhaps this is what is meant by some that the *Course* is like a hologram. If you meditated with the Holy Spirit on one of those holographic-like phrases, paragraphs, or sections it could ultimately be the same as meditating on the whole book.

But I'm not sure if that relates to the way that you say that you have been studying the *Course*. The question is, what is your goal as you study the *Course*? Is understanding it an end in itself for you? Or do you see studying the *Course* as a means to an end, such as a better life in the world or inner peace? Integrating the ideas in the *Course* and practicing its principles in your life are what will bring a transformation in your experience. Merely understanding the *Course* will only bring you understanding of the *Course*!

174. Ask: Why is it so much work to awaken even when you want to? (June 20, 2014)

"Why is it so easy to identify with the ego and it takes so much work to 'awake' even when you want to?" – T

You are born into a consciousness (ego) that is the opposite of Truth (God) in every way. It is real to you and you do not question it until one day maybe you do. Perhaps you question it because on some level you were open to Truth and had an experience that is not of this world. Maybe you question it because it never seemed to you to be all that could be. Or you may question it because you hit a bottom so low that you opened to Truth in desperation. In any case, it's easy to identify with the ego because the ego is what you think is real and true! It's all that you thought you knew.

It seems to take work to awaken (to be aware of Truth) because you have to undo your belief in a thought system (ego) as your reality that is wholly the opposite of Truth. And you do this in the midst of a world that reinforces this opposite-of-Truth thought system rather than Truth. Even if you have directly experienced Truth you do not wholly trust It right away because It is unlike the experience of ego that you have thought was real. In your identification with the ego, lack seems like reality. So Truth, Which is an experience of wholeness like nothing that the world offers, seems too good to be true. And part of your experience of the opposite-of-Truth is a deep-seated, mostly unconscious belief that you are guilty for defying a power over and outside of you. So you don't feel worthy of an experience of boundless love, peace, and joy.

So do you really want to awaken? Yes, you do, because you let Truth into your awareness. And once you did that, your journey to being aware of Truth was set. Now the story for the self in the world with which you have identified will be one of growing your awareness of Truth. But within this process of becoming wholly aware of Truth, sometimes, no, you won't want Truth. It frightens you. It will take a long time to work out your deep-seated belief that the ego, lack, and guilt are reality. It will take experiences of Truth to Which you will open only very slowly because Truth is unlike your experience of the ego and because in your belief in guilt you think that Truth is really out to get you.

The contrast between the opposite-of-Truth and Truth is so stark that your mind could not go from ego right to Truth without going into shock. So the *Course* offers you a gentle process of awakening. Over time you have experiences (miracles) of Truth that first make you aware of It and then develop your trust in It. You have as many of these experiences as you are willing to accept. And as the Truth becomes true for you, you will find the willingness to question the guilt that blocks you from keeping Truth in your awareness.

It is a process. At any given moment you experience as much awareness of Truth as you are willing to experience. Your willingness, and nothing else, determines how aware you are of Truth. And when you want *only* Truth you will experience *only* Truth.

175. Ask: Is it true that there is a peace sweeter than I can imagine? (June 27, 2014)

"Is it true, as the Course *promises, that there is a peace sweeter than the peace I image will be mine when I become financially debt free? Because I can't seem to let that go. I fantasize about being debt free and the peace that washes over me is palpable. But it doesn't last. And the peace of God seems just as elusive. I've been studying the* Course *for about a year and I love the teachings but can't get past this."* – T

Oh, yes, there is a Peace so broad and so deep that there is no correlation to It in your experience of the self and its world. What you imagine you will feel when you are debt free is only the teensiest, weensiest taste of It. No, it's not even that. What you imagine is a peace that comes from the fulfilling of a lack. That's really just temporary satisfaction. The Peace of God (True Being) is far beyond that. It is a Wholeness so complete that lack does not exist There even as an idea.

If *A Course in Miracles* is your first foray into opening to Truth then a year in is just the barest beginning. If you started with some other teaching, or just have had an awareness of Truth in some other way, then you may be further along, but still at the beginning. It will get harder before it gets easier because you have to grow your awareness of Truth, grow your trust in Truth, and work out your obstacles to Truth. And of course all of these have yet to happen when you have just begun!

Peace will come rarely for a long while. Then it will come more often. And then finally it will come to stay in your awareness. It's a process and if you can accept that, and if you can accept that you will be uncomfortable for a while, it will be not-quite-so-hard. There's no sugar-coating this. Looking into a mind that you fear, calling on a Truth that you fear, taking responsibility for a mind that you are used to passively letting the ego run for you, questioning and releasing deep-seated and sometimes cherished beliefs, learning to approach the world from a perspective that is sometimes180 degrees from the way that you look at it now – that's no small feat! It takes time and patience. But you will find peace in the process and in the end peace will be all that you have.

176. Ask: Do you believe in a correlation between head-neck alignment and inner peace? (July 4, 2014)

"My question relates to a recent answer you gave about the feeling of deep peace that you experience. I know from having done some bodywork, including Alexander Technique, that there is a correlation between a certain head-neck alignment and a feeling of deep peace. I see this emphasized strongly in the Zen tradition of meditation as well, where posture is seen to be the means and the end of attainment as well. Judging from your online photos, I can see you also have a very good alignment of the head and neck. Did you work on this consciously, and in any case, do you believe in the importance of this correlation?" – OT

I have never heard of this, so, no, I did not work consciously on my head-neck alignment as a means to attain inner peace. I have worked solely on my mind being open to Truth and to working out my obstacles (guilt, fear) to being aware of Truth.

And, no, I do not believe the correlation is important. I think it possible that one's posture may change as they grow more peaceful. But I do not think that changing their posture will bring them true inner peace. It might, however, bring a bit of temporary relaxation that they might mistake for true peace.

There is a lot of confusion of cause and effect when it comes to attaining inner peace. Students look at what teachers do or how they sit when they meditate or at what they eat, etc. and think, "Ah, I'll do that and I'll be at peace!" They're hoping to find a shortcut that will not be as uncomfortable as looking at the obstacles to peace (guilt and fear) in their mind. But the only source of inner peace is an awareness of Truth. And all that requires is a willingness to be aware of Truth. This willingness is an openness of *mind*. You can have it no matter what you do, how you sit, what you eat, etc.

Behavior (anything the body does, including thinking) always follows from conscious or unconscious thoughts (beliefs). Behavior does not cause thought.

177. Ask: How does one differentiate between feeling spirit and energy from energy work? (July 11, 2014)

"I was doing a meditation the other day that guides you to feel the space around your body and eventually leads you to a state where you are 'no self'. I noticed when I did the meditation that I felt a sensation of energy (lightness, tingling, a distinct presence of energy) and I did have a definite feeling of being something other than my body. My question is how does one differentiate between the feeling of spirit/a connection to truth and the energy that you might feel that accompanies a level of our form (as in energy work such as Reiki)? I had fear arise suddenly that I might be strengthening form instead of connecting with truth..." – MB

If the feeling of being something other than a body was an experience of the dropping of boundaries and an expanded sense of Being then it was an experience of Truth or Formlessness. If you were aware of *only* Being then you experienced what *A Course in Miracles* refers to as a Revelation. If the "something other" was an awareness that you are mind, not a body, but you were still aware of the body or the world, then you experienced a higher miracle. Your experience of lightness, tingling, and the presence of energy were experiences of form. Your experience of not-body, whether a Revelation or a higher miracle, was the cause of these effects-in-form.

There is always an effect in form when you touch Truth either directly (Revelation) or indirectly (miracle). Sometimes it is just taking a deep breath and relaxing. This is probably the most common effect of touching Truth during meditation or even when just touching Truth for a moment throughout the day. I've heard of others experiencing what you described as well as things like hot hands or "chakras" opening. One could also experience a spontaneous healing of the body or mind. After direct Revelations I experienced an almost uncomfortable euphoria. Sometimes the effect-in-form shows up as an expression of fear, like a panic attack or subsequent illness after a Revelation or a higher miracle.

You only need to be concerned if you confuse with Truth what shows up in form as an *effect* of your experience of Truth. The experience of form is not Truth Itself. The body is an idea in your mind and your experience of Truth in your mind affects the ideas in your mind. But these effects, like all form, have no meaning in themselves. Just as smoke reveals the existence of a fire the effects of your mind only attest to the existence of your mind. But it's your mind, not its effects, that is real.

To differentiate between Truth and not-Truth just know that if it happens in form it is not Truth Itself. The cause of form may be your belief in not-Truth or your awareness of Truth.

178. Ask: Is there anything else that you think I could be doing? (July 18, 2014)

"The more I read RG (Releasing Guilt for Inner Peace) *the more it resonates with me. Since I'm retired and no longer have the imposed structure of a job and also divorced and no longer have the daily stress of my former marriage I can easily focus on what's going on with me. I can*

follow my feelings and what shows up is a free-floating, non-specific fear which according to the Course *is guilt. There is no denying it or attributing it to anything outside of me. While I'm not happy about it I do believe this is what's true for me and an authentic way to see myself and live my life right now.*

So I study the Course *by reading. I meditate to invite the ToT (Teacher of Truth) into my awareness which so far has gotten little response. I started the lessons and gave up after 5 out of boredom. I refer to the 7 Rules for Decision Making from to time to time. I reach out to friends including my ex who loves your books. I distract myself by reading history, watching a ton of movies and drink my daily "medicinal" beer. That's me. Is there anything else you think I could be doing?...I do think an honest account of how one student lives his daily life along with your response might be helpful to others who might be getting frustrated."* – ES

The daily practice I recommend is in my book *4 Habits for Inner Peace*. All you need to experience peace is to be aware of Truth. So just do what you want to do each day without judging it and bring your mind back to Truth when you remember to do so. If you find that you cannot do this then you need to look with the Teacher of Truth (Holy Spirit) in your mind at the guilt and fear that are your obstacles to peace.

Recognizing the guilt in your mind is the beginning of undoing it. The next step is to become aware of the unconscious and conscious beliefs that cause your feelings of guilt so that you can undo them with the Teacher of Truth.

179. Ask: I recently resolved an issue at work peacefully but I don't like to judge anyone... (July 25, 2014)

"...I recently started a new position at work in which I am the supervisor of 6 people. 2 of them approached me about their unhappiness with one of their coworkers work ethic they demanded action. It was really hard for me as I just don't like to judge anyone. I did do it in the spirit of love and it did seem to work out pretty well but I was curious of your thoughts. I'm just learning that even in that situation I could be peaceful and not fearful. It was the first experience that I have had that kind of inner peace even in a conflicted situation. I also asked the Holy Spirit for the guidance and saw my onesies with these brothers..." – JW

Since you experienced peace in the situation I'm not quite sure what more I can offer! You must've done something right. Perhaps you still feel conflicted over the idea of "judging" others even though you experienced peace in the middle of what you once considered a situation of conflict.

What you want to sort out in any situation is what is fact and what is your projection of meaning (judgment). For example, it may be a fact that Jane habitually starts work late. That fact has no meaning in itself. And observing this fact is not judging her. It's just observing a fact in the world. And it may also be an observable fact that her lateness violates your company's policies. In this sense you may see her perpetual lateness as "wrong", but neither of these observations would cause you to have a strong emotional charge. A strong emotional charge is the sign that you have judged.

I'm under the impression you did not experience this in the situation that you describe. It is never wrong to judge (to think so would be another judgment!). But believing in your judgments is an obstacle to peace. Your judgments, not the facts, are what cause emotional charges and feelings of conflict. They stem from your conscious or unconscious belief that there is a power over and outside of you (a god) that sits in judgment on you and that will punish you if you do not live up to its standards. Someone else being imperfect only reminds you that you, too, are not living up to your god's standards and so would set off your own guilt and fear of punishment. Your own guilt and fear is what you really see in a situation where you judge. They cause the emotional charge. So ultimately your judgments indicate to you that you need to undo your belief in a god outside of you and over you that you must please or be punished.

You've now had an experience to which to refer when you find yourself again in a situation where you must confront someone with the facts of their inadequate work ethic. And you can learn to discern whether or not you are projecting your own guilt and fear by whether or not you judge them and feel a strong emotional charge.

180. Ask: Is there an affirmation to break through dark fears? (August 1, 2014)

"Could you help with some guidance in the work of quieting fear from thought when facing seemingly unchangeable physical problems, i.e., the slow loss of one's vision or serious health diagnosis in one's child or a close loved one. What can one do consistently in a practical way to combat the frightening feelings that come so tenaciously.....so often in the nighttime? I am wondering if there are honest affirmations or words that might help break the dark fears of the future - and give one a sense of hope and control of the right kind?" – LK

The personal experience is one of limitation, lack, and inevitable losses. Peace comes only from the awareness of the whole, unchanging, eternal Truth ("God" in *A Course in Miracles*) within you. Truth is untouched by anything that does or does not happen in the world. It is wholly apart from the personal experience. So as often as possible remember your experiences of Truth. Use the limitation, lack, and loss of the personal experience to remind yourself to turn inward and remember the Truth. In fact, this is how you can use these experiences to grow your awareness of Truth and peace.

As you remember your experiences of Truth you can say things like: "Only this experience of Truth is real. Everything else falls away."; "Only God is real."; "Only the Truth within me is true."—or some phrasing that helps you to remember the Unchanging and Eternal.

181. Ask: Aren't we addicted to the ego? (August 8, 2014)

"Aren't we addicted to the ego?" – Anonymous

No. But when you think that the ego (personal thought system) is your reality you do think that you need it to live. So you feel that you have a *dependency* on it.

Let's look at the distinction between abuse, addiction, and dependency. These words are often used interchangeably but there is a difference between the experiences.

Abuse refers to using a substance, behavior, or situation improperly, thereby harming or risking harming yourself. This does not necessarily lead to addiction or dependency. For example, most of us abuse food on occasion. You may overeat at a meal or regularly overindulge in a certain food. Or you may get drunk or high, even quite often, without developing an addiction or dependency on alcohol or drugs. Abusing substances can be a passing phase, for example when you are young and want to enhance your fun or when you experience a crisis.

The hallmark of *addiction*, which makes it different from abuse or dependency, is that when one is addicted to a substance they go through painful physical withdrawals when they have been without the substance for a length of time. An addiction is caused by the hijacking of the survival mechanisms in the brain by the substance. The brain becomes conditioned to the substance and responds as though it needs it for survival. So withdrawals are really a misplaced experience of starvation. The body responds as though it is dying without the substance, much as it would without food, when it really is not. Withdrawal does eventually pass, though not necessarily all physical cravings for the substance.

Psychological dependency is the belief that one's well-being is dependent on a substance, person, or behavior (sex, video games, etc.). One does not feel physical withdrawal symptoms if their object of dependency is withdrawn, but they experience an agonizing psychological sense that they cannot live or deal with life without it. Most addicts are also psychologically dependent on the substance that they abuse but not all psychological dependents are addicts. Twelve-step and other recovery programs are centered on learning to deal with psychological dependency even if for the addict withdrawals and possibly physical cravings pass. The dependent must learn to approach life in a manner contrary to the way that their brains are wired and this is why for many recovery is a life-long process.

[There can be a physical *dependency* on drugs that does not involve psychological dependency. One may be dependent on a medication to live (such as an immunosuppressant for a progressive auto-immune disease) or to have any quality of life (such as an anti-depressant for a depressive disorder). One who is dependent on drugs for life or quality of life does not experience either physical withdrawal symptoms or psychological stress if the drugs are withdrawn].

In a sense you could say that the ego is *for* abusing yourself, so you're not *misusing* it when you believe it's you. You are using it the way it means to be used! And you experience relief, not withdrawals, when you release the ego, so you are not addicted to it. But you do seem to have a *dependency* on the ego. However, you seem to *only when your mind seems to be in ego*. Only in ego does ego seem real and only in ego do you feel it necessary to resist your True Being (God). You feel that to let go of the ego is to die. You persist in listening to it, even long after you've learned how much it hurts you to listen to it, because you think that you need it to live. This is why you resist releasing it.

But your existence and the ego are not the same thing. You exist, whole and complete, apart from the ego. Ultimately, this is what you have to learn to release the ego and be at peace.

182. Ask: Does ACIM say anything about tithing? (August 15, 2014)

"...Many people extol the benefits of tithing (usually in the amount of 10 percent or more) to wherever they feel they are being spiritually fed. I'd very much like to hear your views on tithing from A Course in Miracles perspective. I'm sure nothing in either the text, workbook, or manual mentions it (or not that I've come across anyway), but some ACIM teachers recommend it nonetheless. Is there a sound basis for this Course-wise?..." –LH

You are correct that tithing is not mentioned in *A Course in Miracles*. No behavior is necessary for inner peace. If you want inner peace you only have to be willing to be aware of God (True Being). And willingness is of the mind, not of the body.

Like all behavior in the world, tithing is meaningless in itself. Some people tithe as a traditional practice. Others tithe as a practical way to express gratitude. And there are some who view tithing as part of the process of attracting or manifesting wealth in the world.

Tithing reveals an obstacle to peace in your mind if you tithe out of guilt ("I should") or out of a belief that you must make certain things appear in your life to be happy and at peace. But if you tithe because you are used to doing so or to express gratitude then it will not get in the way of your awareness of God.

183. Ask: Will you share how your practice started and has evolved? (August 22, 2014)

"Would you do a blog on how you first started practicing and how it has evolved over the years? I would be very interested to hear that and I'm sure it would be a big help to a lot of people." – WW

My spiritual path began in 1984 with *A Course in Miracles*. I was 20 years old. I had been doing some other psycho-spiritual reading before I found ACIM but ACIM is what grabbed me. Its teaching was really my whole path until study fell away naturally.

In the beginning I did not really practice. Oh, sure, I did the lessons. But I was terrified and I could hardly stand to read them every morning and evening. If I remembered twice a day to do those lessons that were supposed to be done every hour it was a good day! However, much more sunk in than I knew at the time. I repeated the Workbook for another year and didn't do much better

But my "practice" for a long time was really just reading. I was very hungry for ACIM. I read the Text and Manual for Teachers as I did the Workbook. I couldn't get enough of it. Early on I experienced higher miracles and the miracle of a holy relationship. These experiences showed me directly that what ACIM said was true. But I pushed those experiences aside and focused on understanding ACIM. Reading was when I allowed myself to feel the Holy Spirit. And because I had a house cleaning business my mind was free much of the time. So at some point I began to use that time to bring my questions about ACIM to the Holy Spirit (I actually didn't call It "the Holy Spirit" then. I didn't call It anything. I just *called on* It.) I did not always accept Its answers right away. But I was always answered, and usually accepted them within a few days. The answers sometimes came into my mind as unformed thoughts or intuitions. Sometimes the answers came from a book or someone else.

I was probably about five years into this before my trust in the Holy Spirit was enough that I started bringing to It questions about things in the world. Decisions, yes, but the Holy Spirit also functioned as a type of therapist and guide for me. However, I wasn't really practicing the principles of ACIM in my daily life. I read, I meditated in a superficial way, and I asked for the Holy Spirit's help now and then.

I met my wife in '94. She was in a 12-step program and she told me that it was like I had my own program. What she saw was that I was willing to take responsibility for my own thoughts and feelings. But I didn't have peace. My efforts were largely in trying to understand ACIM. Once I was miserable over some guilty reading of ACIM and she said to me, "I've never known anyone who could think about God so much." This really struck me. I realized I was thinking not practicing. But I still didn't put much into practice. I just stopped thinking too much!

Then in the late 90s spiritual study tapered away naturally for me. I got away from all spirituality for about 2 years. (In that time I did take a year to read the Bible from beginning to end but it has never functioned as a spiritual teaching for me). Then one day I picked up ACIM again and I was hooked with renewed commitment. I knew I was not going to let go again. This time, though, my reading of it was very different. I came back to it with fresh eyes. I still read guilt into it, but not as much as before. And where I had once understood pieces of it here and there I now saw the whole message. I saw how every part fit together. It was like for me there was a book within the book. (This eventually became the book *The Message of A Course in Miracles*).

I understood ACIM now because I allowed myself to read it through my experiences of Truth. Over the years I'd had the rare Revelation (only Truth) and the occasional higher miracle (seeing that Truth is true and illusion is illusion but still aware of both) but I had pushed them aside. Now I realized I had to let them fully in or I'd just go in circles merely reading ACIM and not experiencing any real shift toward peace.

This is when I entered what ACIM calls the "period of relinquishment". I found an incredible willingness to follow only the Holy Spirit. I allowed the Holy Spirit to work in me and through me. My trust in the Holy Spirit really deepened during this stage. It became my primary relationship and constant companion. I brought It with me into all of my relationships. My meditations became meaningful as I used them to truly open to Truth rather than to just go through the motions.

There was a direct correlation between my awareness of the Holy Spirit and the peace I experienced. One day I realized that peace had come to stay in my awareness. I was still aware of the ego, but peace never left. And since then it has only grown in my awareness. When others asked me how I stayed centered I thought about it and realized that I did four things to stay centered. These are my *4 Habits for Inner Peace*, which I eventually also wrote a book about. After a while they were just my way of being in the world.

So now there's no "practice" so much as a way of being. It's natural to me to know that what I experience comes from my own mind. So I attend to my mind. Each day is about maintaining my awareness of my wholeness in Truth.

184. Ask: Why become aware of God if we're going back There anyway? (August 29, 2014)

"My friend's friend passed away recently and my friend said, 'I am happy he is home in God now and relieved his pain is over.' But the man who passed did not seem to have any interest in spiritual awareness at all. So is it true that he went home to God? If so, then why go through the hassle of becoming aware of God in the world if you are going to go back there in any case?" - Anonymous

There is a faulty premise behind your questions and it is that in you there is some part of God (True Being; Reality) that left God and that will, upon the death of the body, return to God. But God is whole and complete always (eternal now). No part of It ever leaves It or needs to return to It. This idea is how the ego (personal thought system) makes it seem that the illusion has some reality. No part of illusion comes from Truth (God) so no part of it needs to return to Truth. All of not-Truth is *wholly* illusory.

Your friend's friend did not "return" to God and would not have if he was as aware of God as one can be. No aspect of a self is from God. And all that is real, ever, in any seemingly-individual mind is God. And God is here *right now* untouched by the illusion of an idea in the mind that is unaware of God, is becoming aware of God, or is fully aware of God. What happens in an illusion only affects the illusion.

You do not have to wait for the body to die to be aware that God is already whole and complete in your mind *right now*. There is no "you" to "go on" to become aware of God after the seeming-death of the body. If you want peace *now* you want to open your awareness to God *now* (the Holy Instant). The part of your mind that seems to lack or to have an awareness of God is never real. The need for peace is only a temporary, illusory need. Your choice in every moment is to be in the story of lack or in the awareness that you are already whole in God.

Your friend did not need to wait for his or her friend to seem to "die" to be relieved that his or her friend is no longer in pain. Your friend could have come to the realization that only God is real and that all manifestations of pain are not real. Death does not bring this realization. Nothing happens in death. It is just part of the same illusory story that is called "life".

185. Ask: Can you give examples of personally extending or creating? (September 5, 2014)

"...Please can you give specific examples of how you personally 'extend or create' as Truth? My understanding is that as egos we extend and this is seen in all examples of projecting and then believing our projections as truth. But egos' projections are illusions that end in chaos. For the awakened mind, instead of projecting it "extends or creates" in Truth. Can you translate how as a unified One we constantly create? I recently read that Albert Einstein described himself as someone 'just wanting to know the thoughts of God' When I try to commune with Truth I try to just center myself on Truth so I might be able at some point 'download' intuitive thoughts or feelings from the Truth. Creating peace. Don't know if perhaps this communing with the Truth inside me is the 'extending or creating in Truth'? Can you elaborate?" – SS

As it does with so many terms, *A Course in Miracles* re-defines the word "creation". In the world we think of "creating" as bringing something into being that was not there before. In ACIM, "Creation" means the infinite *extension* of God's Being (Truth). It's really just another way of saying that Truth is one and the same throughout. As you can tell by this definition the experience of Truth is wholly unlike the personal experience, which has multiple levels and variations.

True Extension only happens in Truth so I cannot give you examples of *personally* extending Truth. If my mind is on the personal, or form at all, I am blocking my awareness of Truth's Infinite Extension.

Projection is extension plus denial. It's the same mechanism as extension except you deny that what you see are your own thoughts. You "project" your thoughts away from you onto a meaningless universe of form. The meaning that you project is what makes form seem real to you. They are illusions because they are just ideas and interpretations, not facts.

Extension is something that occurs in the mind. It goes inward, not outward, because it is the recognition that there is no "outward"! You can practice extension (though not True Extension, which only occurs in Truth) by choosing to come from your awareness of Truth in your interactions with the world. In this practice you are aware of the Truth within you and you choose to attend to It and overlook the ego's (personal thought system's) projections of meaning onto the universe of form. Your awareness of Truth therefore extends (grows) in your awareness.

You are no longer projecting because you are aware that your perception of the world is in your own mind.

As for Albert Einstein I suspect that since he was a physicist the universe of form was very real to him and he thought that by understanding its laws he would understand the mind of some god that supposedly made it. But of course all it could lead him to are physical laws that have nothing to do with Truth.

186. Ask: How are others just ideas in my mind? (September 12, 2014)

"A Course in Miracles *tells us:* '*Everyone makes an ego or a self for himself, which is subject to enormous variation because of its instability. He also makes an ego for everyone else he perceives, which is equally variable.*' (T-4.II.2) *I have to admit that I have a hard time seeing how others are just ideas in my mind. There they are, a body, which seems so solid and real to me…*" - Anonymous

The body, like all of the universe of form, is only an empty symbol onto which you project the idea of a "person". For example, my mother died over 10 years ago and yet when I think of her I still get a feeling that I think of as "Mom". It's the same feeling I had when there was a body here onto which to project "Mom". It's really an aggregation of thoughts and the feelings to which they lead that I think of as "Mom". Sometimes it is so vivid that it is as though she is present. So it's pretty clear now that Mom's body is gone that the body could not have been the source of my experience of "Mom". Since I still feel her she must be an idea within me. And since it's the same feeling I had when there was a body here she must have always been an idea within me.

It's the same with anyone who is not in the room with you right now. Think of someone still "alive" but whose body is not with you right now. You get a feeling that you think of as that person. That's obviously coming from you because their body is not present to you right now. So they are only an idea – an aggregation of thoughts and the feelings to which they lead – in your mind. Your experience of them is coming from you. When they are with you their body says and does things, but those actions are meaningless in themselves. You give meaning and a story to those actions based on your story for yourself and your story for them. When you do not know this, you respond to the story in your mind as though it is a fact outside of you over which you have no control. But once you do know this you can deal with your thoughts and change your experience from conflict to peace.

You learn that you are mind, and that everything is an idea in your mind, by watching your mind and seeing how it constructs with thoughts and ideas the world in which you think you live. This does require that you slow down and pay attention to what is going on in your mind. This is the practical way to learn that what you perceive in the universe of form is an illusion – merely a projection of ideas from your own mind.

187. Ask: Is the ache I feel for others a judgment? (September 19, 2014)

"*Is the 'ache' I feel for others a judgment? …What I am experiencing is an overwhelming sadness/ache for others and I sense this is in fact the flip-side of the ego coin and is a form of judgment in its own right. The arrogance of 'feeling sorry for people' perhaps, although it doesn't feel like pity…I feel overwhelmed at times by this 'ache' for others, for the state of the world and so on. I wonder if it is like any other projection that needs to be recognised for what it is, forgiven and released to the Holy Spirit? That said, the ego tells me that if I felt neutral and peaceful over the plight of others I would be cold and heartless. I understand that the pain and suffering of the world is not the Truth, but as a seeming person living 'in it' I can't quite grasp that, although I get the metaphysics of it..." - AM*

You are projecting meaning (judgment – wrong/bad) onto what you see happening in others' lives and responding to your projections of meaning as though they are real. You ache for others because you identify with them. In other words, you are looking out at others from the ego (personal thought system) rather than from an awareness of Truth (Holy Spirit). So you are using these situations to reinforce your belief in the ego in your mind. And, yes, as *A Course in Miracles* teaches, this is a judgment against yourself because the ego is not you.

"To empathize does not mean to join in suffering, for that is what you must <u>refuse</u> to understand. That is the ego's interpretation of empathy, and is always used to form a special relationship in which the suffering is shared. The capacity to empathize is very useful to the Holy Spirit, provided you let Him use it in His way. His way is very different. He does not understand suffering, and would have you teach it is not understandable. When He relates through you, He does not relate through your ego to another ego. He does not join in pain, understanding that healing pain is not accomplished by delusional attempts to enter into it, and lighten it by sharing the delusion."(T-16.I.1)

As long as you see yourself as a "seeming person living 'in it' (the world)" you will not grasp how you can look on the world and see that suffering is not real. You must make the choice to let go of your identification with a self in a body in a world and to learn What is real. In a situation where you are confronted with a story of suffering you can turn away from the story, and therefore the ego in you, and remember that only God (your True Being) in you and in the other is real. This is true empathy. And this is how you can use these situations to remember the Truth instead of to reinforce your belief in the ego.

Of course to the ego your turning away from the ego and its projections appears cold and heartless. And as long as the ego and its projections of meaning seem real to you, you will agree with the ego on this. But as you grow your awareness of Truth you will find yourself overlooking what appears in the world. You will feel compassion for others in that they suffer, but you will know that what they suffer over is not real. In time you will also learn that their suffering is not real, either. But you cannot know this from the ego. You can only know this from an awareness that only the Truth is true.

In anticipation of the emails I will get let me say this about responding to others who seem to be suffering: No, you do not want to say to others that what they suffer over is not real. You do not want to tell them that their own suffering is not real. If you wish to do that you are coming from a competing ego not the Holy Spirit (your awareness of Truth). You just need to know for them that suffering is not real while they still think it is. You will find yourself saying things like, "I can see this really hurts you" or "I'm sorry you are hurting" and leaving it at that. For many, all they want is to be heard and understood. That's all the love that they can accept in their belief that suffering is real. To love others in the world you meet them where they think they are, not where you want them or even know them to be.

188. Ask: Can you take us through how forgiveness has changed for you? (September 26, 2014)

"Wondering if you could just take us through a day in the life for you in regards to 'forgiving'. And maybe how you first started 'forgiving' versus how you do it now. From forgiving the whole world to forgiving a hang nail. Sometimes it seems when I read about child abuse for example, and I say 'it's not real' it kind of feels like I'm discounting the horrible pain the child has gone thru…it's just my projection seems kind of like a cop out or something.....I really do understand it's all a dream, but still. I've been doing my forgiveness work for almost 3 years now and I really don't feel any happier or peaceful and it's starting to zap my motivation.....
  I do what the Course *says:*

1. *Notice it - acknowledge it's you/your projections*
2. *Realize it isn't real/truth*
3. *Release it to the Holy Spirit*

Am I doing something wrong ?" – DC

The reason you cannot forgive is that the world and your projections onto it are still very real to you. You are trying to forgive from the ego.

In the beginning it was the same for me. I finally gave up trying to forgive or to do anything that I thought I read in *A Course in Miracles*. I decided one day that I would focus on what I knew already worked for me: Communing with God (True Being) daily and maintaining my relationship with the Holy Spirit. I did this for a while, and nothing else, and lo and behold forgiveness happened of itself! This is why I emphasize growing your awareness of Truth rather than trying to forgive. Growing your awareness of Truth *is the way to forgive.* You do not forgive the world by looking at it and trying to convince yourself that it isn't real. You forgive the world by looking away from it and toward Truth instead. To let go of the world you must become aware that the Truth is Reality. Otherwise all you've got is the ego and its projections.

So when something comes up that disturbs your peace use it as a reminder to turn your mind to Truth. Don't try to forgive it; just use it to remember Truth. As the Truth becomes true for you the world will become less true for you. Then you will not feel that you are copping out when you say it isn't real. You will truly know that it isn't real.

Now I spend my day maintaining my awareness of Truth and forgiveness happens of itself. In fact, I don't even think in terms of "forgiveness" anymore because there's nothing there to forgive.

189. Ask: What does ACIM say about the future? (October 3, 2014)

"I understand time is an illusion but we still need to deal with the 'world' where we find ourselves. I'd like to know if the Course *says anything about the future." –* J

The future is not here and it never will be. It is only a concept in your mind right now. *A Course in Miracles* points out that the ego (personal thought system) uses this concept to perpetuate guilt:

"By the notion of paying for the past in the future, the past becomes the determiner of the future, making them continuous without an intervening present." (T-13.IV.4)

The Holy Spirit (the awareness of Truth in your mind) knows that you are only right here, right now in the present. So It conceives of the "future" as an extension of the present:

"Healing cannot be accomplished in the past. It must be accomplished in the present to release the future. This interpretation ties the future to the present, and extends the present rather than the past." (T-13.IV.9)

Because the future is only a concept any dream or expectation that you have about the future is a fantasy and nothing more. And all worry about the future is really an expectation of punishment that is rooted in the belief that you are guilty. Fantasies about the future or worry about the future are really just ways of avoiding what is really going on in your mind right now. So when you find yourself caught up in fantasy or worry ask the Holy Spirit to help you look at what is bothering you *right now*. You are either avoiding something painful (fantasy) or expecting punishment (guilty). Both will keep you from being present, which is the only time in which you can be with God (True Being) and work out your obstacles to peace.

When you undo the guilt in your mind you will not think about the past or the future. You will just be present. And, in a practical sense, you will be directed in how to take care of anything now for a future occurrence.

190. Ask: How can people with brain diseases choose the Holy Spirit? (October 10, 2014)

"I would like to know how ACIM *deals with Alzheimer's, dementia and mental illness. These illnesses seem different from say from cancer, paralysis or heart issues. The latter seem to leave room to make decisions with the Holy Spirit. But what about diseases such as the 'brain' related ones mentioned above. How can these patients choose again for Spirit?"* – J

A Course in Miracles does not address specific illnesses because from the perspective of Truth all illusion is illusion. The specific form of an illusion does not make it any less an illusion.

The mind is not in the brain but as long as you identify with a body you will allow your thinking to be affected by the brain as though it is. However, the Truth in your mind goes on untouched in any way by anything that seems to happen in the illusion. Your awareness or lack of awareness of Truth has no effect whatsoever on the Truth in your mind. So if a person's identification with a body keeps them from being consciously aware of the Holy Spirit (the awareness of Truth in their mind) it does not affect the Truth in their minds. They just remain unaware of It.

Remember, your lack of awareness of Truth is temporary. In other words, it only affects what you think of as you in the story that you are that which is in time. That story is an illusion whether you are or are not aware of Truth. It falls away whether or not you become aware of Truth. Only the Truth in your mind is eternal. So no one *has to* become aware of Truth. It's an individual choice of a mind that thinks it is in time and wants to find lasting peace.

191. Ask: Would a "peak experience" be a Holy Instant? (October 17, 2018)

"I was wondering lately how the Course *would describe or define* Maslow's "Peak Experience" *occurrence? I didn't know that I had two distinct* Peak Experiences *before I took a psychology course in college... Nothing since then! Would a "peak experience" be something like the Holy Instant? Thanks."* – CS

What Maslow describes seems to take in many kinds of experiences. So I would say that his descriptions of peak experiences would include, but are not limited to, the Holy Instant.

The Holy Instant is an experience of God (True Being). The ultimate Holy Instant would be a direct Revelation of God in which you experience *only God*. In this experience the world does not exist for you at all, not even as an idea. It is an experience of pure, joyous Being extending infinitely. This is very rare. Most never have this experience. And those of us who do experience direct Revelations have them very rarely.

But as you practice the Holy Instant daily it can show up for you as an everyday miracle, like hearing the Holy Spirit or having peace suddenly come over you. Or sometimes you may have what I call a "higher miracle". In a higher miracle you transcend the world but you are still aware of it. You have an expanded sense of being, beyond the limitations of a self. You are everywhere and you feel joyously connected to everything that you perceive. But you see that the world is nothing. The connection you feel is to *content* – the mind behind the forms that you perceive.

So some of what Maslow calls a "peak experience" would be what I just described as a "higher miracle".

192. Ask: Do the following statements and questions about mind make sense to you? (October 24, 2014)

"...If one has read ACIM *and experienced a number of shifts in identity, do the following statements/questions make sense to you?*

1. IT is what we Are (MIND and mind) = ONE Mind
2. Is the above statement what Jesus (a figure within the mind to point us to the MIND) meant when he said "when two become One, it shall be done". I had experience where the two parts (seemingly) merged or crossed over.
3. Once one realizes that all is Mind, is there a natural merging back into the mind? Or is that still the conditioned mind (ego) demanding attention. It feels like mind wandering again. The running of different fantasy about a personal life and I know that I am hurting myself because at some place I again fulfill the wish (live, die, repeat ??)
4. What stage would this fall into? Once having realized being the Mind, the seeker within (so I don't study like I use to) faded and now I just pay attention to my thoughts. I want to play with them also, but this has led me to a feeling that I have to start all over Forgiving. The secret dream that the Course *refers to is just as demanding but different because one knows the separation never happened. Instead of forgiving the world of form, I am forgiving my perceptions in my own mind. Yet they are perfect if one was to stop and realize. I still mix the ego in with them it seems. Does that make sense?*

5. The personal self does not know what to do to advance her career because I experienced a 'what illusions to choose from' realization. The mind is always waiting for the next thought.
6. There is no personal awakening, so how could Mind realize Itself and continue to pretend to be mind?
7. All the personal yuk stuff resurfaces (only It's in the Mind of the mind). So it seems... new to Salvation and still dealing with my stuff ha ha!!! It is kind of funny. And I get tired of my perceptions pretending to be separate…

…Basically, I want to perceive the Holiness of my Mind all the time. Stable. Having experienced Eternalness I am not fulfilled with anything less than and with this thought I am not as joyous as I have been. I know that IT is there, however I still get caught in my ego thoughts… " – DM

1. Yes, there is one Mind. It is the Mind of True Being. But where the thought of the opposite-of-Truth occurs it seems as though there are many minds split between Truth and illusion. Truth is all that is real and eternal in any mind. Everything else falls away.
2. If you are speaking of a quote in *A Course in Miracles* I could not find it. (I tried all sorts of configurations of your quote in my searchable ACIM and found nothing like it). It is possible that it was a passage referring to your mind no longer being split. However, often when in ACIM such statements are made it is referring to Helen and Bill's unique Holy Relationship where they were at an equal teaching/learning stage, simultaneously learning the same things. They each saw their own Holiness reflected in the other. So it may have been saying that when they accept the Holiness that they see reflected in the other and realize that the seeming separation is not real, their "salvation" will be complete.
3. There is nothing to "merge back into" Mind. Mind is always Mind. The problem is that you believe that you are a self, which is a thought in your seemingly-separate mind. And you believe in all of the other thoughts you have about the self and the rest of the universe of form (also thoughts). And you believe in the thought system of the ego, which is a thought system about the reality of the self. So what must occur is you drop your belief in these thoughts. Then all that will be left is Mind.
4. You are in the" period of sorting out" or you would not be contacting me. Once a person enters the "period of relinquishment" they no longer have a need for an external teacher, except maybe at the very beginning of that stage. It is the stage where you become willing to follow only the Holy Spirit.
Watching your thoughts is the practice that makes you aware that you are mind. Forgiving (releasing your belief in) your ego thoughts is the whole process to peace. So you do not "start over", you continue in that process.
The desire to study will come and go until all studying falls away naturally. Sometimes you will be hungry for study. At other times you will not want to study at all. In those times you are integrating all that you have learned up to that point. When it's time to learn more, the hunger for study will return.
5. Your old motivations for the self fall away when you no longer try to find fulfillment by living through the self. Then you find it difficult to make decisions for the self. So give the self to the Holy Spirit. Say to the Holy Spirit, "Is there a next step for this self's career? If so, I am open to Your guidance." Then let it go and keep your mind open. If there are steps to take, you will know what to do.
6. There is no personal awakening in the sense that a self and its thought system (ego) do not become aware of Truth. But an individual mind can become aware of the Truth in itself apart

from the ego thought system. But becoming aware of the Truth within and accepting that only the Truth is true is a long process where one vacillates between Truth and illusion for a long time as they undo all of the ways that their desire for and belief in illusion shows up. And then, finally, one must become used to a different way of being—as an abstract mind rather than a concrete body/self.

7. You will not be bothered by the ego's perceptions of separation when you no longer believe in them. Then you will see that they are nothing and easily dismiss them. In the meantime, grow your awareness of Truth and the awareness that these thoughts are not real will come naturally.

Yes, once you experience Truth you will not be satisfied without It being wholly in your awareness. And that is the motivation that keeps you going in this long, sometimes difficult process. So as you work this process enter into Truth when you can, and when you cannot, remember that It is here whether or not you are aware of It. Accept that you are in a process that will result in Truth being always in your awareness. Joy will return!

193. Ask: Does ACIM use the word "soul" to mean the same thing as "mind"? (October 31, 2014)

"When I was 10 my grandmother passed away. The music playing was Ave Maria and it made me cry. My mother tried to comfort me by saying, 'Your grammy's soul is in heaven now'. I was miffed and said rather loudly, 'Where was her "soul" before she died? And before she was born!' My mother had no answers.

Now 6 decades later, I look back on that event within the perspective of ACIM and the Holy Spirit. I wonder about the Course's *position in that only the mind is real, there is no birth, life, or death of the illusory body. Are the terms 'soul' and 'mind' similar in these situations? e.g. does ACIM use the term 'soul' to mean the same thing as 'mind'?*

Could the experience at the funeral mass have been an indicator of my mind being in touch with Truth at a time when I believed my body to be 10 years of age?" – J

When most people use the word "soul" they are referring to the ego without the body. They are thinking of the "essence" of the "person". This is also often what they mean when they refer to a person's "spirit", which they think of as individual and unique. They think of this soul/spirit as existing before a person was in a body, that it then went into the body, and that it will leave the body when the body dies. So "soul", or an individual spirit, as these terms are usually used, are concepts for something that does not exist.

A Course in Miracles avoids the word "soul" because it is a controversial word, as I just described. It uses "soul" only when referring to Biblical quotations. In those cases, it is equivalent to "Spirit", Which in ACIM is the Thought of God (or Idea of God) in your mind. (You may wish to read "Mind-Spirit" in the Clarification of Terms after the Manual for Teachers).

You experienced at ten years old questions that many people have. You were not necessarily in touch with Truth but those questions may be what led you to eventually be open to Truth.

194. Ask: Is my life chaotic because I'm working ACIM? (November 7, 2014)

"You have commented several times that when individuals start to seriously work with the Course, *they can experience a lot of upheaval: bankruptcy, divorce, foreclosure on their house, etc. Why is that? I ask because it does seem that every time I really devote myself to* Course *study, 'bad' things in my world start to happen. Then I back away from the* Course *for a bit, primarily because I'm trying to deal with all the issues created. For instance, the last time I was doing Workbook lessons daily, as well as spending time with Holy Spirit twice a day, I experienced a car break down on the highway, the HVAC system in our house died (much earlier than expected), the water heater went right after it (also unexpected according to its age), I was ticketed by a police officer for something I'm pretty sure I didn't do, and I was disqualified for a large rebate I was counting on due to a mistake someone else made. This was all in one month. My life isn't usually this chaotic. What is really going on?*

I should add that it's not all adverse because I do find that I'm coping somewhat better with all the unforeseen events than I may have in the past. And I try to remember to call on HS when I'm feeling fearful and upset. But it does distract me from the Course *as more time is taken in trying to evaluate new purchases, worry about the money to pay for them, decide whether to go to traffic court and contest the ticket, and negotiate with the merchant who gave me the incorrect information about the product I was buying. So I get more anchored in this magical world once again. That doesn't seem to align with the aim of the* Course." *– MD*

What you hear me refer to is a person's life aligning with the changes in themselves as they undo the guilt, shame, fear, and false values on which they built their lives. For example, a woman marries a man she thinks she "should" to please others, they live a lifestyle beyond their means because they feel this show of prosperity is necessary to feel good about themselves, and she stays in a job she hates to maintain that lifestyle. In her pain she starts seeking relief and finds something like *A Course in Miracles* which tells her that she is inherently worthy and does not have to seek outside herself for love and acceptance. As she accepts these ideas it's apparent that she made life choices from a sense of unworthiness. Her outer life is completely out of accord with her new awareness of her inherent value. So she goes through divorce, bankruptcy, foreclosure, and temporary unemployment as her outer life realigns with her inner awareness. In time her outer life will settle down again as an authentic representation of her sense of worth.

What you are talking about is something different. These are just the petty, everyday disruptions to which you are meant to apply the Workbook lessons. Nothing special is occurring, but you are making them special by giving them special meaning. Threatened by your study of ACIM, the ego (personal thought system) in your mind interprets these events as being caused by you working the lessons. So it advises you to stop the lessons rather than to apply them to these occurrences as they are meant to be applied!

Disruptions in the self's life are not going to stop because you are a student of *A Course in Miracles*. Sometimes these disruptions happen in a cluster, but this does not have special meaning. These disruptions are the very classroom in which you are meant to apply ACIM. You can be distracted by them, or, as you said, you can invite the Holy Spirit into them with you. If you do the latter they become the means to remember Truth rather than to forget It.

195. Ask: What authority assigned attributes to God in ACIM? (November 14, 2014)

"Can you tell me if 'God' and 'Father' are the same in ACIM? *Where does the authority come from to assign God attributes other than to say 'God is'. (Frankly, I even wonder where the 'God is' emanates from?) The scriptures have some horrendous qualities designated to God but* ACIM, *although positive qualities, must have come from some knowledge given to Helen? Can you share your thoughts as to where the attributes assigned to God in* ACIM *originated?"* – J

Yes, "God" and "Father" are the same in *A Course in Miracles.* However, as with most everything in ACIM these symbols mean something very different from the way the world commonly uses them. "God" does not mean an authoritative being that brought the universe of form into being. "God" means Reality or Truth, Which is beyond the universe of form. God is the one Being that is. Everything else is an illusion.

"Father" in ACIM refers to God in God's Totality where "Son of God" refers to the Part of God that seems split off from God in a universe of form. This Part of God also seems split within itself between God and not-God. (What seems like "your" mind is a version of this split mind). Keep in mind that God does not really have "parts". "Father" and "Son" and "Part" are designations that are only useful while God still seems apart from you. They are the symbols that you can use to become aware of God within you. Eventually they fall away when you come to realize that there is only one Being and It is God. This is the experience "God is" and it emanates from God within you.

God is all that is real in any mind. And God is in every mind whether one is aware of this or not. Helen Schucman heard the Voice for God (what ACIM calls "Christ" or "Holy Spirit") in her own mind. She labeled this Voice "Jesus" because she needed a tangible symbol for It. This is the Voice that dictated ACIM to Helen. So God is the Authority that assigned attributes to the symbol "God" in ACIM.

The Preface to ACIM tells some of the originating story for ACIM. But you may also be interested in the book, *Journey Without Distance,* by Robert Skutch. It tells the story of how ACIM came to be. It is always important to understand the context in which a spiritual teaching arose. The context should inform your study.

196. Ask: What's the difference between being a sociopath and being detached? (November 21, 2014)

"What's the difference between a sociopath and the kind of detachment you seem to teach is desirable?" - Anonymous

A sociopath is someone who has a disorder that makes them unable to feel empathy for others. They are amoral (without morality) because they cannot understand the consequences of their actions on others. Psychologists report that sociopaths are actually deeply enraged. Anger is a defensive response so they are deeply fearful. Their ego's (personal thought system's) view of the world is very real to them.

The detachment that I write about is the natural result of you being aware that only the Truth is true. So you no longer respond to the world with the emotions you did when the ego's (personal thought system's) interpretations of the world were real to you. In the awareness that only the Truth is true you feel whole. This is the same as saying that you feel an abundance of

Love. So the self in your mind behaves in ways that are more likely to be considered "moral" by the world. You remember what pain was like so the self expresses compassion to others even though you know that pain is not real. You do not make others' pain your pain but the self responds to their expressions of pain because the pain is real *to them*.

There is a misperception that "detachment" means "coldness". And it is true that some unhealthy people may perceive you as "cold" when you choose to no longer play emotional games with them or you put up healthy boundaries to which they are not accustomed. But when you come from Truth healthy people will find you warm and loving.

197. Ask: Why can't both God and the world be real? (November 28, 2014)

"Why does it have to be "non-duality"? Why can't duality be real? Why can't both God and the world be real?" - Anonymous

It's not that it "has to be" non-duality. It's just the way it is! Truth, or Reality, Which is what is meant by "God" in *A Course in Miracles*, is an experience of Being extending infinitely and eternally. There is nothing else in the experience. It is whole and complete in Itself. It is *one* both in the sense that It is whole and that It is All-That-is.

Once you have this experience, either in direct Revelation (only God) or in a higher miracle (an awareness that only God is real while still being aware of the world), you understand that Reality is really beyond the world that you thought was reality. It reveals to you that the world has no more substance than vapor.

But aside from the experience itself, which is really the only thing that will convince you that there is only one Reality and It is God, logic shows that something cannot be something else and still be itself. For example, an apple cannot be an orange and still be an apple. Nor can it blend with an orange and still be an apple. A hybrid applange would not be an apple. It would be its own thing.

So it is with God. Formlessness (God) cannot be form and still be Formless. Wholeness (God) cannot lack and still be Whole. Limitlessness cannot be limited and still be Limitless. Truth cannot be not-Truth and still be Truth. There can only be one Truth, or Reality. And It cannot oppose Itself and still be Itself. That's why it "has to be" non-duality.

Keep in mind that you experience duality only because you are in denial. You seem to be split against yourself. And this is what gives you the sense that there is an inside of you and an outside of you (the world, a god), right and wrong, Heaven and earth, subject and object, etc. when actually your Reality is an undivided Whole. When you experience This it is because denial has fallen away.

198. Ask: Can you clarify the terms mind, awareness, etc.? (December 5, 2014)

"You say that we are mind but I read others who say mind does not exist. Then there are terms like awareness, consciousness, and perception that seem to be used in different ways by different teachers. I get very confused. Can you clarify?" - Anonymous

You are correct that these terms are used by spiritual teachers in various contradictory or interchangeable ways. I cannot clarify how anyone else uses them. But I will clarify how I use them.

Before I do that, however, I want to point out that these contradictions can be useful if you are a serious student of spiritual material. Words are symbols and will never mean the same thing to everyone. Discerning how a teacher uses these words can be a way of both deepening your understanding of their teaching and your own understanding of the ideas that the words represent. So bring your confusion to the Teacher of Truth (Holy Spirit) in your mind and look at them. How do you use these words? How does the teacher that you are studying use them? Is there a difference? If so, what does it show you about what you believe? What does it reveal about their teaching? How is their teaching different from what you already believed? How is it different from what else you've studied? If you do not *think* about what you read, you are not *studying*, you are just *reading*.

I use the term "Mind", when capitalized, to refer to the aspect of Being through Which Being knows Itself. In Truth, *to know* and *to be* are the same experience. So for me Mind and Being are synonymous. Mind/Being is formless, limitless, and timeless. It simply *is*. When teaching about Truth it makes sense to me to speak in terms of "mind" rather than "being" because the obstacles to being aware of True Being are thoughts, ideas, and beliefs. These are what make it necessary to speak of Mind as an "aspect" of Being as though What is One has parts.

The part of Mind where the idea of Its Own opposite seems to be I call the "split-mind". The split-mind seems to be split-off from Mind, seems to be split between Truth (Mind) and illusion (awareness, consciousness, perception and their object, the universe of form), and seems to be split within itself into billions of different versions of itself. When speaking of it in a seemingly-individual form, as "mind", I use the lower-case "m". Mind in this context no longer *knows* its Own Being. Instead it *thinks* (which is a form of *doing* rather than *being*). What it thinks about is what it is aware of, is conscious of, or perceives, either Truth (Mind) or illusion (the universe of form). So it is further split into "subject" (mind) and "object" (universe of form) as its thoughts are projected away from it. It identifies in particular with one of its projected thoughts, a self (body/personality), which it thinks surrounds it.

However, every mind is really still a part of Mind and can become aware of this. So your awareness (consciousness, perception) can transcend your belief in form-as-reality and realize that formless Mind is reality. You do this first by becoming aware of the Truth (Mind/Being) in your mind and allowing this awareness (which I call the Teacher of Truth or Holy Spirit) to help you change your thoughts so that they are aligned with Truth. By attending to your mind and its activity you eventually realize that mind, not the forms it observes, is reality and is also the source of what it observes. You become aware of both the one split-mind that is the source of the universe of form and of the Eternally Unified Mind (Truth) beyond even that. In time, your awareness of the Eternally Unified Mind reaches a point where you are ready to stop *all* thinking with the thought system in your mind that is about being a self in a body in a world (ego/personal thought system). At this stage you perceive the nothingness of form. Your seemingly-individual mind no longer seems to be apart from the universe of form or from Mind.

This highest awareness (consciousness, perception), however, is not True Being Itself. It is a transitional stage that prepares your mind to drop all awareness (consciousness, perception) and form. You are ready for the "last step" in which your mind will blend wholly with Mind. In True Mind/Being there are no thoughts or other forms, so no awareness (perception, consciousness) and no subject-object. Just Mind/Being extending without limit.

So, the way I use the terms, awareness, consciousness, and perception are activities of the mind that can be used to stay in denial of Mind. Or they can be used to return mind to Mind, at which point they must fall away.

199. Ask: Why do I keep passing out into peace? (December 12, 2014)

"When I read the text, the manual and/or the lessons, I invariably fall asleep with the book open in front of me, often even when I'm fresh soon after waking. I first read the Course *nearly 30 years ago. Ever since, it happens each time I read the* Course, *including your* 'Message of...' *versions of them. It does not happen when I read them with a group. But this falling asleep— more like passing out—is often a remarkable experience because when I wake I experience a sense of release, clarity, energy, and a great welcome for what is happening in the present. It's something more than merely waking from a nap or even from a deep night's sleep. The words of the* Course *seem to have so much power that they virtually sort through my thoughts and find a new place, such that 'my' thoughts seem to be set aside. The result is that I feel a great sense of peace even though I'm perplexed why I seem to pass out while reading. Is this an experience you've had, and is there a way that I can be conscious of its purpose and value?"* – GB

When I was first a student of *A Course in Miracles* I would read a paragraph in the Text and fall asleep. I could not keep myself awake, no matter the time of day or that I was an otherwise vigorous and energetic 20 year old. This was clearly a form of resistance because it totally interfered with my studying. But what you describe does not sound like a form of resistance. It seems like your unique way of absorbing the *Course*.

I have not heard of this before. But I have heard from others that they sometimes have dreams at night that seem to lead to a similar experience though they do not always remember the dream or the dream itself seems unremarkable. Something is going on in the unconscious in these experiences. And you stated the purpose and value of them yourself: "*...I experience a sense of release, clarity, energy, and a great welcome for what is happening in the present... The result is that I feel a great sense of peace...*"

200. Ask: Why do I have sudden thoughts about perceived attacks in the past? (December 19, 2014)

"Let's say I'm going about my business feeling no stress, conflict or pain and suddenly, 'out of the blue' comes some disturbing thought about a person/incident from the past which feels like I'm under attack, requiring me to defend and counterattack etc. I haven't seen this person for years, they're not in my life but there they are. While I believe that circumstances and people don't create feelings in us but rather we project our feelings onto them (it's entirely my movie), what I don't get is the suddenness, and absence of current context for these thoughts. Why now?..." – ES

What you describe is when something of which you are not conscious, or not fully conscious, triggers a memory of a person or circumstance. It may be some object your eyes light upon, a snatch of music or another sound, a body memory, or a train of thought that you had not been consciously following. It may also be that if the ego (personal thought system) in your mind feels threatened by your spiritual practice and experiences it recalls people and incidents to

distract you. It may use the "rewards" of feeling a victim as soon as you, often unconsciously, glance its way. Sometimes these memories come up because of a chemical change in the body that induces feelings that cause you to recall when you had those feelings before.
So there is a current cause for the thoughts. You are just not consciously aware of it. In any case the cause is not important. What's important is these memories still evoke a strong emotional reaction in you. This indicates that you still have unconscious beliefs in guilt and fear to undo. So these memories, no matter how they are evoked, give you an opportunity to undo your obstacles to peace.

201. Ask: Will you read "A Course of Love"? If not, why not? (December 26, 2014)

"....Last week I was reading Jon Mundy's magazine on the Course*.... In his mag, there was an advertisement notice that there was a new book out,* A Course of Love*, www.acourseoflove.com...Have you heard of this book? Will you read it? If you will not read it, why not? I am curious to get your opinion about its close similarity to only knowing the Truth and meditating just on the Truth..."* – SS

I heard of this book many years ago and I continue to get advertisements for it. But, no, I will not be reading it. The need to study fell away from me naturally many years ago. Since then I find reading spiritual material to be superfluous and, frankly, rather tedious. I can only liken this to reading a recipe for a dish I make every day. After a while the recipe becomes unnecessary and turning to it actually gets in the way of making the dish quickly and efficiently. So when I read spiritual material now I feel, "too many words". They are not necessary for me to experience Truth and they are a distraction from experiencing Truth. I get all I need from turning inward and communing with the Eternal Quiet.